EDUCATIONAL LEADERSHIP AND CHANGING CONTEXTS OF FAMILIES, COMMUNITIES, AND SCHOOLS

EDUCATIONAL LEADERSHIP AND CHANGING CONTEXTS OF FAMILIES, COMMUNITIES, AND SCHOOLS

Eighty-ninth Yearbook of the
National Society for the Study of Education

PART II

Edited by

BRAD MITCHELL AND LUVERN L. CUNNINGHAM

Editor for the Society

KENNETH J. REHAGE

19 NSSE 90

Distributed by THE UNIVERSITY OF CHICAGO PRESS ● CHICAGO, ILLINOIS

The National Society for the Study of Education

Founded in 1901 as successor to the National Herbart Society, the National Society for the Study of Education has provided a means by which the results of serious study of educational issues could become a basis for informed discussion of those issues. The Society's two-volume yearbooks, now in their eighty-ninth year of publication, reflect the thoughtful attention given to a wide range of educational problems during those years. In 1971 the Society inaugurated a series of substantial publications on Contemporary Educational Issues to supplement the yearbooks. Each year the Society's publications contain contributions to the literature of education from more than a hundred scholars and practitioners who are doing significant work in their respective fields.

An elected Board of Directors selects the subjects with which volumes in the yearbook series are to deal and appoints committees to oversee the preparation of manuscripts. A special committee created by the Board performs similar functions for the series on Contemporary Educational Issues.

The Society's publications are distributed each year without charge to members in the United States, Canada, and elsewhere throughout the world. The Society welcomes as members all individuals who desire to receive its publications. Information about current dues may be found in the back pages of this volume.

This volume, *Educational Leadership and Changing Contexts of Families, Communities, and Schools*, is Part II of the Eighty-ninth Yearbook of the Society. Part I, which is published at the same time, is entitled *Textbooks and Schooling in the United States*.

A listing of the Society's publications still available for purchase may be found in the back pages of this volume.

Library of Congress Catalog Number: 89-063574
ISSN: 0077-5762

Published 1990 by
THE NATIONAL SOCIETY FOR THE STUDY OF EDUCATION

5835 Kimbark Avenue, Chicago, Illinois 60637

First Printing, 5,000 Copies

Printed in the United States of America

v

Acknowledgment

The National Society for the Study of Education is grateful to the editors of this volume, Professors Brad Mitchell and Luvern L. Cunningham, and to the several authors who have contributed chapters to the book. This in-depth exploration of recent developments in families, communities, and schools leads to a new array of significant challenges to educational leadership. Working from the perspectives that have developed from their research, the authors have prepared essays that add new dimensions to the calls for reform in the programs for preparation of administrators, to the discussions about restructuring schools, and to a renewed emphasis on the study of educational administration as a field of professional practice.

Bringing out a volume that attempts to break new ground makes a considerable demand on those who agree to participate in the project. The Society is greatly indebted to all whose work has made it possible to bring this volume to completion.

Table of Contents

Section One
Introduction

Section Two
Children, Youth, and Educational Leadership

Section Three
Families, Communities, and Educational Leadership

Section One
INTRODUCTION

CHAPTER I

Educational Leadership and Administration: Retrospective and Prospective Views

LUVERN L. CUNNINGHAM

The National Society for the Study of Education (NSSE) has often focused on issues of leadership and administration throughout its nearly ninety-year history of producing yearbooks on educational issues confronting the nation. Explicit reference to administrators first appears in 1908 in the title of the Seventh Yearbook, Part I, *The Relation of Superintendents and Principals to the Training and Professional Improvement of Their Teachers.* Five years later, in 1913, Parts I and II of the Twelfth Yearbook were devoted to the supervision of city schools and rural schools. In 1914, high school administration and secondary school instruction were the subjects of Part I of the Thirteenth Yearbook. Topics directly germane to the administrative function did not appear again until 1934 in the Thirty-third Yearbook, Part I, *The Planning and Construction of School Buildings.*

The Forty-fifth Yearbook, Part II, *Changing Conceptions of Educational Administration* (1946) was the first yearbook in which chapter authors concentrated on educational administration as a field of study and practice. *Behavioral Science and Educational Administration* (Sixty-third Yearbook, Part II, 1964) also treated administration as an established function, even a discipline, essential to schooling and informed by knowledge from a broad range of the behavioral sciences. *Leaders in American Education* (Seventieth Yearbook, Part II, 1971) contained biographical and autobiographical essays on the lives of eleven selected educational leaders, ten men and one woman. It is the only yearbook in which the term "leader" appears in the title.

Obviously, the content of all yearbooks has been pertinent to the work of administrators. Most volumes often have broad policy

1

significance and important implications for administrator training and practice. *Social Forces Influencing American Education* (Sixtieth Yearbook, Part II, 1961) is a classic example. *The Courts and Education* (Seventy-seventh Yearbook, Part II, 1978), *Policy Making in Education* (Eighty-first Yearbook, Part I, 1982), *The Ecology of School Renewal* (Eighty-sixth Yearbook, Part I, 1987), and *Critical Issues in Curriculum* (Eighty-seventh Yearbook, Part I, 1988) are more recent examples.

In this volume, the authors wrestle with the changing contexts that surround the work, the roles, and the responsibilities of educational leaders for the next generation of children and youth. What we have learned and are learning about children, their families, their teachers, their schools, their communities, and about how children learn and how they are taught is important for how we plan to organize and administer tomorrow's schools. The focus is on how educational leadership relates to ideological, institutional, and individual transformations that occur in abundance as society evolves. It is a volume where the authors audit some dimensions of the human condition relevant to teaching and learning and extract meaning and significance for those who expect to lead and administer our schools.

Contemporary Developments in the Field

All professions, and the institutions that prepare persons to enter them, are undergoing intensive internal and external review. Professional fields of practice such as accounting, medicine, theology, social work, business, nursing, and education are being scrutinized by the media and others at an unprecedented scope and pace. Educational administration is not above the rabble. Principals and superintendents have been cited in the spate of national reports over and over again as both the Achilles heel of American education and the Adonis for improved performance of the nation's schools. One example is the series of reports produced by the Carnegie Corporation of New York. *A Nation Prepared: Teachers for the 21st Century* (1986) and *Turning Points* (1989)[1] both contain criticisms of the professions of teaching and school administration and proposals to revitalize teacher training and transform educational organizations especially at the middle-school level.

Beginning in the mid-1980s, through initiatives of the University Council for Educational Aministration and the Danforth Foundation, the profession of educational administration conducted a self-examination, focusing initially on the preparation and licensing of school administrators. A National Commission on Excellence in Educational Administration, formed in 1985 under the leadership of Daniel E. Griffiths, was charged with assessing the status of educational leadership in the United States and with formulating proposals for improvement. Early in 1987, the Commission published *Leaders for America's Schools*.[2] One of its recommendations called for the establishment of a national policy board. The board was created in 1988-89 with financial support from the Danforth Foundation. Its headquarters is at the University of Virginia. The first report of the National Policy Board for Educational Administration was published in May, 1989 and included an extensive agenda for reform focusing on the recruitment, selection, and preparation of educational administrators.[3] Although some observers felt the agenda was "old wine in new bottles," it became evident that national attention had been placed on the administrative and leadership functions of education. A major proposal in the report was to form a national professional standards board to develop and administer a national certification examination and encourage states to require candidates for licensure to pass the national examination. If such a board is established it will parallel the National Board of Professional Teaching Standards, a 1988 outgrowth of proposals included in *A Nation Prepared: Teachers for the 21st Century*, the 1986 report of the Carnegie Forum on Education and the Economy.

In the mid-1980s, the Danforth Foundation increased its investment to strengthen preservice preparation and continuing education of principals and superintendents. The preservice initiatives involved the selection of a small number of universities willing to revamp their preparation programs in general and another small number of institutions willing to revise, update, or otherwise transform their programs for principals. Over a period of three years more than thirty universities took steps to strengthen their programs with Danforth support. These Danforth Foundation grants followed the pattern of the W. K. Kellogg Foundation in the 1950s where seed monies were provided to a small number of universities to stimulate research, underwrite the development of preparation programs, and provide fellowships for promising students of administration. Clearly, educational administration as a field of study and of practice faces profound and unique opportunities, as do those who are concerned with the professional preparation of administrators.

Beginning in the 1970s and continuing through the 1980s, a frenzy surrounded the need to improve capabilities of practicing school administrators. The Eighty-second NSSE Yearbook, Part II, entitled *Staff Development* (1983) provided an appropriate assessment of the status of staff development and new programs and practices especially for teachers. Changes inside the schools and in the world outside the schools, a theme of this volume, were well underway. Skills taught or otherwise acquired through earlier forms of preservice education and continuing professional education were not adequate. Consequently, state departments of education, professional associations, in-service entrepreneurs, colleges, and universities tried desperately to conceptualize fresh approaches to the professional preparation of superintendents and principals. School districts struggled to come to grips with the problem. Networks of school districts for staff development were created. School study councils, which began in the 1950s, shifted much of their emphasis away from "study" to professional development for teachers, principals, and superintendents. Subgroups within state and national associations of administrators were created to concentrate on particular needs. Today, many of these groups are highly energized and totally committed to deal with improved competence in educational leadership.

One noble example is the rapid creation and development of principals' centers and academies. The Harvard Principals' Center was an early entrant. In fact, through the Harvard Center, a National Directory of Principals' Centers has been formed, with help from the Danforth Foundation. The Directory produces a newsletter and other forms of formal and informal communication. Its philosophy includes emphasis on the development of individual programs of professional development for principals and offers suggestions as to how individual administrators can take charge of their own professional futures. These centers for principals, and their counterparts for superintendents, are part of a recent grass roots spontaneity in the tradition of American ingenuity.

As important as these investments of time, dollars, and energy are, they appear to be falling short of meeting ever intensifying and changing demands for administrator competency. Changing demographics, technological innovation, the need for collaboration and cooperation, and the prospect of reconstituting institutions, take the measure of men and women in educational leadership positions today.

A Break with Tradition

This yearbook departs from preceding ones devoted to administration and leadership. Rather than concentrating on functional tasks, organizational theory, or other behavioral science perspectives, we have chosen to center attention on changes occurring within student populations, their families, communities, and schools themselves. The premise is that cultural changes are so rampant that attention to administrative functions such as budgeting, finance, school law, organizational theory, curriculum development, and supervision lacks transformative power. Similarly, the art, science, study, and practice of leadership must encompass contemporary demands placed on principals and superintendents. *Education in School and Nonschool Settings* (the Eighty-fourth Yearbook, Part I, 1985), foreshadowed many of the meaningful changes administrators now face, especially those at the building level.[4] The thesis of the 1985 volume is that learning occurs in many places. Classrooms are an essential part of human development. They provide the most extensive and sustained experience in the common knowledge and skills citizens are likely to have. However, this yearbook assumes that policymakers must recognize that education takes place in many settings, is lifelong, and warrants policies reflecting ". . . an understanding that varied learning environments can be linked in ways that promote improved education for all children and youth."[5] Schools are the central, but not the only, formal location for learning. In the past, state and local policies urged principals to concentrate their efforts on the children in school. School systems were designed vertically, as bureaucratic patterns of organization dictated. Linkages with other educational settings were treated casually, if at all, and certainly were not considered essential for the building administrator to establish. The church, the school, and the home were understood to be the three separate institutions basic to human development. Each institution made its contribution but each was expected to do its work independently, without entanglements. Indeed, the constitutional separation of church and state drove a nearly impenetrable wedge between religious organizations and the public school, producing at times a tense coexistence. Parent-teacher organizations were invented to expedite and enrich communication between schools and families, and as important as they have been, they have fallen short of connecting these two dynamic settings for learning.

Authors of this volume respect the integrity of institutions contributing to learning but they value linkages, formal and informal, that enhance the general well-being of children and youth. They understand, too, what institutions are becoming as well as what they have been. Families, once centers of love, affection, and caring, marked by interdependence among members, now often exhibit independence and distance, where hostility and violence are sometimes common. Children arriving at the schoolhouse door are extraordinarily different in terms of family experience, language, race, and ethnicity, all traditional indicators of diversity. But their numbers also include children marked by depression, and by learning impairment produced by improper prenatal diets of their mothers including drug and alcohol consumption. More and more frequently, especially in our cities, children with the AIDS virus arrive in school ready and eager to learn. Some children and youth are already chemically dependent, drug pushers, and victims of a treacherous drug economy for which there is a seductive beginning but only a disastrous end. Caught up in the frenzy of differing expectations, driven by mounting pressures to become competitive and to produce persons who can fuel voracious manpower demands, schools must still respond on a day-to-day basis to the basic, primary needs of those enrolled. Schools are not what they once were and maybe can never be again.

The Context of Reform

The 1980s and 1990s may be heralded as the age of reform. Calls for change in education came from many sources including the education professions. But the most strident appeals for improvement have been made by leaders from business joined by political figures at all levels. *Investing in Our Children* was the title of a major 1986 report from the Committee for Economic Development (CED), a private, nonprofit, nonpartisan research agency supported for the most part by business corporations.[6] Authors of the report note: "It is a national tragedy that despite the existence of many excellent schools, there are classrooms and even entire schools in which students are being prepared not for success in later life, but failure."[7] Challenges from the business community encourage educators to apply what is known about good education to every classroom in the nation. Business leaders are called on to work with local school districts, develop local business-school partnerships, encourage employees to serve on school boards, permit working parents and other employees to participate in school affairs, and support initiatives to increase funding for the public schools when needed. The report admonished educational leaders to allocate current resources more effectively, to spend more on instruction and less on bureaucracy and administration.[8] The sentiments of the CED report were echoed independently by dozens of powerful business executives throughout the mid and late 1980s.

Business leaders found an ally in higher education leaders. On the eve of the 1988 presidential election, the Business-Higher Education Forum urged the successful candidate to make the development of human resources "a national priority of the first order."[9] The forum is comprised of university presidents and corporate executives who analyze social policy problem areas and make recommendations to political, business, and educational leaders. Recommendations issued in September 1988 were directed to preschool needs, traditional K-12 educational institutions, job training organizations, and undergraduate and graduate institutions. Arguments for change were rooted in two premises: (1) that the large number of reform reports earlier in the decade contained several hundred inconsistent and disconnected proposals for change; and (2) that the often cited dependency of the economy on sound education of young people was too narrowly cast and should give way to the realization that there is a clear need for all people "to learn their way through full and satisfying lives."[10]

Business leaders were prominent organizers of school im-provement groups, task forces, alliances, and commissions at national, state, regional, and local levels in the 1980s. The pace and intensity of business involvement in public education seemed to surpass efforts of an earlier period documented by Raymond Callahan, who assessed the relationships between business and education beginning with the arrival of the "efficiency expert" in about 1910.[11] Business leaders touted the importance of schools adopting efficient principles of business management and implored school principals and superintendents to be trained in sound business practices. Callahan maintained that weak educational leaders succumbed to business pressures with disastrous results. He called it an American tragedy in education:

And when all of the strands of the story are woven together, it is clear that the essence of the tragedy was in adopting values and practices indiscriminately and applying them with little or no consideration of educational values or purposes.[12]

Some business efficiency arguments recently have been coupled with the need for a talented, specialized work force thought necessary for American global competitiveness. Callahan's cautions appear to be unheeded. It is likely that schools and business leaders will maintain an essential interdependency. Schools need the legitimacy and business support; business needs educated workers. The ties appear to be binding tighter and tighter despite the pleadings from enlightened leadership in other sectors of public and private life.

THE FORGOTTEN HALF

Superintendents and principals heard other social policy messages in the 1980s. The title of still another reform report, *The Forgotten Half*, attached that label to the large percentage of the nation's students who do not go on to higher education.[13] These non-college-bound youngsters face problematic, uncertain futures. The report notes that half of our youth are in danger of being caught in a massive bind that denies them full participation in our society and the full benefit of their own talents:

Indeed, one of the cruelest myths of contemporary life is the claim that our economy is healthy because unemployment is relatively low. Employment data obscure the radical job market changes of recent years, the increase of one-parent families, the growing number of working poor and part-time workers, as well as the large numbers of people who have simply stopped looking for work.[14]

The commission that released this report, like others, was chaired by a well-known and influential public leader, Harold Howe II, senior lecturer at the Harvard Graduate School of Education and former U.S. Commissioner of Education. Its recommendations are followed by some excellent implementation strategies. The report is filled with poignant reminders that Americans think quite differently about the college bound than they do about the non-college-bound. Public policy and resource allocations lean heavily in favor of those who want to and do succeed in going to college. Monies flow into building and maintaining large higher education institutions, many of them research universities, with expensive law and medical schools, attracting students from the upper socioeconomic half. Scholarships and other stipends, many of them public, are available to students in the "remembered half" rather than to those in the "forgotten half."

Many calls for reform are issued on behalf of special populations such as those described in *The Forgotten Half* and more recently in a

Carnegie Foundation report on young adolescents entitled *Turning Points*. Early childhood education, day care, preschools, even infant education are other examples where educational leaders are drawn into a political milieu frought with problems related to ideology, delivery systems, age grouping, and resources.[15] Extensions of traditional compulsory education age ranges are now under review. In fact, many public as well as some private schools offer services to nontraditional age groups. Preschools and day care are now available to parents through many school districts. Special programs such as those for teen parents and second-chance offerings for dropouts are widespread.[16]

Efforts to reach out to more and more populations are endorsed, and in some cases, supported by federal policy, such as the Family Support Act of 1988. This legislation is unique in two respects. First, it commits the federal government to provide increasing levels of support for education, training, and employment programs for Aid to Families with Dependent Children (AFDC) as well as for the support services (e.g., child care) necessary to enable recipients to participate in these activities. Second, it mandates collaboration between human service agencies and school districts.[17] Local schools that provide programs for eligible recipients must also offer child care.

ENTER THE POLITICIAN

Despite attempts to shelter it from the rough and tumble environment of everyday politics, education has always been of political interest especially to leaders in business and industry. As it is presumed that good education is central to a sound economy, Vincent Ostrom argued in the Sixtieth NSSE Yearbook, *Social Forces Influencing American Education*, Part II (1961), that a strong, vibrant educational system is essential to an effective political system. Ostrom maintained that learners, the recipients of public education, are in no position to bear the costs of their learning.[18] The costs must be covered by someone else. The political system negotiates and produces those resources and learners are thus dependent on the commonweal. "Education shapes the capabilities and potentialities of its political community, and the political community determines the scope and character of education as a public service."[19]

The 1970s and 1980s were notable for the forceful entrance of governors into educational politics. Florida was an early "reform" state. Under funding provided by the legislature, Governor Reuben Askew appointed a large citizens' committee in 1971 and commissioned a report to the people of Florida on ways to improve the state's schools. The committee produced a comprehensive study filled with recommendations many of which were enacted into law in 1973. The new legislation received a mixed reaction among Florida superintendents and principals, especially provisions for building-level site management, local school advisory councils, and annual reports of school progress. Florida reform legislation in 1973 was an early example of state-level political interest in schools. Today, nearly every state has enacted its own educational improvement legislation, often labeled a "reform package." A number of states, many in the southeast, were well on their way to reform when the celebrated report, *A Nation at Risk*, was released by the U.S. Secretary of Education in 1983.[20] Governors Alexander in Tennessee, Riley in South Carolina, Clinton in Arkansas, Hunt in North Carolina, and Kean in New Jersey led the way, each exhibiting strong personal leadership and effective relations with their legislatures and statewide interest groups. They earned national reputations, moreover, as friends of education. Many other governors were active too, earning some credit for tending the untidy vineyards of educational politics. The National Governors' Association endorsed many extant reform ideas and introduced some new ones in its 1986 report on education entitled *Time for Results*.[21] The governors were particularly outspoken on choice and parental involvement, sparking national interest and contributing to legislative action across the states.

Indeed, one of the most widely debated reform proposals of the 1980s has been "choice." It also captures the attention of superintendents and principals. Several states, following the leadership of Minnesota, enacted some form of choice legislation. Choice opens up a series of options for learners and their parents under a free educational market approach. Choice, first advanced by Milton Friedman in the 1950s, was linked to vouchers in the 1970s and generated controversy within educational leadership circles. Vouchers with a designated monetary amount were to be given to parents to be spent on public or private schooling. In the 1980s, proponents of choice have not stressed the voucher concept, for the most part because the idea has not received enough political support. Many school board members as well as other educational leaders are concerned about choice initiatives. They fear parental choice is yet another subtle mechanism designed to dilute or kill off public schools just as vouchers threatened to do. They are skeptical, too, about its leading to further segregation of schools and large-scale collective bargaining problems in the years ahead. Choice imposes new accountability demands on local schools whether the options available to parents are intradistrict or interdistrict. Options in the form of magnet schools or alternative schools have been available in some districts since the 1960s, often related to plans to remedy segregation. Interdistrict options are newer and we do not know enough to assess their merits and demerits. It is evident that as parents and students exercise choice, the prospects of gaining or losing students at the building level and the district level introduces a new perspective on quality not common to the public school ethos. Schools and school districts that lose students are obviously in trouble. Tarnished reputations and loss of state revenues follow; they are less attractive places to teach, making recruitment and retention of competent personnel a serious problem. Schools and school districts attracting students will have problems of growth, a matter much less troubling than decline. In either case, the lives of administrators are affected.

Timar and Kirp suggest that state efforts to manage school improvement represent only the first, albeit the most visible, dimension of school reform.[22] It is up to leaders on the firing line, on a day-to-day basis, to fulfill the implementation phase of reform. No wonder prospects for the future of public education seem so bewildering to most principals and superintendents.

RESTRUCTURING AND TRANSFORMING SCHOOLS

Numerous reform proposals contain provisions for restructuring and transforming schools and school systems. The two reports issued by the Carnegie Corporation cited earlier call for restructuring the schools to provide a professional environment for teaching, to reshape the teaching force, and to introduce a new category of "lead teachers" who are to be active leaders in the redesign of schools, especially at the middle-school level. Such proposals engender apprehension about loss of power and status among school leaders as restructuring stimulates interest in acquiring power and status for other members of the educational family.

Empowerment is a term often linked with the rhetoric of restructured schools. *Visions of a Better Way: A Black Appraisal of Public Schooling*, an essay by the Committee on Policy for Racial Justice, was published by the Joint Center for Political Studies Press in 1989.[23] The report urges the black community to exert leadership and make a conscious effort to achieve change through the empowerment of parents, teachers, and students. Closer bonds between schools and families are encouraged. Readers are reminded the school does not exist in a void. It is not an isolated institution. Rather, it is community anchored and owned. Authors emphasize that the crisis in education is also a crisis in democracy and signals, as has no other report, the catastrophic effects of school reforms that promote a narrow view of "excellence" devoid of social justice concerns for black children and their families.[24] The positive contributions of Head Start are highlighted and an appeal is made for continuous funding of this important program for children of the poor. At the same time, the evils of tracking and ability grouping are revisited with a call for their abandonment. In urging the black community to take action, the report emphasizes that the needs of poor people and minorities in America are often neglected or overlooked, and those people negatively affected must take the lead in paving the way for justice and equality. The essay is reasoned and factual, devoid of rhetoric, and offers reasonable appeals for large-scale restructuring. The report is respectful of the school as an institution, asking only that it contribute effectively to the well-being of all black children and poor children of all races.

Challenges to Educational Leadership

Educational leadership faces a number of serious challenges in a world that is changing rapidly, among them institutional decay, problems of equity, the impact of technology, and the need for collaboration among agencies serving children.

INSTITUTIONAL DECAY

Respect for public education is not universally held. In the 1960s and 1970s calls were sounded for "deschooling" society, dismantling in effect a 350 year old institution. Few will deny that schools face major problems, some the product of historic weakness such as control vested overwhelmingly in white, Anglo-Saxon, Protestant, male school administrators and school board members. Few will contest the assertion that there are large numbers of good schools across the country. Nevertheless, concerns persist about ineffective schools concentrated in poor urban and rural areas as well as about those youngsters in the "forgotten half" who are found in most every school. *Working in Urban Schools*, a 1988 publication of the Institute for Educational Leadership, documents the dismal working conditions found in many urban communities. "Unsupportive leadership, lack of respect, low participation in policymaking, limited opportunities for collegiality, lack of recognition, and inadequate professional development activities seem to be the norms for urban school teaching." In urban areas, however, these issues take on a different and debilitating scale given the resource problems, the bureaucracy, and the special needs of students.[25] The decay of the human spirit, diminished energy, and professional lives devoid of self-esteem as well as esteem for the school as an institution are the legacies of urban education. The human condition is matched in many settings with archaic, worn out, dysfunctional school facilities. Libraries, classrooms, science laboratories, theaters, practice rooms, playgrounds, even restrooms are dismal and inadequate. The human infrastructure and the physical infrastructure are in joint decay, each contributing to the other.

EQUITY

Issues of equity and instances of inequity still abound in American culture and its institutions. Schools are no exception. Gender and racial discrimination persist, although constitutional remedies were achieved in the 1950s and 1960s. Granted some progress has been made, substantial improvement many would say, there are still gross inequities in financing education. Pay scales and fringe benefits vary widely, especially between and among school districts. Access to administrative positions for females and minorities is still restricted and remnants of stereotyping and inaccurate representation of gender and racial issues in curriculum and instructional materials continue to exist. Some of the seemingly intractable problems are embedded in school district organization, and to some extent in attendance areas. The existence of "have" and "have not" school districts persists in all states except Hawaii. The 1989 decision of the Kentucky State Supreme Court declaring the state system of financing schools to be unconstitutional may stimulate a wave of new interest in attacking inequity among school districts through school district reorganization. The spate of fiscal equity lawsuits of the 1960s and 1970s may be revived, bringing other equity problems into view simultaneously.

Unbalanced representation of females and minorities in the governance and management of education may join fiscal equity on center stage. Fewer than 4 percent of the nation's school superintendents and school board members are from minority groups. Less than 4 percent of the superintendents are female; about 30 percent of school board members are female. The numbers of minorities in other administrative positions are stable, although there is a decline in the numbers of minority secondary school principals. Similar statistics are found in the governance and administration of higher education. Given the incredible changes in demography, the question is how long can these conditions persist. Unfortunately, racial prejudice and discrimination continue to challenge America's ethic of freedom and social justice for all.

TECHNOLOGY

Technology is driving societies in the Western world. Its pace of growth is accelerating with no evidence that it will decelerate. Consequently, the impact of technology on institutions is unsettling, reducing predictability, leading at least one well-known business analyst to advocate learning to love change and thrive on chaos.

Meyrowitz has probed the impact of television, a communications technology with a half-century history, on the socialization of age groupings within the society. He observes children are not childlike anymore. There has been a blurring of distinctions between children and adults across age groups. In the shared environment of television, children and adults know a great deal about one another's behavior and knowledge, too much, in fact, for them to play out the traditional complementary roles of innocence and omniscience.[26]

Computer applications within education have grown over the near half-century existence of digital mechanisms for the transfer of information. Instructional uses of computers and allied technologies seem nearly unlimited. The same is true for their applications to institutional management and governance. As architects of schools and classrooms of the future note over and over again, the physical, instructional and organizational features of learning settings in the future will be starkly different from those we know now. The point is that advancements in technology will continue to intrude on individual, family, and institutional life, especially on schools, calling for new competencies on the part of administrative leaders in education. Even the work settings and work practices of professional educators will be modified, substantially altering their relationships with the learners. Schein suggests the work settings for most professionals in all fields are or will be transformed.[27]

COLLABORATION

Collaboration between and among agencies serving children and youth promises to be a prominent part of the work of educational leaders in the future. Phelps foreshadowed the importance of collaboration and cooperation in the interests of youth in *Toward Adolescence: The Middle School Years*. She noted that agencies were beginning to understand how to build bridges between public and private sectors and construct networks of services and approaches to meet the needs of young people.[28]

More recently, federal policy has demanded collaboration for agencies to qualify for federal monies (e.g., the Family Support Act [FSA] of 1988). FSA forces collaboration at state and local levels involving departments of human services and education at the state level, and county commissioners and school boards at the local level. States have had to produce implementation strategies as well as rules and regulations for the administrator.

A new vocabulary is emerging. Collaboration, cooperation, compact, council, consortia, alliance, federation, and network are terms that apply to cross-sector and boundary-spanning structures springing up across the country even without federal or state mandates. Such new associations are responsive to the realization that needs of children and youth are no longer satisfied by schools and schooling alone. Young people's problems often exhaust the resources of a single agency or a single set of professionals trained to work with this age group. Chemical dependency, abuse syndromes, teenage parenthood, teenage suicide, depression, truancy, delinquent behavior, hunger, malnutrition, and poverty are widespread today in rural and urban communities alike. These problems push beyond the boundaries of professional competence and of agency or institutional missions, thus making collaboration necessary.

Programs of interprofessional education, both prelicensing and continuing, are being offered in many places. Ohio State University pioneered an interprofessional education program in 1973. Prelicensing interprofessional courses, interprofessional continuing education conferences and institutes, and interprofessional policy analysis developed over the years to the point where hundreds of preprofessionals and practicing professionals are served annually. A companion focus on interprofessional practice is responsive to the growing importance of interprofessional and interinstitutional collaboration and cooperation.[29]

Collaboration imposes new demands on individual professionals and institutions. New skills are required. So are personnel policies that encourage and support collaborative work and activity. Collaboration must find its way into job descriptions as well as into rules and regulations governing employee responsibilities. Above all, it creates new expectations for administrative leaders including the competence to lead across many sectors of interest and responsibility. Moreover, it imposes extraordinary time demands in the work life of the enterprise. Despite such problems, as well as issues of turf and accountability, for example, it is clear that interinstitutional cooperation has to occur pending the reconstitution of public and private institutions that will bring them into closer correspondence with human need.

Concluding Statement

Educational administration is a turbulent field in a hostile environment. Historic images of administrators "in control" and "in charge" are dimming if not closed. Administrators of the past were busy managing people and resources, addressing problems routinely, satisfying parents and other constituencies, concentrating on budgets, buildings, and buses, and somehow sustaining themselves through many years of professional service. This is less the case now, although traditional administrative tasks still must be done.

It is not our intent to belittle the traditional work of administrative leaders. Instead, the authors of this volume attempt to take a fresh look at the challenges for educational leadership in a changing world. Broad and deep cultural patterns shape the study and practice of educational administration. As a subject of scholarly study it no longer can afford applications of paradigms and perspectives from other behavioral sciences. We must explore more deeply and more rigorously how administrators and administrative action influence real life in real schools. As a field of professional practice, educational administration can no longer afford false dichotomies such as labor and management or home and school. Educational leaders for tomorrow's schools must be equipped to embrace paradox and to seek opportunity as society despairs over another lost generation. We trust this volume provides something new to consider for the sake of children and families on the margin of societal transformation.

FOOTNOTES

1. Carnegie Task Force on Teaching as a Profession, *A Nation Prepared: Teachers for the 21st Century* (New York: Carnegie Forum on Education and the Economy, 1986); Carnegie Council on Adolescent Development, *Turning Points: Preparing Youth for the 21st Century* (New York: Carnegie Corporation, 1989).

2. Daniel E. Griffiths, Robert T. Stout, and Patrick B. Forsyth, eds., *Leaders for America's Schools: The Report and Papers of the National Commission on Excellence in Educational Administration* (Berkeley, CA: McCutchan Publishing Corp., 1988).

3. National Policy Board for Educational Administration, *Improving the Preparation of School Administrators* (Charlottesville, VA: University of Virginia, 1989).

4. Mario D. Fantini and Robert L. Sinclair, "Linking School and Nonschool Education: Public Policy Considerations," in *Education in School and Nonschool Settings*, ed. Mario D. Fantini and Robert L. Sinclair, Eighty-fourth Yearbook of the National Society for the Study of Education, Part I (Chicago: University of Chicago Press, 1985).

5. Ibid., p. 267.

6. Committee for Economic Development, *Investing in Our Children, Executive Summary* (Washington, DC: Committee for Economic Development, 1986), p. 1.

7. Ibid., pp. 5-6.

8. Ibid.

9. Business-Higher Education Forum, *American Potential: The Human Dimension* (Washington, DC: American Council on Education, 1988), p. 9.

10. Ibid., p. 2.

11. Raymond E. Callahan, *Education and the Cult of Efficiency* (Chicago: University of Chicago Press, 1962).

12. Ibid., p. 244.

13. Commission on Work, Family, and Citizenship, *The Forgotten Half: Pathways to Success for America's Youth and Young Families* (Washington, DC: William T. Grant Foundation Commission on Work, Family, and Citizenship, 1988).

14. Ibid., p. 1.

15. W. Norton Grubb, *Young Children Face the States: Issues and Options for Early Childhood Programs* (New Brunswick, NJ: Center for Policy Research in Education, Rutgers University, 1987).

16. Andrew Hahn, Jacqueline Danzberger, and Bernard Lefkowitz, *Dropouts in America: Enough Is Known for Action* (Washington, DC: Institute for Educational Leadership, 1987).

17. William T. Grant Foundation, *New Partnerships: Education's Stake in the Family Support Act of 1988* (Washington, DC: William T. Grant Foundation), p. 9.

18. Vincent Ostrom, "Education and Politics," in *Social Forces Influencing Education*, ed. Ralph W. Tyler, Sixtieth Yearbook of the National Society for the Study of Education, Part 2 (Chicago: University of Chicago Press, 1961), p. 26.

19. Ibid., p. 30.

20. National Commission on Excellence in Education, *A Nation at Risk: The Imperative for Educational Reform* (Washington, DC: U.S. Government Printing Office, 1983).

21. National Governors' Association, *Time for Results* (Washington, DC: National Governors' Association, 1986).

22. Thomas B. Timar and David L. Kirp, "Education Reform in the 1980s: Lessons from the States," *Phi Delta Kappan* 70 (March 1989): 504-511.

23. Committee on Policy for Racial Justice, *Visions of a Better Way: A Black Appraisal of Public Schooling* (Washington, DC: Joint Center for Political Studies, 1988).

24. Ibid., p. 31.

25. Thomas B. Corcoran, Lisa J. Walker, and J. Lynne White, *Working in Urban Schools* (Washington, DC: Institute for Educational Leadership, 1988), p. 127.

26. Joshua Meyrowitz, "The Adultlike Child and the Childlike Adult: Socialization in an Electronic Age," *Daedalus* 113 (Summer 1984): 44.

27. Edgar H. Schein, *Professional Education* (New York: McGraw-Hill Book Co., 1972), chap. 2.

28. Edith Blakeslee Phelps, "Youth Groups and Agencies," in *Toward Adolescence: The Middle School Years*, ed. Mauritz Johnson, Seventy-ninth Yearbook of the National Society for the Study of Education, Part 1 (Chicago: University of Chicago Press, 1980), pp. 111-113.

29. Frederick R. Cyphert and Luvern L. Cunningham, "Interprofessional Education and Practice: A Future Agenda," *Theory Into Practice* 26 (Spring 1987): 153-156.

Section Two
CHILDREN, YOUTH, AND
EDUCATIONAL LEADERSHIP

CHAPTER II

Loss, Belonging, and Becoming: Social Policy Themes for Children and Schools

BRAD MITCHELL

We humans tend to believe our lives follow certain patterns. As we see others age and as we grow older, we sense changes in physiological and cognitive development. It seems we are born to mature. Western society in particular, seems infatuated with issues of physical and mental hygiene and "healthy" human development. The transformation of the human condition is a prevailing theme in the arts, literature, and the social sciences. Some would argue that human development is the root metaphor of the social sciences.[1] Certainly, the maturation of humankind pervades the work of the great social scientists of the industrial age—Charles Darwin, Karl Marx, Adam Smith, John Dewey, Frederick Taylor, Jean Piaget, Margaret Mead, and Max Weber.

The broad and growing spectrum of social scientific inquiry provides a diversity of perspectives on one bedrock phenomenon—human development. Levels of analysis may vary from individual to collective development. Operational definitions about aspects of human development often differ as to what distinguishes a child from an adult or growth from maturation. Yet, the concept of development still dominates the traditional social science disciplines—economics, psychology, sociology, history, political science, anthropology, and education.

Economists often attempt to chronicle and assess trends in decisions regarding resources in order to predict how an organizational, industrial, local, regional, national, or international economy is "developing." Economic indicators such as gross national product and money market flows are designed to provide benchmarks on the growth and the stability of a nation's economy. Psychologists probe the physiological and psychological attributes of human behavior in order to understand how well a person is "maturing." Mental health indicators such as substance abuse rates and treated mental disorders are used to size up the nation's psychological well-being. Political scientists scan the polity in order to describe how the battle over power and influence is "evolving." Voter participation rates, socioeconomic status, residence, age, and gender, often are correlated to determine whose interests must be served before the next election. Sociologists explore issues of collective cohesiveness and security in order to gauge how well society is "shaping up." Crime rates and delinquency indices often are analyzed to discover any potential threats to public safety and community progress. Historians and anthropologists strive to make sense of changes in the human condition over time and space. Cultural artifacts such as books, tools, architecture, and graves provide these social scientists with indicators about how and how well individuals or groups lived out their lives.

We educators tend to seek out and apply a wide array of analytic perspectives. The study of the teaching and learning process, as well as of the physical, emotional, and cognitive development of children and youth, slices across the social science disciplines. However, regardless of which social science paradigm is used, educators identify academic performance as the fundamental litmus test for every student's progress through the educational system.

Growth, transformation, maturation, evolution, and progress are all synonyms for development. Why has this one concept monopolized how we look at our individual and collective lives? It often has been suggested that angst over our own mortality forces us to focus on human development.[2] Through critical and continuous self-inquiry, it is presumed that we might discover the mystery of our existence. Closely related to this argument is the notion that the scientific study of how humans grow might produce knowledge that will allow us to control nature[3] and conquer death. At the very least, inquiry about the nature of being human enables us to cope with some of life's most nagging anxieties—ambiguity about role relationships and requirements, necessity of performing unpleasant tasks, and uncertainty about the unfolding text of one's own life.[4]

Essentially, the modern interpretation of human development rests upon three rather simple themes—loss, belonging, and becoming. Human growth and maturation is judged largely on how one confronts change (loss), relates to others (belonging), and seeks the future (becoming). Images of loss, belonging, and becoming have sculpted both our vision of human development and our efforts to build a better world through social policy.[5] Moreover, schools and schooling are the cultural inventions[6] through which our society deals with the more problematic outcomes associated with the interplay of loss, belonging, and becoming. Somehow over the past 150 years, the mission of public schools came to be understood as repairing debilitating loss, promoting the right forms of belonging, and creating an acceptable sense of becoming. Many of the tensions and paradoxes educational leaders face today arise from the fusion and fission of these three themes of social policy and human development.

I am interested in how images of loss, belonging, and becoming are shaping social policy and school reform in late twentieth-century America. In particular, I want to explore what challenges the collusion and collision of these three themes place on educational leaders for tomorrow's schools. Thus, this chapter is organized as follows: (a) a critical explanation and examination of loss, belonging, and becoming as central themes in human development and social policy for public education; (b) a look at the implications of these three themes on how we govern, administer, and operate public schools; and (c) a discussion of how recent social policy and school reform responses to loss, belonging, and becoming relate to the sociohistorical pursuit of educational equity and excellence.

Loss, Belonging, and Becoming: Humanity at the Crossroads?

Why can't things be like they were? Does anybody love me? Do I belong here? Why am I alive? What purpose do I serve? What am I seeking? Such questions creep inside virtually everybody's lived experience. As Judith Viorst wryly writes in her best-selling book, *Necessary Losses*,[7] the lives of human beings are marked by a series of painful, yet necessary, losses. For example, marriage designates the dissolution of one family and the creation of a new one.

A cultural emphasis on loss often is related to an infatuation with being at risk. We are a nation attracted to risk. We have grown to seek out and embrace threat. The evening news constantly reminds us of the various risks we have accepted in our lives without breaking stride—acid rain, AIDS, earthquakes, terrorism, stock market crashes, high cholesterol. Where once we participated in slumber parties on Friday nights, the modern teen generation holds slasher parties. Blood and gore ooze out of our video tape machines as we order pizza and rent teen mutilation movies with titles such as "I Spit on Your Grave," "Horror High," and "Nightmare on Elm Street." The love of risk usually evolves from a sense of loss. We feel separated from our parents and our children. We believe the former mortgaged the latter's future while we helplessly watched. We grieve the separation from the prosperous future promised us by our elders. Loss dominates our point of view on belonging and becoming. How can we belong in a world that has lost any sense of common destiny? How can we yearn to become something in a time that teeters on the threat of instant destruction? The loss of a sense of personal authority to make a difference quickens the retreat to bureaucracy. Let us rely on the reliable other—a predetermined, prestructured cornucopia of ordered roles and relations. We face an AIDS epidemic? No problem. We shall have the surgeon general lead the education and public health bureaucracies in a swift and efficient organizational response. We face a drug abuse epidemic? No problem. We shall have the president appoint a drug czar to lead the education and law enforcement bureaucracies in a swift and efficient organizational response. We face a homeless epidemic? No problem. We shall have the Secretary of Health and Human Services lead a swift and efficient organizational response. Of course, none of these actions would be necessary if we had not lost a sense of sexual responsibility and civic virtue.

Why worry about loss? Why do we strive so diligently to protect ourselves from the inevitability of loss? Are we raising children who numb themselves to the prospect of loss? Is it not a natural outcome of human development and social progress? Why do we not celebrate loss? Spring does always follow winter. As the clouds empty, rainbows appear. In order to belong we must lose a sense of personal identity. In order to become we must separate ourselves somewhat from what we once were. Why such a knee-jerk reaction to loss? Why is it such a dominant theme in human development and social policy?

Rapid and repeated episodes of loss often lead to surplus powerlessness.[8] In other words, instead of coping with recurring loss, we choose to ignore it. The psychological and sociological repercussions of such a behavioral response promote a cultural mindset of fatalism and disempowerment. Instead of understanding loss, we eschew it. Instead of learning from loss, we develop pathological behaviors of powerlessness. A sense that it can never be as good as it once was dooms the next generation, the becoming generation, to a legacy of surplus powerlessness. There is no resilient sense of empowerment in a culture obsessed with notions of economic, civic, and moral mortality.

Loss cannot be confronted in a vacuum. It must be tied with efforts to belong and to become. We perceive loss when we feel we do not belong or something does not belong. We perceive loss when we recognize that what we wish to become is not possible. Certainly, as Viorst reminds us, there are necessary losses in the journey of belonging and becoming. A grown child no longer belongs to the parent in the same way but such a shift in relational status is necessary for the next step of becoming. Yet an unhealthy fixation on loss impedes belonging and becoming. A teenager who loses a close friend to suicide may experience disconnection from others and from the future. The avoidance of a related suicide comes not only from just managing the sense of profound loss, but also from the cultivation of conditions that enhance the prospects of a renewed sense of belonging and becoming.

A sense of belonging often is a very important factor in how and how well we deal with loss. There is security in belonging. Humans can deal with losses such as death, physical illness, and professional failure as long as they know they belong to someone or something. Thus, loss and belonging often weave together as life unravels. Belonging and becoming are aligned as well. The security inherent to belonging may allow and encourage one to take the risks associated with becoming. Attentive parents know how much children need to feel support before they can be challenged to become something more. The ties between belonging and becoming used to rely heavily on factors such as age, sex, race, religion, and birthplace. If one belonged to the "right" age group, gender type, race, religion, or community, then the "right" destiny would prevail. Labels of belonging, such as blue collar and white collar or the red bird and blue bird reading group, once were very influential in what the future might bring.

Today, there is really only one widely recognized factor that shapes belonging and becoming—knowledge and the capacity to use it. Knowledge workers[9] do not belong to an organization because of where they were born or the presence or absence of a Y chromosome.

Unlike our fathers and mothers and their fathers and mothers, we can deal in the coin of the realm without concern over who we are, where we come from, whom we know, and what we look like. Supposedly, all we need for economic success in a postindustrial age is a mastery of a specialized knowledge base and the capacity to learn. In a high tech world, our bodies *become* more and more separated from our work.[10] One no longer has to belong to become and no one has to become something in order to belong. A hyper-technical world may finally bring a classless society but the price may be the abandonment (or loss) of traditional and vibrant forms of belonging.

Of course, America will continue to have its share of haves and have nots, but failure to *become* one of the haves will not be due to traditional barriers such as racial discrimination, rigid social hierarchies, or chauvinism. Instead, fault will be placed primarily on the individual's initiative and partially on genetic heritage. Especially this will be the case if we truly reform the American education system and make it capable of effectively and efficiently producing all the knowledge workers needed for a national, regional, and global competitive economy.

In a strange twist of logic, the classic American dream has not been lost. The old admonition still rings true: work hard in school and you shall become economically successful. The difference now is that the pursuit of the American dream is no longer a matter of choice, but an act of survival. In a highly competitive global economy where the only real edge is knowledge, governments feel compelled to compel all their citizens to seek, serve, and create new knowledge. The pursuit of national economic interest becomes the main reason for belonging.

Peter Drucker, in his most recent book, *The New Realities*, points out that prior to the industrial age most people sought salvation through faith. In a caustic world where one could experience profound loss without any sense of hope, religious faith served as a tonic for troubled souls. There was great solace from a belief in an afterlife free of loss, full of joyous belonging and perfect becoming. A troublesome potential consequence of the salvation-by-faith mentality is an insensitivity to some of the more difficult dilemmas inherent to our poisoned and turbulent planet. In their 1989 book, *New World New Mind*, authors Ornstein and Ehrlich speculate that a salvation-by-faith approach to life limits individual responsibility:

To this day some powerful monotheistic religions invoke God as an excuse for not facing and doing something about the changes that human beings have brought to the planet. Thousands of years after the pharaohs the concept of an afterlife still helps to slow the recognition of dangerously changing environments. It focuses the mind of the faithful on the fate of individuals in another world rather than on the fate of the life-support systems (and therefore of societies) in this one.[11]

Drucker also argues that the social dislocations associated with the industrial age forced people to seek out a new form of salvation. Belief in the "power of social action to create a perfect society"[12] became the new doctrine of becoming. The credo of salvation through perfect society helped boost Marxism as a serious political ideology by the last quarter of the nineteenth century. The basic tenets of Marx's scientific socialism called for an everlasting society, full of social and individual perfection.

By 1917, Vladimir Ilyich Lenin's vision of salvation by socialism uprooted Russian religious and governmental orthodoxy. The Soviet experiment was portrayed to the world as the natural and logical next phase in the laws of historical development—a system of community based on "infallible" methods of problem resolution and future planning. Throughout Russian society, almost overnight, Lenin's portrait replaced candle-lit religious icons. It was a visual reminder framed in red bunting that salvation by faith had given way to salvation by society. Yet, three generations later the rhetoric of "Perestroika" seeps through the world's capitols and even the prospect of a "Soviet style" perfect society seems grounded on the rocks of short-term economic interest.

Acceptance of Peter Drucker's basic argument leads one to conclude that we now face a void in how we commonly conceive the interplay of loss, belonging, and becoming. Salvation by faith and salvation by society lack any real power as day-to-day creeds for living even though there has been some resurgence in church going and community volunteerism over the past decade.[13] Such trends tend to be faint echoes of lost crusades. Peter Drucker is not optimistic about how the void might be filled. He writes:

There may well be new messianic movements. The disappearance of the belief in salvation by society and in the second coming of a secular revolution may call forth new prophets and new messiahs. But these new messianic movements are likely to be anti-society and based on the assertion that there can be salvation only outside society, only in and through the person, perhaps even only in and through withdrawal from society.[14]

Salvation by "knowledge workers" seems to be the most likely candidate to breach the abyss left by the collapse of Lyndon Johnson's "Great Society." The perfection of the individual as an entity capable of synthesizing, analyzing, and creating knowledge over and over again is quite an attractive option. The world faces an energy shortage due to capricious use of finite resources? Find two knowledge workers in the mountains of Utah who have discovered a cold fusion process to rid the globe of any energy concerns as long as plentiful water supplies exist. People are dying of heart attacks due to poor eating habits and the ingestion of nicotine? Find a new wave and flamboyant doctor who has discovered a way to build an artificial heart that can run on two "C" batteries. The two superpowers have built a nuclear arsenal capable of destroying the world a million times over? Find physicists across the nation who are willing to take billions of federal dollars in the search for a strategic defense technology that will zap nuclear missiles in the vacuum of space. Salvation by knowledge worker makes faith in a trouble free afterlife and belief in a perfect society seem almost too limiting. The creation of knowledge capital on demand is widely seen as the salvation of a planet depleted in natural resources and rich in the gleeful pursuit of economic self-interest.

Earth supports some 300 million tons of people.[15] The Soviet Union and the United States house roughly twenty-five thousand strategic nuclear warheads combined.[16] Threats to the planet's ecological balance abound—acid rain, depletion of the ozone layer, build-up of CO_2 (the greenhouse effect), oil spills, unmanageable toxic waste, pesticides, and the destruction of African and South American rainforests. Robert Ornstein and Paul Ehrlich discuss the issue of world salvation not in terms of religious faith and perfect society, but in terms of changed perceptions. They write:

Humanity, until very recently, lived almost entirely on its "income"—on solar energy captured by green plants in fields, on farms, and in forests by the process of photosynthesis. Now, thanks to cultural evolution, humanity is living largely on its "capital"—nonrenewable resources. Homo sapiens was the recipient of a one time bonanza whose use has shaped our societies and attitudes as nothing ever did before. The capital that we inherited included fossil fuels, high grade mineral ores, rich agricultural soils, ground water stored up during the ice ages, and above all, the millions of other species that inhabit the Earth along with us. Our total inheritance took billions of years to assemble; it is being squandered in decades.[17]

Essentially, Ornstein and Ehrlich argue that humans and human collectives take a short-term, reactionary perspective when confronted with a dramatic threat to their security (i.e., a perceived potential loss to how they want to belong and what they want to become). Ornstein and Ehrlich suggest we are "losing control of our future"[18] because our biological and cultural patterns of evolution favor the attributes of limited perception and quick reflexes. Our capacity to transform the world is quickly outdistancing our ability to understand it. In other words, we are not conditioned to "see" the repercussions on our own well-being of the death of a tropical rainforest—a place thousands of miles away most of us have never visited and perhaps never will. Our systems of perception and our world are mismatched.[19] Despite mounting nuclear arsenals popping up all around the world, we assume that the fail-safe mechanisms of yesterday will work for tomorrow. Our cultural codes of living tell us the best way to confront the threat of loss is to assume the future will be like the past. New threats may emerge, but our responses to them remain remarkably the same. We readily accept traditional notions of loss, belonging, and becoming because they help us cope with threats to personal and planetary development. We employ images of loss, belonging, and becoming to "caricature"[20] reality.

In an age where humanity knows it has the knowledge to annihilate itself almost instantaneously, simple and superficial portraits of short-term realities are highly prized. How many of us have purchased a commodity where we saw advertising claiming that only a few items remained? Was there ever really a shortage of Cabbage Patch dolls? We elect presidents and other governmental leaders who promise immediate economic growth (becoming), no new taxes (loss), and guaranteed social security (belonging) even though the nation faces huge budgetary and trade deficits. The nightly news shows a shattered DC-10 in an Iowa cornfield, so we switch our reservations to airlines with fleets of 727s but we continue to fly and we pass through metal detectors at the airport with little thought of why they are there. As the 727 lumbers down the runway the image of the Iowa cornfield recedes in the mist of memory and we look toward our destination with a renewed sense of confidence.

Loss, Belonging, and Becoming: Salvation by Education

Every culture must deal with loss, belonging, and becoming or face the risk of regression, if not extinction. In order to grow and develop, individuals, groups, communities, states, and nations must feel secure. Numerous theories of human development[21] point to the critical importance security plays in the shaping of self. The integrity of personhood generally depends on how and how well loss is experienced, relationships are formed, and future opportunities are envisioned. Schools and schooling often are the key cultural inventions used to transmit appropriate signs of loss, belonging, and becoming. This is especially the case where families or other traditional institutions of belonging (e.g., churches, clubs, workplaces, community organizations) are perceived as too weak and fragmented to nurture and maintain "social capital."[22]

Drucker in *The New Realities* and Ornstein and Ehrlich in *New World New Mind* place education on the pedestal of global transformation. Salvation by education is promoted by the authors as the rightful successor to salvation by faith and salvation by society. In a world where knowledge rules, the process of education becomes the ultimate supplier of power. Drucker notes: "An economy in which knowledge is becoming the true capital and the premier wealth-producing resource makes new and stringent demands on the schools for educational performance and educational responsibility."[23] Since the 1983 release of *A Nation at Risk*, more and more civic, business, political, and educational leaders have accepted the maxim of "economic salvation through educational excellence." American society has become quite sensitive to an immediate scarcity of capable knowledge workers. This sense of impending loss has prompted considerable school reform activity, which in turn has started to reshape opportunities for student belonging and student becoming. For example, several states are considering legislation to reduce the welfare benefits of the parent if the child does not attend school within acceptable guidelines. This form of forced education shares the same logic of the compulsory attendance laws enacted over a hundred years ago at the pinnacle of the industrial revolution—the perceived economic need for competent workers supercedes certain individual rights and privileges.

Ornstein and Ehrlich's call for educational renewal is based on a different logic. They want to "take a fresh look at how we are educating our young"[24] in order to save the planet. In fact, the rationale for needing to sustain economic prosperity expressed in *A Nation at Risk* and *The New Realities* is seen by Ornstein and Ehrlich as "old mindedness" and constitutes the real threat to spaceship Earth. They encourage all those who "pray at the altar of perpetual growth"[25] to rethink the ultimate consequences of excessive resource exploitation and material acquisition. Thus, Ornstein and Ehrlich desire an educational system that cultivates "new minded" approaches to loss, belonging, and becoming. They suggest that instead of being so sensitive to immediate personal and economic loss, we should be educated to look at long-term, collective well-being. Instead of accepting traditional patterns of belonging (e.g., gender stereotyping and socioeconomic status), they argue for an educational system that teaches how human evolutionary and social history has shaped different human minds differently. Instead of promoting the belief that the future is a simplified caricature of past realities (e.g., new technologies will be invented to handle any threats to health, safety, and happiness), they seek a curriculum that will empower a society to adapt to loss more through critical cultural evolution rather than through blind faith in technological wizardry.

Ornstein and Ehrlich want an educational system where loss, belonging, and becoming are walking sticks that help people make adaptive responses to new situations in difficult terrain instead of "default switches" that ignore the negative consequences of unfettered economic progress. The curriculum they propose focuses on humanity and not prosperity. At the close of their chapter on educational reform, they write:

There is now enough material from studies of human development; cognitive psychology; decision analysis and the physical, biological and social sciences in general to develop a new curriculum to deal with the problems of the new world. The basic tools are already available, albeit often buried in irrelevant material. The key goal of a new curriculum will be to encourage students to think about the nature of their own minds and the limitations on their own thinking, about underlying physical and biological principles that govern the world, and about long-term trends in that world, as easily and as continuously possible in their schooling . . . So refashioning how people are educated could have enormous import for the future of our species.[26]

Whether you accept the logic proposed by Drucker or by Ornstein and Ehrlich is not as important as the recognition that both points of view call for a renewed look at how the human development and social policy themes of loss, belonging, and becoming should be manifested in the formal education of children and youth. Drucker sees this endeavor as important in order to perpetuate American ideology and interests in a "transnational" world.[27] Ornstein and Ehrlich perceive the issue as one of global justice and human grace.

Regardless of which viewpoint gains the most popularity, educational leaders must address the new realities a new world places on old-minded schools.

LOSS AND PUBLIC EDUCATION

In an incisive and provocative article, David Cohen explored the role of loss in the historical development of social policy for public education. Cohen particularly probed how a sense of lost community spurred the growth of public schooling during the mid-to-late nineteenth century. He observed:

Beginning in the second quarter of the nineteenth century there developed an acute sense that society was coming unstrung, that common values and cohesive institutions were eroding. This sense of loss powerfully influenced social policy. It evoked the belief that families were failing and produced efforts to shore them up or to replace them with new institutions. . . . It evoked the belief that primary institutions—families, churches, and communities—had lost their ability to pass a common culture along and this became a powerful inspiration for the development of public education.[28]

Over a century later, policymakers are still preoccupied with portraits of lost community, lost family cohesiveness, and a lost generation of disconnected children and youth. On the campaign trail to the 1988 presidential election, George Bush announced he was haunted by the loss of hope in the eyes of inner-city youth he met. We believe we have lost many things in the twentieth century: the stable and nurturing family, full-time motherhood, childhood innocence, cohesive community, winnable wars, rugged individualism, virtuous political leadership, personal responsibility, the middle class, separate gender roles, true religions, economic competitiveness, and schools that make a difference. Popular literature tells us to accept our losses as natural conditions of modern life (e.g., Viorst's *Necessary Losses*), to return to a sense of spiritual commitment and responsibility (e.g., Robert Bellah's *Habits of the Heart*) or to rediscover a sense of community (e.g., Scott Peck's *A Different Drum*).[29]

E.D. Hirsch's phenomenal 1987 best seller, *Cultural Literacy*,[30] laments the loss of a commonly held common culture in modern pluralistic America. The pursuit of cultural literacy is a monotonous refrain in American history. As the new home for millions of immigrants and scores of ethnic and racial groups, the United States has had to build mutual order out of a pluralistic chaos time and time again. The immigrant's experience in a new world is full of a sense of loss. Loss usually is associated with being separated from something or someone. Loss also is an inevitable condition of change and modernization.

As Cohen pointed out, American social policy has tended to confront numerous forms of loss through the establishment or reestablishment of tradition and order. The public school system historically has been perceived as the efficient and effective conduit of tradition and order because of its compulsory nature and its bureaucratic ethos. Throughout American history and particularly in the last forty years, policymakers have turned to the public schools to rectify any damages associated with real loss or the risk of loss. The GI Bill helped America cope when the end of World War II brought a loss of employment for massive numbers of ablebodied young men. The Elementary and Secondary Education Act of 1965 bolstered governmental authority in an era where discriminatory social policy lost legitimacy and the social order experienced radical ruptures. The "excellence in education" reform movement of the 1980s came at a time when demographic realities clearly told America it could no longer afford to lose the potential economic contributions of children from economically impoverished families. Cohen was right: a national sense of loss and social policy for public education have formed a double helix bond in the sociohistorical development of modern America.

Educational leaders must deal with loss all the time. The loss of academic standards. The loss of the common core curriculum. The loss of teacher authority, principal authority, school authority, parental authority. The loss of nonunionized angels of teaching virtue. The loss of large numbers of households with school-age children. The loss of local control. The loss of middle- and upper-class student talent to private education. The loss of public and policymaker confidence in public education. The loss of safe schools free from the threat of mass murderers. The loss of children and youth to substance abuse, suicide, teenage parenthood, gangs, prisons, hotels for the homeless, and illiteracy. How do educational leaders respond to loss? More bureaucratic control and accountability? More support services and less coordination? A return to tradition? An expansion of equality?

Virtually every principal and superintendent is hired under a context of loss. The calls for fresh leadership tend to follow certain scripts. Parents decry the loss of order and control in the school and they seek stronger leadership, especially on matters of student discipline. Board members sense a loss of control of the district to the teachers' union so they embark on a quest for a "no-nonsense, pro-board" superintendent. The public loses confidence in the ability of the schools to produce desired outcomes. Local business leaders bemoan the decline in the numbers of "employable" high school graduates. School reformers suggest the public schools have lost a common sense of direction and purpose.

Even in good, or so-called effective schools, a transition in upper or middle management usually is accompanied by a fear of not wanting to lose hard fought gains. The new superintendent might not support a recently implemented testing program. The new principal might not maintain multigrade teaching assignments. Board members may not want to risk losing the rapport that management has established with teachers. The rookie principal must not initiate drastic changes early lest she risk alienating a highly qualified and committed staff.

The management of public schools has been and continues to be predicated on identifying and dealing with discrete episodes of loss. Loss, by itself, is not necessarily a dysfunctional problem frame.[31] Concerns arise, however, when attention on loss unduly displaces attention on gain. Educational leadership oriented to loss minimizes risk and seeks a quick return to stability. Gain-oriented leadership finds opportunity in risk and pursues long-term development. Regardless of the leadership orientation, the management of loss remains the central function of educational administration.

Teacher contract negotiations often are acts of managing loss. Management representatives and union leaders usually enter the negotiation process reflecting on what they lost or failed to gain in the last master contract agreement. In order to maintain or regain legitimacy with their respective constituents, they seek recovery. Unfortunately, recovery is not renewal. Recovery is short-sighted and old-minded. Recovery fits our cultural obsession with loss but it is deadly for just and proactive educational reform and for social evolution. Many superintendents fear losing credibility with the school board, especially when master contracts are up for renewal. Thus, it is not in the vested self-interest of superintendents to be perceived as pro teacher. Yet, even a superintendent labeled as pro teacher can overcome the stigma by consistently espousing classic union caricatures such as teacher militancy, excessive self-interest, and protectionism.

A perceived loss in school order and control is perhaps the principal's greatest and most frequent fear. A typical response is to purchase authority. Mass locker searches bring the authority of uniformed and armed law enforcement officials inside the academically disordered world of a drug-infested high school. Lost authority may push the principal to purchase more off-duty police for the football games, more former professional athletes for antidrug talks at school assemblies, more isolation boxes for unruly students. Unfortunately, real authority cannot be purchased. A school culture must be cultivated where a sense of direction is clear, personal responsibility is common and quality control is paramount.[32]

The organizing principle of schooling is knowledge of loss. How much has student A retained of subject B from grade C to grade D? How many days has student E been absent? (Due to school finance formulas, most schools lose funding when attendance rates drop.) Which students with deficient competencies will be placed in whose classrooms? Which teachers do not have lesson plans on file? How many children in the school lack sufficient language and literacy skills? For whatever reasons, public schools in America focus on the weakness or deficits of learners and teachers rather than their strengths. The pace of curriculum and the assessment of student performance is usually a function of the perception of what is missing or lacking. Drucker observes:

When teachers call in the parents of a ten-year-old, they usually say: "Your Jimmy has to work on the multiplication tables. He is way behind." They rarely say: "Your Mary should do a good deal more writing to do even better what she already does well."[33]

A consistent and well-documented finding from child development research is that performance cannot be based on attention to weaknesses; performance is built on recognized strengths.[34] Moreover, child development experts tend to agree that the recursive attitudes expressed by adults about a child's performance largely shape the child's image of his or her performance capability.[35] In other words, a child learns to believe and accept the opinions adults hold about him or her. Students tend to perform as they are construed. How many times has the labeled "slow learner" lived up to the expressed expectation? On the other hand, children who are the most verbally articulate receive a disproportionate share of the teacher's verbal interaction and therefore become even more articulate.[36] Thus, a school system, school, or classroom that focuses on loss in order to build performance places the learner at a developmental disadvantage and threatens to reduce the desire to learn. Unfortunately, the current school reform movement is awash in a sense of loss—declining test scores, capable females and minorities seeking occupations besides education, rising illiteracy rates. The natural response is to tighten the curriculum and standardize pedagogical practice. Yet, child development research tells us there is a greater chance of a student feeling incompetent when exposed to a narrow curriculum and dogmatic instruction.[37]

One only needs to review accountability and assessment policies and practices to discover that we govern and organize public schools around the notion of loss. As goes evaluation, so goes the curriculum. Numerous types of students have experienced the negative consequences of an unreasonable orientation on loss—females, minorities, native Americans, children with special needs. America can no longer afford to lose these children, who, like all children, deserve an educational experience that exploits their strengths rather than their weaknesses.

Educational leaders must become more aware of how a cultural sense of loss shapes social policy for public education. A bit of critical scrutiny is needed to ensure that a loss mentality will not direct rhythms and patterns of human growth and development. If educational leaders truly want to affect the future, especially in the nurturance and education of children, then they must forge the political will to confront an American culture obsessed with notions of loss and deficiency. They also must value and consult child development research when they attempt to restructure school organization, curriculum, and pedagogy. They might consider the wisdom Margaret Mead provided the world nearly forty years ago:

By recognizing that Americans will reach for solutions that are optimistic and open-ended, will repudiate suggestions that are limiting, will tend to see things in black-or-white terms, often simply reversing a past position rather than arriving at a higher level of abstraction—by recognizing all this we can build a new climate of opinion in which we shall be able to include, simultaneously, the recognition of the regularity of the growth process for all human beings, the regularities of the cultural process within each culture and the individuality with which each human being has grown with his particular physical endowment within his particular culture, his particular period of history, and his particular situation.

We can then ask, out of knowledge of these processes, and out of our twentieth-century American hope for an open-ended and improving world, whether we can devise pediatric and educational procedures that will make it possible for adults who understand their culture and the limitations it lays upon them to bring up children who will be as much stronger, as much more aware, than their parents as they will need to be if they are to carry the load of developing a world community.[38]

An awareness of loss coupled with an awareness of child and cultural development will empower educational leaders to help mold just and hopeful social policy for public education. Children, especially children who live on the margins of society, have nothing more to lose.

BELONGING AND PUBLIC EDUCATION

Culture begins when people form groups. For tens of thousands of years humans lived in small groups where everybody knew everyone else and understood his or her relationships to others. Even though they led distinctive lives, they all knew basically the same things and they could keep track of virtually all the relationships among the group. Under such a context, our early ancestors could clearly and precisely answer the question: Who cares for me and for whom should I care? Tribal relations were predicated on a universally known sense of belonging. Rituals, symbols, and ceremonies were created and sustained in order to ensure group cohesion and individual loyalty. It is interesting to note that the average size of the prehistoric village ranged around 100 people—the same number of people that sociologists identify as the maximum number with whom a human being can reasonably interact beyond a superficial level.[39] In many high schools, teachers must interact with between 120 and 180 students each day. Moreover, it is hard to imagine one person (i.e., the principal) keeping track of the 12 million possible relationships between 5,000 people—the size of some high schools in large cities.[40]

Understanding the dynamics of belonging is an essential attribute of leadership. Yet, factors such as group size may not allow even the most resourceful and tenacious leader to build a solid set of productive and interdependent relations. Of course, the bureaucratic organizational structure was invented as a rational response to the dilemmas associated with large-scale human population and uncertain role relationships and requirements. Max Weber's description of the prototype bureaucracy came from his studies of the highly populated Prussian army and Catholic Church.[41] Weber found that in the face of multiple and multiplying social interactions, people seek security and constancy. Bureaucracy, like any organizational form, designs patterns of belonging. Rosabeth Moss Kanter notes:

The ideal typical bureaucracy, in order to secure rational control and reliability, is built on security, routinization, fixity of procedure, and constancy of stimuli and response. By such mechanisms as the regularization of promotion, the instituting of tenure and seniority, and generally fixed wages and salary which are unrelated to financial fluctuations and only slightly related to individual performance, the organization eliminates sources of uncertainty and inconstancy.[42]

Public schools, in general, are run like bureaucracies. With over 37 million students and 3 million adult employees, the American public school system faces enormous challenges in the creation and maintenance of patterns of belonging. Techniques of bureaucratic management have enabled public schools to put diverse people with different skills and knowledge through a common socialization process. In a phenomenological sense, bureaucratized schools value and shape "other-directed" learners who are more interested in what others think of them and in how they fit in the web of interpersonal relationships than in fulfilling personal achievement needs and wants.[43] This description of the American schooling experience runs counter to the long-espoused cultural creed of rugged individualism. The idealized American self as a lone wolf ready to compete with anyone is not highly prized in the public school bureaucracy. In Japan, the concept of personhood is based on a definition of self that is more "other-sensitive" than "other-directed." "Kanjin shugi" is the Japanese phrase for the definition of self in terms of interpersonal relations.[44] Japanese culture stresses that the individual's identity is determined by the nature and quality of reciprocal relationships. The need for personal achievement is not tied to seeking acceptance but to gaining respect from significant others.

The essential imperative for a proper sense of belonging in an American public school is to be other-directed and to promote the efficacy and effectiveness of the collective. The collective can be the classroom, the school, the peer group, the academic department, or a host of other subgroups related to the public school bureaucracy. The modern public school employs a variety of strategies and tactics that consistently compare learners against each other—normed achievement testing, grading on the curve, social promotion, ability grouping, graded reading levels, etc. Public schools also employ a number of bureaucratic ploys to reduce pressures to change existing rules, roles, and relationships—specialization and differentiation, collusion and the discouragement of personal responsibility.

Specialization and differentiation of curriculum and pedagogy allow the public school to make incremental adjustments to external demands or challenges. As James Thompson pointed out over a generation ago, complex organizations such as public schools accommodate change through increased specialization of functions and personnel.[45] For example, a decline in public confidence in the quality of secondary education prompted dozens of state legislatures to extend high school graduation requirements in math, science, English, and social studies and to expand the high school curriculum to include the new specialization of "computer literacy." Such a reform strategy focused discussion on structural additions to the public school bureaucracy and avoided, for at least a little while, any serious examination of the nature, purpose, and function of secondary education in America.

Bureaucratic organizations often try to coopt deviant or defiant individuals or subgroups. At a bare minimum, principals want students to attend school regularly, to comply to formal authority, and to place some attention on academic performance. It is widely assumed that students who fail to behave along these lines do not belong in the dominant culture of the school. The list of supposed deviant or defiant students traditionally included black males, progeny of "blue collar" families, native Americans, children and youth with special needs, and drug abusers. Public schools have dealt with these groups by either coopting them or excluding them. The strategy of bureaucratic collusion is not limited to just these groups of students. There is a rich vein of sociological studies of schools that clearly demonstrate the power and influence of student peer groups in shaping the schooling experience.[46] Several of these studies point to how the school bureaucracy works in collusion with student peer groups to maintain at least the resemblance of order and control.[47] Starting in elementary school, students seek to gain acceptance and recognition from their referent peer group, largely along lines of class and culture. By the age of adolescence, most students accord more status to their peer group than to their teachers.

In the last decade there have been several excellent descriptive studies of schools that touch on how the norms of bureaucratic life relate to the norms of peer group culture (e.g., Sara Lawrence Lightfoot's *The Good High School*, Peter McLaren's *Life in Schools*, Powell, Farrar, and Cohen's *The Shopping Mall High School*, Gerald Grant's *The World We Created at Hamilton High*, and Philip Cusick's *The Egalitarian Ideal and the American High School*.[48] These five studies make several salient points about how the interaction of bureaucracy and student peer groups largely determines the appropriate forms of belonging in public education. These points are:

1. The bureaucratic division of the school and school day allow students the time, space, and energy to build peer groups.

2. The meritocracy aspect of school bureaucracy· and the shared culture aspect of student peer groups largely reflect the resources and social status of parents.

3. As children grow older, their peer group role becomes more important than their student role.

4. Student peer groups, especially in grades 7-12, influence, if not control, the nature and scope of participation in many extracurricular activities.

5. Academic performance is not as strongly normed as bureaucratic compliance and peer group recognition. Academic success is not essential to belonging in the school bureaucracy or the referent peer group.

It is unclear whether or not educators can build learning communities where academic performance and individual creativity can overcome the bureaucratic and peer group norms that promote excessive forms of other directedness. Unlike the Japanese concept of kanjin shugi, the development of personhood in the American public school does not emphasize self-criticism and self-discovery through reciprocal and respectful relationships.

James Coleman sees modern American society as deficient in the social capital needed to raise strong, happy, and confident children. Social capital refers to "the norms, the social networks and the relationships between adults and children that are of value for the child's growing up."[49] Access to an abundance of social capital can provide children and youth with the kinds of attitudes, motivations, and conception of self they need to grow and develop. Social capital formulation depends on patterns of belonging that promote self-directedness and responsibility for others. It is unclear whether the norms of school bureaucracy and student peer group enhance or impede the creation of social capital.

We have learned from decades of child development research that children benefit substantially from a sense of continuity and constancy in their environment.[50] Children need a secure one-to-one relationship with a caring adult. As Urie Bronfenbrenner has repeatedly stated, children need someone who is crazy about them.[51] A continuous and consistent sense of interconnectedness is not a central feature in how we organize a student's total school experience. Children often are bumped from one grade to the next, one teacher to the next, and one subject to the next with little regard to their developmental need for continuity and consistency. Once again, principles of bureaucratic management win out over principles of child development.

Educational leaders must take a hard look at which norms of belonging dominate the public school experience of most students. Belonging based on mindless compliance or superficial acquaintance will not produce self-directed and highly motivated learners. As employees of a large public interest bureaucracy, we educators tend to lose sight of the delicate and intimate dimensions of human belonging. A "people processing" mentality can keep school administrators from openly discussing how structural and behavioral factors may inhibit a sense of belonging within and across students. Yet the development of interpersonal trust and reflective self-criticism is possible in schools. Lightfoot's search for good high schools uncovered a place where a strong and strongly cultivated sense of belonging allowed for institutional and individual criticism and discovery. She writes:

Among students, faculty and administrators there was a clear recognition of the unevenness and weakness of their school. Criticism was legitimized, even encouraged. The stark visibility of their institutional vulnerabilities was related to a deeply rooted tolerance for conflict, idealism, and feelings of security.[52]

Security comes through consistent and continuous nurturance of belonging. Norms of educational effectiveness such as a shared sense of purpose, self-directed learning, and attention on high quality academic work depend on building a collective sense of belonging. Neither bureaucratic norms nor student peer group norms fit well with a developmentally based approach to belonging. Size and resource efficiency concerns also limit the likelihood that every student will find a teacher who is crazy about him or her. In the past we could rely on many teachers to go beyond the job description and forge deep, continuous, and consistent relationships with students needing a boost in a personal sense of belonging. Today, however, many teachers do not develop such bonds with their students due to the fear of legal liabilities, burnout, excessive job demands, and union directives. Unfortunately, we now have more students who need the irrational involvement of caring adults. Educational leaders must pursue social policy strategies that allow and support greater teacher involvement in the lives of students and their families. Innovative experiments such as intervention assistance teams, on-site case workers, and parent education programs need to be implemented on a greater scale with appropriate shifts in teacher roles and responsibilities. For example, why can't career ladder programs allow some teachers to spend a bit less time in the classroom and provide leadership in home-school relations and family counseling?[53]

The development of a stronger sense of belonging is an important social policy theme for public education. Those who govern and administer schools must be willing to confront dysfunctional bureaucratic norms and to reshape teachers' work. Schools should not belong to bureaucrats nor should they belong to student peer groups divided according to class and culture. As an authentic learning community, the school must build an ethos where belonging revolves around the norms of shared purpose, self-directed learning, and critical reflection.[54] Of course, the essence of human belonging really comes down to the constant cultivation of love and forgiveness.

BECOMING AND PUBLIC EDUCATION

Belonging and becoming are mutually reinforcing, but they are not always perceived as such in the ways we organize and administer public schools. In fact, we often overlook the dynamic interplay of belonging and becoming. For example, we know adolescents learn through and with peers, yet we structure their junior high days around the specialized knowledge of six to eight teachers. Preparation for the highly fragmented and differentiated world of high school takes precedence over the power of peer learning in adolescent development.

When you really think about it, we only seek to become something once we feel a secure sense of belonging. Even the basic desire to survive relates to the desire to reproduce and reproduction is the primary mode of belonging. We all initially belong to someone else through an umbilical cord. We become by how we belong. A 1979 report from the Carnegie Council on Children entitled *Small Futures* highlighted the importance of work relationships for a child's sense of becoming. The report stated:

Participation in and contribution to the process of production are an indispensable condition of social membership. . . . To a substantial degree it is through their works that people are connected, for better or for worse, to the society at large and also substantially through work that people judge and assign prestige to others and esteem to themselves. That classic question of adult to child, "What do you want to be when you grow up?" is no trivial one, for both a child's sense of the future and, we have speculated, a child's situational code are tied to the answer.[55]

Everything is in a state of becoming. We review our past in search of cues for what we are to become. We judge the present by how well it fits with our image of where we want to be. Our cultural myths, religions, and schools depend upon the concept of becoming. Myths glorify our wonder in the mysteries of the cosmos—where we came from and where we are going. Myths also serve a pedagogical function.[56] They can teach us how to live a lifetime, how to ripen, how to become. The development of religion is wedded to cultural, historical, and social desires about the destiny of humanity. Through religion we strive to understand, if not control, environmental forces that might inhibit a graceful process of becoming (e.g., death, illness, prejudice, ignorance, and injustice). Finally, our schools are designed to cultivate competencies we hope will enable us to survive, cope, and perhaps, even prosper as our individual and collective lives unfold.

As mentioned earlier, many people find our world in a state of disarray. Salvation by faith and salvation by society have lost their luster. Capitalism, socialism, and a slew of other "isms" have proffered an infinite variety of paths to social bliss. Yet, we grow cynical at all the contradictions. Capitalism needs poverty. Socialism needs welfare. Communism needs mediocrity. The perfect society is balanced delicately on imperfect features. We have lost, or at least temporarily misplaced, a common and thriving sense of becoming.

Today's children inherit the rules of a game they did not invent. Human becoming for the first half of the twentieth century fundamentally related to the drive for industrialization and bureaucratization. Out of this sociohistorical context came two rules of becoming that still dominate the ethos of most public schools: (a) competitive academic achievement marks developmental success, and (b) blind conformity to authority provides stability and ensures order. The world and schools we created in the 1930s, 1940s, and 1950s were founded primarily on these two rules. Cultural and bureaucratic forces translated these rules into behavioral actions. Low trust and predetermined productivity characterized our organizational and school lives. The rules of the game were secure as long as the economy grew 3 percent per year and the next generation believed it could do better than the preceding one.

Pre-Reagan America could afford to lose those children who did not accept, did not have the capacity to follow, or were culturally isolated from the rules of competitive achievement and blind conformity. Their active participation would not have threatened the rules of the game anyway. We face a different story today. Corporate leaders across the country have called for a new and extensive investment in the children who reside in the shadows of society.[57] The investment mentality encompasses some of the rules of the past. If we "invest" in children we doom them to a pathological relationship of manipulation between themselves and their parents and grandparents. Such a strategy will lead to low trust and predetermined productivity all over again. Instead, we must collaborate with our children to shape a context that enhances their power to restructure economic, political, and social relationships. We must remember Margaret Mead's insights about the necessity for building a world community but also about the difficulty of doing so. If educational leaders fail to act on this challenge, tomorrow's children will be so preoccupied with survival and self-interest that issues of mutual growth and development will be largely ignored.

Conditions of Child and Family Well-Being

So what are our children becoming? Two commonly accepted premises of human development may help us address this question. First, the child is assumed to be the parent of the adult. In other words, it is widely argued that adult status and the patterns of adult behavior are shaped in childhood. Second, the family is considered as the core factor in the developmental well-being of the child. Family can provide a context of continuity and consistency children need to thrive.[58] Thus, one could reasonably conclude that a fair assessment of what children are becoming in America would include an exploration of the conditions of childhood and the conditions of family.

A mind boggling number of statistical indicators could be consulted as one strives to understand the present and future status of family and child well-being. I have identified five indicators for each that educational leaders need to understand and monitor. The ten indicators are presented in list fashion below followed by a discussion of their implications for schools and school leaders.

CHILD WELL-BEING INDICATORS

1. Every day nearly 1,000 children are abused and nearly 3,300 children run away from home.[59]

2. Eighty-five percent of the one million dropouts each year possess low basic skills.[60]

3. Nationally, black students are 1.5 to 2 times as likely to receive corporal punishment than white students. Blacks are 3 to 4 times more likely to be suspended from school than whites.[61]

4. The numbers of disconnected youth can be assessed by what is known as the inactivity rate, that is, the number of people ages sixteen to nineteen who are not in school, the military, or employed relative to the number in their age group. In 1983, the inactivity rate for white male teens was 17.8 percent as compared to 8.3 percent in 1978. For white females, the rate rose from 17.8 percent to 24.2 percent during the same time period. For black males, the rate jumped from 17 to 34 percent, and for black females from 34 to 48 percent between 1978 and 1983. Essentially, 3.44 million American youth spent at least some of 1983 disconnected from school, work, or the military.[62]

5. People over 65 comprise 12 percent of the population but receive 27 percent of all federal dollars. The elderly receive nearly 48 percent of federal dollars when spending on national defense, interest on the national debt, and foreign aid is excluded.[63] Americans over fifty years of age control 70 percent of the total net worth of U. S. households.

FAMILY WELL-BEING INDICATORS

1. One of five families with children under eighteen are single-parent, female-headed homes.[64]

2. Since 1980, federal programs and entitlements for poor children and families have been cut $50 billion while the national defense budget has gained $624 billion.[65]

3. Every day nearly 3,000 children see their parents granted a divorce.[66]

4. The two fastest growing households in America are dual-income adults with no children and single-parent females with children in need of welfare assistance.[67]

5. Each year 700,000 babies with low birth weight are born to young mothers who do not or cannot provide adequate prenatal nutrition. There is a strong correlation between low birth weight and future learning disabilities. Excessive alcohol use in pregnancy often leads to mental retardation and fetal alcohol syndrome in offspring.

An increasing number of newborns come from women using drugs, particularly cocaine and crack, resulting in a broad range of developmental problems.[68]

What news can we derive from these ten indicators of child and family well-being? First, it is clear that an intergenerational transfer of wealth has transpired between young and old. The demographic reality of a huge number of aging baby boomers and the economic reality of a two trillion dollar deficit place tomorrow's children between a rock and a hard place. A person six years old or younger has a six times greater likelihood of being poor than a person sixty-five or older. The elderly are getting richer at the expense of the young, especially children of the poor. More and more educational leaders face a political reality of communities inhabited by growing numbers of middle aged and elderly people who vote in high percentages and do not hold a vested self interest in public schools. The nation's children are a voteless constituency and they come increasingly from racial and ethnic groups traditionally not well supported by American society.

Second, the selected well-being indicators demonstrate that educational leaders inherit a number of social problems (e.g., developmentally disadvantaged, low birth weight children; children with academic, social, and emotional development problems due to the trauma of divorce; abused and alienated children and youth) that could be better confronted with preventative actions in health, family, and employment policy. Educational leaders must forge tighter political alliances with colleagues from health, human services, and community development to confront avoidable future academic problems.

Third, there are millions of today's children who are not connected formally with schools and who need a strong sense of belonging and becoming. Educational leaders cannot write these adolescents off and try to save the younger ones exclusively. The nation's yearly cohort of dropouts cost society $240 billion in lost future earnings and taxes.[69] They represent a problem that will not magically go away. Leaders across all sectors of education (preschool to higher education) must work better together, especially at the state level, to reduce political infighting. The "education family" must stop trying to top one another, blame one another, and unduly replicate each other's roles and functions. We spend over $328 billion a year on education in America. It is a big-stakes, high-profile business. Educational leaders need to worry less about who gets the lion's share of these monies and worry more about how these resources can be better used to enhance the destinies of all children, especially children at the boundaries of society. Lisbeth and Daniel Schorr have noted that effective intervention and prevention programs are led by people who "adapt or circumvent traditional professional and bureaucratic limitations when necessary to meet the needs of those they serve."[70]

What are children becoming? They are becoming debt payers. They will have to pay for a federal deficit generated from excessive military expenditure over the last decade. They will have to pay for the support of the elderly. Health care costs make up nearly 11 percent of the gross national product, roughly twice the percentage that goes to education. Some of them will pay through mental, physical, and developmental disabilities for the substance abuse habits of their parents. Some of them will pay through physical and mental abuse for the economic and employment stresses experienced by their parents. Many of them will pay through problems in academic, social, and emotional development for the breakdown of the family due to factors such as divorce. All of them will pay through the decline in environmental well-being for the convenient, but nonbiodegradable diapers their parents placed on their tiny bottoms.

Social policy for public education must look more at what children are becoming rather than what has been lost. We cannot and probably should not strive to recapture a Donna Reed/Lake Wobegone America where all the women are strong, all the men are good looking, and all the children are above average. Educational leaders need to focus more on belonging and becoming and less on loss. The recent report by the Carnegie Council on Adolescent Development captures the tone and direction all educational leaders must adopt. The problem of disrupted belonging and becoming for children between ten and fifteen years of age is framed in the "Foreword" to the report:

There is a crucial need to help adolescents at this early age to acquire durable self-esteem, flexible and inquiring habits of mind, reliable and relatively close human relationships, a sense of belonging in a valued group and a sense of usefulness in some way beyond the self. . . . Most young adolescents attend massive, impersonal schools, learn from unconnected and seemingly irrelevant curricula, know well and trust few adults in school and lack access to health care and counseling. Millions of these young people fail to receive the guidance and attention they need to become healthy, thoughtful, and productive adults.[71]

Somewhere along the way, learning in public schools became a matter of compliance to adult authority.[72] Becoming became a mindless series of rituals of conformity. Today, the rules of the game have shifted. Authority cannot be forced compliance. It must evolve from mutual responsibility. Teachers must assume the disposition that they can make a difference in their students' lives. Students must assume the disposition that teachers can profoundly influence their lives.[73] Educational leaders must assume the disposition that they can help create a learning community ethos that promotes the norms of shared authority, self-directed learning, and critical self-assessment.

Splintered Realities

The world, our "global village," is pressing on without benefit of a generative and connective metaphor. Instead, we face a world of splintered realities where attention spans are short and dreams are delimited. Nothing seems to be holding us together (except, perhaps, survival-oriented economics). We no longer readily accept the power of myth and metaphor to transform our lives. Virtually every literate society has operated on the proposition that education presupposes a vision of the future. Education depends on metaphors associated with loss, belonging, and becoming. In human development, the word and the world are inseparable. Words and the capacity to use them empower us to organize and reproduce culture. Words provide each of us a sense of identity, a sense of place, and a sense of worth. Words can emancipate and oppress. The family and the school are the cultural inventions designated as the time and space where children embrace splintered realities through the development of language.

The irony of our age is that the seemingly infinite power of tele-communications and information technologies is impotent when culture and consciousness are not enlightened through literacy. We have no theory in educational administration and leadership to deal with the intricate patterns and splintered realities associated with the development of culture and mind through language. Leadership invents the world through words. Leaders change the facts of the world through a mutual act of empowerment called literate communication. Similar to Bronfenbrenner's concept of an ecological approach to human development, I would like to see notions and theories of educational leadership be sensitive to the "progressive, mutual accommodation between the developing person and the changing properties of the immediate and broader contexts in which the person lives."[74] A transformative theory of educational leadership begins with the recognition that human learning is a creative and communicative act which transcends the boundaries of the school and the classroom.

Perhaps the greatest challenge for educational leaders is to play the role of mid-wife in the transition to the twenty-first century. Schools are still considered the key "alterable variable" in societal develop-ment. Government does not have a good track record in trying to change how individuals and families behave. Thus, schools remain the epicenter for societal rebirth. Yet, there are many who argue that no new age is to be born. Instead, our collective sense of loss, detachment, and despair prompts numerous social observers to suggest that we are near the end of the ride. The year 1989 will be remembered as the year when many cherished ideas seemed to come to an end, namely, communism, public schools, and nature. Gorbachev met capitalism. East met West at the Berlin wall. Public schools met parental choice. Nature met man. In the late summer of 1989, a best-selling book and a widely read journal article captured the nation's intelligentsia. Both Bill McKibben's book, *The End of Nature*, and Francis Fukuyama's article entitled "The End of History" boldly suggest that humankind has reached the end of the line. From McKibben's perspective, our ability to reshape and destroy our natural habitat has come to the point where nature no longer has a mythical omnipresence.[75] From Fukuyama's point of view, the struggle over which political and economic ideology will dominate the world is over and the Western notion of liberal capitalism has won. He writes:

The end of history will be a very sad time. The struggle for recognition, the willingness to risk one's life for a purely abstract goal, the worldwide ideological struggle that called forth daring, courage, imagination, and idealism will be replaced by economic calculation, the endless solving of technical problems, environmental concerns, and the satisfaction of sophisticated consumer demands.[76]

Have we reached the end of history and the end of nature? I think not. However, I do feel we believe we have *lost* the capacity to improve the world through collective action and new ideas. Education is the "alterable variable" we must choose to engage if history and nature are to remain viable metaphors for human development. Notions of history and nature stem from how we perceive loss, belonging, and becoming. Our conception of history encompasses how we choose to confront loss, reconnect, and seek newer worlds. Our conception of nature helps us find out who we are, how we relate, and where we are going. We now need to find a conception of educational leadership where loss, belonging, and becoming are seen as the bedrock metaphors of human growth and development. I trust we do not see the day where educational leaders accept the end of history and merely serve as technical problem solvers and service "sophisticated consumer demands."

Children, Schools, and Change

Many school board members, superintendents, principals, and teachers' union leaders, governors, legislators, and business executives are ill-prepared for the tremendous challenges facing them as they tackle changing cultural and social policy notions of loss, belonging, and becoming. American society, once again, is trying to reform itself through reshaping its children. This strategy leads to policies and administrative tactics that promote standardization, compliance, measurable performance, order, and control. The short-time horizon of public policymakers inhibits any real consideration about society's long-term commitment to children. Public schools often are governed, administered, and run with little attention to widely accepted and well-documented principles of child and adolescent development. Many people feel educational excellence and educational equity are at worst incompatible and, at best, important but overly expensive mutual aims. Passive, externally directed students are expected. Matters of attendance, discipline, and public relations consume a large part of supervisory and administrative resources. Bureaucratic organization and functional specialization are still standard modes of operation in public schools. The influence on individual academic performance by student peer group interaction is tolerated but largely ignored as a legitimate and alterable pedagogical resource.

Tomorrow brings the promise of change. Images of loss, belonging, and becoming will continue to influence social policy for public education. Hopefully, this chapter has pulled together some important and timely knowledge about these three themes of social policy and human development. Yet, the real issue is whether or not we have the wisdom and the will to identify and balance notions of loss, belonging, and becoming when we strive to restructure education for tomorrow's families and children.

FOOTNOTES

1. Richard H. deLone, *Small Futures: Children, Inequality, and the Limits of Liberal Reform* (New York: Harcourt Brace Jovanovich, 1979).

2. Allan R. Buss, "Piaget, Marx, and Buck-Morss on Cognitive Development: A Critique and Reinterpretation," *Human Development* 20 (1970): 118-127.

3. Ibid.

4. Rosabeth Moss Kanter, "The Organization Child: Experience Management in a Nursery School," *Sociology of Education* 45 (Spring 1972): 186-211.

5. David K. Cohen, "Loss as a Theme in Social Policy," *Harvard Educational Review* 46 (November 1976): 553-571.

6. William Kessen, "The American Child and Other Cultural Inventions," *American Psychologist* 34 (1979): 815-820.

7. Judith Viorst, *Necessary Losses: The Loves, Illusions, Dependencies and Impossible Expectations That All of Us Have to Give Up in Order to Grow* (New York: Simon and Schuster, 1986).

8. Michael Lerner, *Surplus Powerlessness: The Psychodynamics of Everyday Life and the Psychology of Individual and Social Transformation* (Oakland, CA: Institute for Labor and Mental Health, 1986).

9. Peter F. Drucker, *The New Realities: In Government and Politics, in Economics and Society, in Business, Technology, and World View* (New York: Harper and Row, 1989).

10. Shoshana Zuboff, *In the Age of the Smart Machine: The Future of Work and Power* (New York: Basic Books, 1988).

11. Robert Ornstein and Paul Ehrlich, *New World New Mind: Moving toward Conscious Evolution* (New York: Doubleday, 1989), p. 54.

12. Drucker, *The New Realities*, p. 11.

13. U.S. Department of Education, Office of Educational Research and Improvement, *Youth Indicators 1988: Trends in the Well-Being of American Youth* (Washington, DC: U.S. Department of Education, 1988).

14. Drucker, *The New Realities*, p. 15.

15. Ornstein and Ehrlich, *New World New Mind*, p. 44.

16. Ibid., p. 171.

17. Ibid., p. 45.

18. Ibid., p. 10.

19. Ibid., chapter 4.

20. Ibid.

21. A representative sampling of compendium works on child development include: Elliott Medrich, Judith Roizen, Victor Rubin, and Stuart Buckley, *The Serious Business of Growing Up* (Berkeley, CA: University of California Press, 1982); Vance Packard, *Our Endangered Children: Growing Up in a Changing World* (Boston: Little, Brown and Company, 1983); Robert J. Trotter, "You've Come a Long Way, Baby," *Psychology Today* 21 (May 1987): 34-45; Edward Zigler and Kirby Heller, "Strengthening Social Policies in Behalf of Children and Families," in Robert Boger, Gaston Blom, and Larry Lezotte, *Child Nurturance, Volume 4, Child Nurturing in the 1980s* (New York: Plenum Press, 1984), pp. 3-19.

22. James S. Coleman, "Families and Schools," *Educational Researcher* 16 (August-September 1987): 32-38.

23. Drucker, *The New Realities*, p. 232.

24. Ornstein and Ehrlich, *New World New Mind*, p. 198.

25. Ibid., p. 185.

26. Ibid., p. 233.

27. Drucker, *The New Realities*, chapter 9.

28. Cohen, "Loss as a Theme in Social Policy," p. 554.

29. Robert Bellah, *Habits of the Heart: Individualism and Commitment in American Life* (Berkeley, CA: University of California Press, 1985); Scott Peck, *A Different Drum* (New York: Simon and Schuster, 1987).

30. E. D. Hirsch, *Cultural Literacy: What Every American Needs to Know* (New York: Vintage Books, 1987).

31. Martin Rein and Donald Schon, "Problem Setting in Policy Research," in *Using Social Research in Public Policymaking*, ed. Carol Weiss (Lexington, MA: Lexington Books, 1977), pp. 235-251.

32. William R. Torbert, "Educating towards Shared Purpose, Self-Direction, and Quality Work: The Theory and Practice of Liberating Structure," *Journal of Higher Education* 49 (1978): 109-135.

33. Drucker, *The New Realities*, p. 237.

34. Ibid., chapter 16.

35. Jay Belsky, Richard Lerner, and Graham Spanier, *The Child in the Family* (Reading, MA: Addison-Wesley, 1984).

36. Ibid.

37. Ibid.

38. Margaret Mead and Frances Cooke Macgregor, *Growth and Culture* (New York: G. P. Putnam's Sons, 1951), pp. 22-23.

39. Ornstein and Ehrlich, *New World New Mind*, p. 62.

40. Ibid.

41. Max Weber, *Max Weber on Capitalism, Bureaucracy, and Religion: A Selection of Texts*, ed. Stanislav Andreski (London: Allen and Unwin, 1983).

42. Kanter, "The Organization Child," p. 193.

43. Ibid.

44. Harumi Befu, "The Social and Cultural Background of Child Development in Japan and the United States," in *Child Development and Education in Japan*, ed. Harold Stevenson, Hiroshi Azuma, and Keiji Hakuta (New York: W. H. Freeman and Company, 1986), p. 22.

45. James Thompson, *Complex Organizations* (New York: Scott Foresman, 1967).

46. Philip Cusick, *Inside High School: The Student's World* (New York: Holt, Rinehart and Winston, 1973).

47. Philip Cusick, *The Egalitarian Ideal and the American High School* (New York: Longman, 1983).

48. Gerald Grant, *The World We Created at Hamilton High* (Cambridge, MA: Harvard University Press, 1988); Sara Lawrence Lightfoot, *The Good High School* (New York: Basic Books, 1983); Peter McLaren, *Life in Schools* (New York: Longman, 1989); Arthur Powell, Eleanor Farrar, and David K. Cohen, *The Shopping Mall High School: Winners and Losers in the Educational Marketplace* (Boston: Houghton Mifflin, 1985).

49. Coleman, "Families and Schools," p. 36.

50. Zigler and Heller, "Strengthening Social Policies in Behalf of Children and Families," pp. 13-15.

51. Urie Bronfenbrenner and Heather Weiss, "Beyond Policies without People: An Ecological Perspective on Child and Family Policy," in *Children, Families, and Government: Perspectives on American Social Policy*, ed. Edward Zigler and Sharon Kagan (New York: Cambridge University Press, 1983).

52. Lightfoot, *The Good High School*, p. 309.

53. Brad Mitchell, "Emergent Literacy and the Transformation of Schools, Families, and Communities: A Policy Agenda," in *Risk Makers, Risk Takers, Risk Breakers: Reducing the Risks for Young Literacy Learners*, ed. Jo Beth Allen and Jana Mason (Portsmouth, NJ: Heinemann, 1989).

54. Torbert, "Educating toward Shared Purpose, Self-Direction, and Quality Work," p. 112-116.

55. deLone, *Small Futures*, p. 188.

56. Joseph Campbell and Bill Moyers, *The Power of Myth* (New York: Doubleday, 1988).

57. Committee for Economic Development, *Investing in Our Children: Business and the Public Schools* (New York: Committee for Economic Development, 1983).

58. Zigler and Heller, "Strengthening Social Policies in Behalf of Children and Families," pp. 13-16.

59. "The Children's Hour," *U. S. News and World Report*, 7 November 1988, p. 40.

60. Anthony Carnevale, Leila Garner, and Ann Meltzer, *Workplace Basics: The Skills Employers Want* (Alexandria, VA: American Society for Training and Development, 1988), p. 6.

61. National Coalition of Advocates for Students, *Barriers to Excellence: Our Children at Risk* (Boston: National Coalition of Advocates for Students, 1985).

62. Charles L. Betsey, R. G. Hollister, Jr., and Mary Papageorgiou, *Youth Employment and Training Programs: The YEDPA Years* (Washington, DC: National Academy Press, 1985).

63. Peter Brimelow, "Consuming Our Children?" *Forbes Magazine* 138 (November 14, 1988): 225.

64. Mitchell, "Emergent Literacy and the Transformation of Schools, Families, and Communities," p. 299.

65. Marian Wright Edelman, *Families in Peril: An Agenda for Social Change* (Cambridge, MA: Harvard University Press, 1987), p. 43.

66. "The Children's Hour," p. 40.

67. Coleman, "Families and Schools," p. 34.

68. Harold Hodgkinson, *All One System* (Washington, DC: Institute of Educational Leadership, 1985).

69. Mitchell, "Emergent Literacy and the Transformation of Schools, Families, and Communities," p. 304.

70. Lisbeth Schorr and Daniel Schorr, *Within Our Reach: Breaking the Cycle of Disadvantage* (New York: Doubleday, 1989), p. 258.

71. Carnegie Council on Adolescent Development, *Turning Points: Preparing American Youth for the 21st Century* (New York: Carnegie Corporation, 1989), pp. 12-13.

72. Richard Elmore, "Reform and the Culture of Authority in Schools," *Educational Administration Quarterly* 23 (Fall 1987): 60-78.

73. Ibid.

74. Bronfenbrenner and Weiss, "Beyond Policies without People," p. 393.

75. Bill McKibben, *The End of Nature* (New York: Random House, 1989).

76. Francis Fukuyama, "The End of History?" *National Interest*, No. 16 (Summer 1989): 18.

CHAPTER III

Children, Youth, and Restructured Schools: Views from the Field

BRAD MITCHELL   —

The call rings out across the land—it is time to restructure schools. The newest phase and phrase of the "excellence in education" movement proclaims restructured schools as the required reform strategy for educational and economic salvation. Education *re*formers are fixated on the "re" prefix. Their rhetoric is based on the *re*cognition that the *re*generation of American economic competitiveness depends on how well we *re*focus and *re*direct the public education system to *re*structure schools and *re*design schooling to *re*produce a well-educated and *re*vitalized workforce. Opponents of educational reform frequently express (but sometimes repress) feelings of resistance, reluctance, resentment, or repulsion. Moreover, educational reforms often are reactive responses to the rearrangement of pertinent social, political, and economic relations. For example, the launch of Sputnik in 1957 reaffirmed the growing concern that the United States needed to revise assumptions about the military and technological might of the Soviet Union. The event prompted American policymakers to reestablish superiority through well-funded scientific research and to reorganize mathematics and science education from kindergarten to college.

Under the auspices of the National Defense Education Act, America's renewed resolve to confront a perceived Soviet threat led to a realignment of resources for schools and colleges. The "re" prefix was alive and well in public education then and it still kicks up a storm today. Public schools rely on a repertoire of educational practices governed by the "re" prefix—grade-level *re*tention, standardized tests based on the concept of statistical *re*gression, *re*mediation, *re*habilitation, subject area tests focused on short-term memory *re*call, reading exercises designed to *re*tell stories and *re*do written work, and student discipline strategies centered on positive *re*inforcement. Of course, there also are some unpopular and undervalued "re" words such as revolution, rebellion, reflection, religion, and retrenchment.

52

So what great insights are revealed when we pay attention to the power and the placement of the "re" prefix in the American public school experience? Perhaps the prevalence of "re" words in school reform may relate partially to the social policy themes of loss, belonging, and becoming discussed in chapter 2. According to the *Oxford English Dictionary*,[1] the "re" prefix serves three purposes in modern day language. First, it may be used to modify a word to suggest a reversal of a previous action or a restoration to a previous state (e.g., revitalize, restore, renew, recover, reconstruct). The "re" prefix also can express the act of reconnecting two or more things (e.g., refit, rebridge, reseal). Finally, it can denote a change from one state or quality to another (e.g., reconstitute, redefine, reinterpret, rearrange).

As discussed in the preceding chapter, loss tends to be associated with separation and the desire to *restore* order; belonging centers on cultural and interpersonal *relationships* that often enhance a sense of security; and becoming involves the *redefinition* of self within a series of *reconstituted* contexts. Even a seasoned etymologist might release a small sigh at the apparent fit between the "re" prefix and broader cultural notions of loss, belonging, and becoming. The word "reform" has three distinct meanings as well. In its most literal sense it means to form again, renew, restore, reestablish (loss). Reform also can express a change in arrangements and relationships (belonging). It often is used to denote a conversion into another and better form (becoming). Thus, an amateur etymologist employed as a professor of education might argue that educational reform in the guise of restructured schools is: (a) designed to return schools to an earlier and more ideal organizational form; (b) aimed at changing the roles, rules, and relationships between schools and other educative institutions (e.g., family, church, and community); or (c) committed to reshaping schools and schooling based on what we know about teaching and learning and human development.

I am interested in examining the similarities and differences across each of these three interpretations of restructured schools. My database will come primarily from descriptive accounts of real life from real people who learn and work in real restructured schools. The ultimate purpose of this chapter is to get beyond the limits of the "re" prefix and to explore how schools are transformed and how they can become transformative. I want to see the patterns of school culture[2] that encourage and empower teachers and learners to seek new forms of connectedness, where learning is not compliance to authority[3] but a never-ending process of self-determination and self-accountability. The notion of schools as self-governed communities of learners is not at all new. Yet, it looks like we are taking up the issue again as one century falls from the tree and another begins to bloom. Perhaps the discussion on restructured schools should begin with one simple but provocative question: What is school restructuring and why is it such a popular reform proposal?

Restructured Schools: What, Why and Where?

The crusade for restructured schools has taken many forms. Some reformers seek a shift in power and authority relations between and among principals and teachers. Career ladders for teachers is a popularly espoused strategy for restructuring schools based on modifications in working conditions and instructional roles and responsibilities. The implementation of such a plan in Rochester, New York, has sparked considerable national attention.

Closely related to the career ladder strategy is the push to "professionalize" teaching through graduate-level teacher education and the establishment of stronger ties between schools and colleges of education. Nearly 100 colleges of education housed in major research universities have formed an alliance under the title "Holmes Group"[4] to promote school restructuring through the recruitment, professional education, and selection of a new breed of teachers. The approach is based on a long-held principle of partisan politics. All astute political executives, whether a governor or a president, realize that if they inherit an executive branch run by people loyal to the opposition party they must "change the organization by changing who is employed by the organization."

Other reformers are more interested in changing how schools are managed. The concept of site-based management is attracting a great deal of attention.[5] This restructuring initiative assumes that teachers and principals will produce better outcomes if they are given more managerial authority over the operation of the school. Dade County (Florida) is generally considered the litmus test for restructured schools through site-based management. In Dade County, each school receives its budget in one lump sum, subject to the managerial discretion of the principal and instructional staff. The district also waives policies and regulations that threaten to impede change at the school site (e.g., mandated class sizes, length of school day, number of minutes taught per subject). In general, site-based management (also sometimes called shared decision making) is founded on four principles: (a) bureaucratic constraints must be overcome if educators are to serve a diverse clientele effectively; (b) all curriculum and instructional decisions should be made as close to the classroom as possible; (c) individual schools should be held accountable for results; and (d) authority and control of the teaching and learning process should be at the school level.

The hottest current proposal for school restructuring is expressed in two words—parental choice. Very early in his presidency, George Bush endorsed the right of parents to choose the schools their children attend. In 1988, Minnesota cracked the seal by adopting a comprehensive open enrollment plan. The Minnesota plan allows parents to choose virtually any school district in the state and students who transfer take approximately $3,300 with them in state aid. Over the last two years, roughly twenty-four states have adopted some form of choice or have established task forces or study groups to explore such proposals.[6]

A fifth commonly advocated strategy to restructure schools would tighten the coordination of student support services within schools and across human service agencies. The argument for this approach rests on the belief that most schools serve most students well, but they seldom meet the needs of students on the margins of society (e.g., children of the poor and the disempowered). Interagency collaboration and restructured student support services are hailed as the new and better ways to serve "at-risk" students and to enhance their transition to productive adult lives. Recent federal efforts at welfare reform mandate tighter coordination of services and more employment-oriented educational programs for children of people on public assistance (i.e., Family Support Act of 1988). Under the banner of the "New Futures" project, the Anna Casey Foundation has put up $25 million to help five middle-sized urban areas restructure children and youth services and to employ "case workers" in schools to serve as advocates and accountability agents for "at-risk" students.

Of course, there are dozens of other school restructuring experiments across the country that do not receive as much media attention, among them Theodore Sizer's Coalition of Essential Schools, pilot schools centered on "state-of-the-art" information technology and educational software, school improvement programs based on the application of the latest research on teaching and learning. Yet, educational policymakers, particularly at the state level, are most interested in the five strategies for school restructuring already discussed:

1. Change working conditions and teacher roles and responsibilities (e.g., career ladders).
2. Change who will become tomorrow's teachers and let them serve as the catalysts for school renewal (e.g., graduate-level teacher training).
3. Change the management structure of schools and allow teachers more discretion over curricular, instructional, and resource allocation decisions (e.g., site-based management).
4. Change the market of potential clients by giving parents more choice as to where their children will attend school (e.g., magnet schools, alternative schools, and open enrollment districts).
5. Change the nature and coordination of student support services in the school to serve better the needs of at-risk students (e.g., caseworkers housed in schools).

The list of current policy options regarding restructured schools reads like the classic set of organizational change strategies expressed in the first chapter of a rudimentary text on business administration. The logic is simple and succinct: organizations change when there are significant changes in employment relations, personnel, managerial structure, market, and core/support functions. Unfortunately, schools are complex cultures with little affinity for quick fixes and isolated reforms. Yet, state policymakers continue to strive to restructure schools as quickly and as efficiently as possible. Why? The realities of educational politics demand it. Public education is a high-profile and high-stakes game. Consider the following "realities":

1. Education is the single largest budget item in most states (roughly 50 percent of the total). Over $180 billion is spent annually on public elementary and secondary education.
2. Educational expenditures comprise about 7 percent of the gross national product.
3. Nearly one million high school students fail to graduate each year, costing over $250 billion in lost future lifetime earnings and taxes.
4. Since 1949, per pupil cost has increased fourfold, in real terms, while SAT scores have declined from a 969 composite average in 1961 to around 895 in 1988.[7]
5. From 1972 to 1982, school enrollment dropped 14 percent while the number of teachers increased 1.4 percent.

6. Over $350 billion is spent each year on all of education, public and private, precollegiate and collegiate. This figure represents approximately one-third of the total amount of money spent on education around the world.[8]

There are at least five reasons why proposals to restructure schools are currently so popular. First, the idea of organizational restructuring fits corporate America's image of effectiveness and competitiveness for a postmodern age. Bestselling books on organization management, such as *In Search of Excellence*,[9] *Theory Z*,[10] and *In the Age of the Smart Machine*,[11] point to the need to transcend the limitations of bureaucratic structures. Moreover, business leaders see schools as a critical factor in the production of well-educated future producers and consumers. The antiquated school bureaucracy is seen as ill-fitted to shape the character and the capacity of tomorrow's knowledge workers.

Second, most proposals for restructured schools are relatively cheap, promote public confidence, and do not really question the authority and legitimacy of professional educators to run the schools. Most career ladder plans do not expand personnel budgets but reallocate extant funds across new position categories. Parental choice plans usually rearrange how public monies reach school districts. Site-based management schemes take the same dollars and merely designate different people to determine how some of the funds will be expended. Virtually all of these proposals keep educators firmly in control of a public school system still divided into three levels (elementary, middle, and secondary), still processing large numbers of students through self-contained classrooms, and still dividing up knowledge in isolated subject matter areas taught over discrete units of time. Sizer observes:

We're still talking about testing everybody and putting the screws on the existing system even more. The problem is the existing system. And until we face up to that unpleasant fact—that the existing system has to change—we're not going to get the kinds of changes that everybody wants.[12]

The rhetoric of school restructuring, however, does "sell" well in a climate of stormy public and policymaker opinion. After nearly a decade of attention on school reform, educators still face a crisis of confidence. The number of dropouts continues to grow, illiteracy rates are still too high, and drugs still linger in the shadows of the schoolyard. School restructuring holds the promise of being the reform that will finally make a difference. Moreover, a reform proposal such as site-based management can be stretched to cover virtually every malady of an ailing community and school district. Consider the public relations value inherent in the following task force report from a Louisiana school district:

> The site-based management effort will make a difference for our students. The effort will get East Baton Rouge Parish schools in compliance with the desegregation court order, pupil and teacher absenteeism will go down, test scores will go up, vandalism will go down, community support will go up, dropouts, suspensions and expulsions will go down, morale of teachers will go up and overall accountability will be improved.[13]

A third explanation for the current fervor over restructuring schools emerges from a quick glimpse at the history of educational reform over the past quarter century. The reform pendulum has swayed several times between the push for centralization and the push for decentralization. The Elementary and Secondary Education Act of 1965 was designed to promote educational equity within and across all states. Traditional wisdom among makers of social policy is to pursue equity through centralized authority. At the core of Lyndon Johnson's "Great Society" initiative was the belief that social equity demanded the central authority of the executive, legislative, and judicial branches of the federal government. States' rights advocates responded to the perceived intrusion of the federal government through a myriad of strategies designed to promote the legitimacy of decentralized authorities (e.g., local school boards, cities, townships). Early in the 1980s, the federal government again sought to centralize educational authority under the theme of excellence. *A Nation at Risk* proposed a common set of educational aims, a core curriculum, and a more comprehensive system of school assessment.[14] In recent years, we have seen more and more state and local educational authorities consider reform proposals calling for empowered teachers, enhanced local control, and extended parental choice. Clearly, the question of who will run America's schools continues to occupy a central place in politics and government.

A fourth factor in the renewed emphasis on school restructuring is the growing pressure for new forms of school organization to exploit the power of information technologies. Interactive video discs, more flexible educational software, and local area computer networks are just some of the ever-increasing prospects in information technology. The potential educational uses of information technology fit well with recent theories and research findings emerging from scholarly work in artificial intelligence, cognition, and cognitive development. For example, computer technology provides the coordinated instructional capacity to deal with Howard Gardner's theory of multiple intelligences.[15] Gardner proposes that human beings possess not one, but seven relatively autonomous intellectual abilities. These intellectual abilities include the verbal and logical skills traditionally stressed in schools, as well as musical intelligence, spatial intelligence, physical intelligence, and social intelligence. Computers can enhance the educator's understanding of and access to these multiple intelligences simultaneously.

The fifth and most salient reason for the rebirth of broad discussion on the need to restructure schools relates to the changing conditions of children and families in America. Schools are not designed to deal with the new realities of growing up in this country. Due to laws and regulations regarding compulsory attendance and the length of the school day and year, children are required to spend over seven thousand hours of their early existence in elementary school classrooms. Of course, the total number of hours in school often pales in comparison to the time spent watching television and time expended separate from any adult supervision.

In the absence of strong bonds with caring adults, children, especially adolescents, often fulfill their need for belonging through participaton in peer groups. Peer culture influences significantly how individual status is gained and maintained. Resistance to school and adult authority tends to be a positive status symbol in many peer cultures. Thus, a youth is unlikely to accept an adult-oriented school culture at times when self-esteem is fed through peer group attachment.

William Glasser addresses problems of youth alienation in his notion of control theory.[16] Glasser argues that schools are not *structured* to satisfy the basic human needs of belonging and becoming (see chapter 2). He proposes that schools discover ways to redirect student energies aimed at subverting schooling and give them choices in *structuring* their own learning experiences. Growing up in today's America can be a terribly disempowering experience. A dominant public school culture based on notions of deficit, detachment, and denial dim the prospect of a thriving and hopeful childhood, especially for children of the urban poor. Based on impressions from field visits to a number of urban schools around the country, former *New York Times* education reporter, Gene Maeroff, writes:

The lack of success of minority students in urban schools is so prevalent that the expectation of failure is as much a part of many classrooms as the textbooks that the children struggle to read. Remediation is a permanent state of being rather than a temporary intervention.[17]

Neither are schools prepared to confront directly the new realities facing the American family. Educators bemoan the disruptions of school life related to changes in family well-being—emotionally insecure children of divorce, limited parental participation in school due to the growth in dual-income households, student discipline problems associated with turbulent home environs. Programs are added to the school to deal with these "perceived" family pathologies in an incremental and isolated fashion (e.g., peer counseling, parental education courses, home-school community agents, latchkey services). Unfortunately, many conditions and changes in family life are perceived by many educators as generating unreasonable stresses and demands on them. As a result, the family often is seen as the cause of the school's or the teacher's inability to help certain children and youth grow and develop. Some school restructuring proposals, such as expanded parental choice and coordinated student/family support services, are based on the assumption that the school is okay but the family either needs to be repaired (another "re" word) or held more accountable for its own educational well-being. In an important but largely overlooked book, *Worlds Apart: Relationships between Families and Schools*, Sara Lawrence Lightfoot warns educators to avoid the arrogance and closed-mindedness associated with the "missionary zeal" to invade the household and fix it. She writes:

Most important, the moves out into the community reinforce the asymmetry of the relationship between home and school (i.e., reinforce the power and dominance of the school and the vulnerability of the family) and distract our attention away from *the school* as the setting that needs to be *restructured* and changed to adapt to the strengths, weaknesses, and skills of the children it serves. Professional educators must redirect their focus to life inside schools, a setting that includes the responsible participation of parents rather than searching out the origins of pathology beyond the school walls. This turning inward (with welcome arms spread wide to receive and include parents) helps teachers look at their own behaviors and institutional norms as contributing to patterns of disruption and failure with children and uses parents as colleagues in helping to develop alternative classroom structures and interactional strategies that will meet the child's needs.[18]

If one accepts Lightfoot's logic, *real* restructuring begins with a commitment to explore how the social and cultural contexts of the school impede or enhance a sense of belonging from the perspective of the student and his or her family. Choice without voice is a hollow victory for parents. Under an open-enrollment plan the parent may choose a new schoolhouse door, but there is no better guarantee that there will be a greater say in how the learning experience of the child is structured once inside the school. Joseph Murphy writes about a new era of educational equity where each student is exposed to the curricular and instructional assets needed for personal and academic development. Current school restructuring plans, especially ones involving parental choice, do not allow the voice of the learner or his or her advocate to influence how the educational experience will be delivered. Perhaps the concept of choice with voice is where a school restructuring initiative should begin.

Choice with Voice: Views from the Field

This chapter is designed to be a companion piece to chapter 2. As mentioned previously, notions of loss, belonging, and becoming have shaped the ways we see humans develop, as well as the educational structures dedicated to human development. A sense of belonging seems to be at the epicenter of cultural and individual transformation. Yet, public schools have become large, impersonal places where children and youth seek an unfulfilled sense of belonging and see little connection between what they are requested to do in the classroom and the world they experience immediately outside school as well as the world that awaits them tomorrow. Out of the plethora of proposals for restructuring, I propose that educational leaders place special attention on three:

1. building schools for tomorrow that transcend traditional distinctions between learning in and out of school;
2. focusing on early adolescents, ages ten to fifteen, and providing them formal educational experiences within small and intimate "learning communities"; and
3. bridging the chasm between school and home literacy, and promoting student success on the basis of their strengths in literacy rather than their weaknesses.

LEARNING IN AND OUT OF SCHOOL

As Lauren Resnick so eloquently points out in her 1987 AERA

presidential address, we have tended either to ignore or unduly discount the similarities and differences between learning inside and outside the school. Resnick notes:

. . . schooling focuses on the individual's performance, whereas out-of-school mental work is often socially shared. Schooling aims to foster unaided thought, whereas mental work outside school usually involves cognitive tools. School cultivates symbolic thinking whereas mental activity outside school engages directly with objects and situations. Finally, schooling aims to teach general skills and knowledge, whereas situation-specific competencies dominate outside.[19]

Put simply, Resnick reminds us what John Dewey told us long ago— learning is cooperative, experience-based, practical, and not confined to a specific context. Resnick's view of learning is quite pertinent for a world where knowledge work (i.e., knowledge creation, synthesis, manipulation, and dissemination) is expected to dominate. Her four distinctions between learning in and out of school should be one of the first analytic frameworks considered by leaders of a school restructuring effort. Even if you disagree with the validity of one or more of the distinctions, the important thing is to ask the broader question: How and how well does formal schooling fit with the learning needed for productive living?

YOUNG ADOLESCENTS AND SMALL COMMUNITIES FOR LEARNING

In June 1989, the Carnegie Council on Adolescent Development released a very important report, entitled *Turning Points: Preparing American Youth for the 21st Century*.[20] Unlike virtually all the other major reform reports of the 1980s, *Turning Points* is solidly based on an incisive and objective view of child and adolescent development. The report does not get caught up in the "re" prefix mentality of relentless revitalization and repair of bad schools, bad teachers, and bad administrators. Instead, *Turning Points* relies on the "trans" prefix to outline an agenda for middle-school transformation. The report asks middle schools to embark on a transition from the large and impersonal to the small and the intimate. Specifically, *Turning Points* encourages middle schools to do the following:

1. Create small communities for learning where a sense of belonging is strongly cultivated for "intellectual development and personal growth."
2. Teach a core academic program that emphasizes critical literacy and community service.

3. Ensure success for all students through the elimination of achievement-based tracking and the promotion of cooperative learning and instructional flexibility.
4. Empower teachers and other school leaders to make decisions about the educational experiences of early adolescents through school-based governance structures and processes.
5. Reengage families in the education of young adolescents by working with them in mutually respectful and well-supported roles and relationships.
6. Connect schools with communities to hold both accountable for each student's success and to establish better and more effective coordination of student support services and after-school activities.

Building a sense of belonging and becoming among young adolescents is the central message of *Turning Points*. Through small learning communities and restructured teacher roles, it is assumed that students will bond more with adults connected to the school and that they will feel the school belongs to them and they belong in the school. Gene Maeroff writes:

[A learning community of] 200 to 300 students with a faculty of its own that is shared with no other school—even though schools *may coexist* on separate floors in the same building—can be an intimate institution in which students see the same small cadre of teachers over and over again. Time must be built into the schedule for teachers to meet regularly for several hours a week with small groups of students to talk about life and its problems.[21]

Educational leaders must not balk at the word "small" and other old-minded homilies such as "impractical and too costly." No new middle-school building need be built. Bricks and mortar may remain the same, but the patterns of belonging inside the school will shift dramatically. The basic premise of *Turning Points* is that young adolescents will not automatically seek self-gratification or unhealthy peer group associations if they feel adults in the school care about who they are and feel responsible for their intellectual and emotional development. The exposure to and socialization of the middle-school student to a six-class-period, six-teacher day may help them cope with the logistical realities of high school, but it will not necessarily prompt a strong sense of belonging at a time in their emotional and social development where they need a solid anchor of personal identity. Clearly, educational leaders must make school restructuring in the middle-grade years a high priority.

SCHOOL AND FAMILY LITERACY: TIES THAT BIND?

"Going to school" is the most private and the most public experience in the life of most people. Education is an intensely intimate phenomenon even when it is experienced in the context of a collective. Literacy learning encompasses our mind, soul, body, past, present, and future. Becoming literate is an extremely public enterprise. Most of us achieve literacy through a system, structure, and strategy called school. Our peers view us and we view them when we stumble and when we succeed as we recite our ABCs in supposed unison. We learn how to be citizens and develop our civil literacy in a fishbowl called the self-contained classroom. We learn how to express ourselves in both written and oral form in social clusters called ability groups. The unique literacy needs of the individual learner often are not sufficiently confronted as the "system" strives to fulfill a public purpose, to protect the public interest, and to produce a literate citizenry.

There is a continuous and deep stream of research evidence to suggest that school factors are just as important as home factors in the development of literacy in children and youth. Yet, the traditional approach to family literacy programs is to prepare parents to conduct school-like activities in the home and to assist children with their homework. Such an approach assumes certain parents lack the necessary skills to promote school success in their children. Recent theory and research from a social-contextual framework suggests schools should draw on parents' knowledge and cultural strengths to enhance literacy learning for their children. Essentially, the social-contextual approach to literacy development is especially effective for growing numbers of children and families from working class, minority, or non-English-speaking contexts. Family literacy programs should be designed to involve children and their families in collaborative curriculum development so that literacy becomes a meaningful aspect of family and community life as well as a means for shaping the social context. Auerbach describes two innovative and effective family literacy programs:

In Pajaro Valley, parents and children are involved in a project in which they read, discuss, and write children's stories together. Critical for this project is the positive value placed on the use of the home language both as a vehicle for communication within the family and as the foundation for children's academic success. Also important is the linking of reading to students' lives through a process of dialogue: readers share personal reactions and feelings, relate the story to their own experiences, critically analyze the events and ideas in the stories, and discuss real-life applications of this understanding. The process of sharing Spanish children's literature becomes the foundation for then asking children and parents to write their own stories about significant events in their lives. This kind of family literacy work draws on parents' cultural strengths and encourages critical thinking about key issues in family life.

Another project designed to build home and school links is the Chinle Navajo Parent-Child Reading Program. In this project, children bring books home and share them with their parents, either by reading or telling the stories. Children also write their own books based on Navajo stories they have heard from their parents and grandparents. In the process, the home culture is validated and promoted through literacy work; the parents' cultural knowledge contributes to rather than conflicts with school learning.[22]

Educational leaders can learn a great deal from a social-contextual approach to literacy development. All literacy is context specific. Schools, as formally authorized purveyors of the formally authorized literacy, must work with and not work on families who do not easily transact in the cultural capital of the dominant forms of literacy. Literacy is the fundamental skill for knowledge work, and America needs all the knowledge workers it can get. At the core of any school restructuring effort should be a rigorous and reflective exploration of how and how well school and family literacy relate. Both contexts for literacy development need to respect and to build upon their respective strengths.

Restructuring Schools: Leadership Challenges

Other than in the title of this chapter, I purposefully have tried to avoid using the phrase "restructured schools," preferring instead the phrase "school restructuring." The former denotes a static, reactionary view of the world where one best system of schooling is replaced by another one best system. In a way, it is like plastic surgery. Once the surgeon resculptures your face, you assume you have a functional and stable facade until the next time reconstruction is deemed necessary. The phrase "restructuring schools" possesses and expresses a much more vibrant and flexible message. The constant emergence and interplay of new voices (e.g., a new batch of students every year) in the school organization demands that social and cultural contexts transform continuously. The scholarly work of Seymour Sarason on the dynamics of school culture is quite specific on this point.[23] Culture is flowing structure. Group and individual behavior shapes and is shaped by rituals, ceremonies, symbols, icons, roles, rules, and relationships.[24] From this point of view, site-based management really means a local school leadership attentive to the changing patterns and connections of cultural life. Put simply, good school leaders constantly are involved in restructuring their schools.

Culture depends on authority to exist. It is the primary duty of the educational leader to ensure that the authority of the school is not a product of coercion or negotiation. Yet, more often than not, principals are personally expected to produce specific cures and miraculous transformations without much shared authority emanating from school or community. They are charged with the responsibility for the maintenance and growth of the school organization; yet, they often are denied access to or ignore central channels of school authority (e.g., student peer groups, informal teacher leaders, teacher dispositions about their capacity to change the lives of their students).[25] School authority must be constructed mutually among people who embrace and are not overwhelmed by loss, who possess and nurture a sense of collective belonging, and who seek and sustain a shared vision of collective becoming. The challenge to educational leadership is to cultivate a context where children and adults can take risks with little or no threat of retribution or loss of reputation (some more of those dreaded "re" words). A further challenge is to discover how to encourage individual creativity/autonomy and collective effectiveness/accountability.[26] Educational leaders need to question traditional notions of student development—clear aims, linear progress, and success defined and measured by levels of attainment. Instead, leaders of schools must "insinuate themselves into the lives of students in ways that make the schools places where students want to be."[27] Good principals, especially at the elementary school level, make the pursuit of a collective sense of belonging their first priority.

For too long, educational leaders have purchased authority from courts and legislatures (e.g., compulsory attendance, desegregation plans, school finance formulas). For too long, leaders of a diverse array of special interests have targeted schools as the dispensers of desired remedies and resources (e.g., teacher collective bargaining rights, special additive or pull-out programs funded through categorical aid, markets for publishers of textbooks and tests). One of the unfortunate consequences of purchased authority and political pluralism is that the concept of a mutually supportive school and community no longer exists. Nor do we often think of school as a cohesive and coherent community in and of itself.

John Dewey warned us of the consequences associated with a rift between the cultural concepts of school and community.[28] Choice alone cannot build a school community. Voice is required. Active and responsible dialogue must be nurtured and sustained through the voices of all participants in the school, particularly children and youth. As Glasser and a host of others remind us, the student *structures* her or his learning experience. The student is involved in a constant process of school restructuring inside his or her head and heart. The essential challenge for educational leadership is to help childen and youth realize what is of value to them in life. Time in prison and unwed parenthood should not be the rituals of belonging for large numbers of adolescent Americans.[29] School restructuring actions must confront such cultural rituals with a respect for the dynamics of larger social contexts and an appreciation for the power of the individual to transform their own lives when they see authentic choice with voice.

FOOTNOTES

1. *The Compact Edition of the Oxford English Dictionary* (London: Oxford University Press, 1971).

2. Anthony Wilden, *The Rules Are No Game: The Strategy of Communication* (London: Routledge and Kegan Paul, 1987).

3. Stephen Arons, *Compelling Belief: The Culture of American Schooling* (New York: McGraw Hill, 1983).

4. Holmes Group, *Tomorrow's Teachers: A Report of the Holmes Group* (E. Lansing, MI: Holmes Group, 1986).

5. For a nice synthesis of research on site-based management initiatives, see William Clune and Paula White, *School-Based Management: Institutional Variation, Implementation, and Issues for Further Research*, Report Series RR-008 (New Brunswick, NJ: Center for Policy Research in Education, September, 1988).

6. "Fixing the System from the Top Down," *Teacher Magazine* 1 (September/October, 1989): 54.

7. "Are We Spending Too Much on Education?" *Forbes* 138, no. 14 (December 29, 1986): 72-76.

8. Ibid.

9. Thomas Peters and Robert Waterman, Jr., *In Search of Excellence: Lessons from America's Best-Run Companies* (New York: Harper and Row, 1982).

10. William Ouchi, *Theory Z: How American Business Can Meet the Japanese Challenge* (New York: Avon, 1981).

11. Shoshana Zuboff, *In the Age of the Smart Machine: The Future of Work and Power* (New York: Basic Books, 1988).

12. Theodore Sizer, quoted in "Fixing the System from the Top Down," p. 55.

13. East Baton Rouge Parish School Redesign Plan, *At the Crossroads* (East Baton Rouge, LA: E. Baton Rouge Parish Schools, March 1, 1988), p. 1.

14. National Commission on Excellence in Education, *A Nation at Risk* (Washington, DC: U.S. Department of Education, 1983).

15. Howard Gardner, *Frames of Mind: The Theory of Multiple Intelligences* (New York: Basic Books, 1983).

16. William Glasser, *Control Theory in the Classroom* (New York: Harper and Row, 1986).

17. Gene Maeroff, "Withered Hopes, Stillborn Dreams: The Dismal Panorama of Urban Schools," *Phi Delta Kappan* 69 (May 1988): 638.

18. Sara Lawrence Lightfoot, *Worlds Apart: Relationships between Families and Schools* (New York: Basic Books, 1978), pp. 206-207.

19. Lauren Resnick, "Learning In School and Out," *Educational Researcher* 16 (December 1987): 16.

20. Carnegie Council on Adolescent Development, *Turning Points: Preparing American Youth for the 21st Century* (New York: Carnegie Corporation, June 1989).

21. Maeroff, "Withered Hopes, Stillborn Dreams," p. 638.

22. Elisa Roberts Auerbach, "Toward a Social Contextual Approach to Family Literacy," *Harvard Educational Review* 59 (May 1989): 176-177.

23. Seymour Sarason, *The Culture of the School and the Problem of Change* (Boston: Allyn and Bacon, 1971).

24. Ibid.

25. Richard Elmore, "Reform and the Culture of Authority in Schools," *Educational Administration Quarterly* 23 (Winter 1988): 60-78.

26. William R. Torbert, "Educating toward Shared Purpose, Self-Direction, and Quality Work," *Journal of Higher Education* 49 (1978): 109-135.

27. Maeroff, "Withered Hopes, Stillborn Dreams," p. 638.

28. John Dewey, *The School and Society* (Chicago: University of Chicago Press, 1902).

29. Maeroff, "Withered Hopes, Stillborn Dreams," p. 634.

CHAPTER IV

Rethinking Policy for Children:
Implications for Educational Administration

MICHAEL W. KIRST AND MILBREY MCLAUGHLIN,

WITH ASSISTANCE OF DIANE MASSELL

America's children and youth[1] and their educational prospects are profoundly affected by the context of their lives and their relative location in the larger society. Among the related set of elements that shape children's experiences one can include the level of family income, parental[2] employment, family structure, racial and ethnic background, health care, the availability of alcohol or other substances, and family support systems such as child care or mental health services.

In recent years substantial changes in these components have redefined the contours of childhood. For instance, a growing number of children have come to experience poverty and often other incidental[3] risks that seem to be cumulative, such as poor physical health, lower academic achievement, and lower self-reports of happiness. In addition to the growing number of children in poverty, more and more children from single-parent families and from minority and limited-English-proficient backgrounds are entering the public schools. At the same time, many of the income-support programs and other programs that serve children and youth have experienced declining or limited resources. Aid to Families with Dependent Children and other such programs do not cover the eligible population. Increasingly schools must meet the needs of growing numbers of at-risk children and youth. Yet schools were not set up to serve such students and have historically not served them well.

Educational leaders, especially school administrators, need a better grasp of the educational implications of the everyday lives of children, and a new strategy for bringing together the various public and private organizations to help. The current fragmentation across children's services represents a fundamental failure to confront the comprehensive needs of children, youth, and adults. Those responsible for providing services to children have neglected to begin with the simple, provocative question: What is it like to be a child who needs help? The

69

current top-down policy approach operates from the organizational perspective of the multiple providers. We outline here the changing conditions and needs of children to form a basis for analyzing the effectiveness of the current services delivered to them. We then move to the conditions of the services as they presently exist, and to prescriptions for improving and reconceptualizing policies and administrative approaches. Finally, we delineate the role of the schools in this new conceptualization.

Analyzing the Conditions of Children as a Prelude to a New Policy

The context of childhood has undergone considerable change in the last few decades. Since 1969, an expanding cohort of children has come to experience poverty,[4] a condition that increases the likelihood of health and academic risks; furthermore, economic status is the best single predictor of adult self-sufficiency.[5] Family structure has also shifted dramatically. The once common pattern of two biological parents—one working outside and the other inside the home—is found in a diminishing proportion of families. The numbers of children from racial and ethnic minority backgrounds have increased relative to the majority population, greatly so in some states and locales.

To explore these changes and their consequences, Policy Analysis for California Education (PACE) recently sponsored a major report on the conditions of children and youth. In the following section we use the aggregate national statistics drawn from the PACE report and others to examine these conditions. Although any particular element may vary considerably by region and state, these numbers provide a fairly accurate portrait of the general trends.

Poverty. Today nearly 20 percent of children in the nation live in poverty, up from 14 percent in 1969.[6] The median income of families in the bottom income quintile (20 percent) has eroded over time from $9,796[7] in 1977 to $8,919 in 1986, and the gap between the incomes of the poorest and wealthiest families has grown. The decline in real income to those in the lower quintile has been accompanied by gains for those in the two top income quintiles (40 percent). Race and ethnicity, gender, and family structure are strongly associated with the likelihood of poverty. In California, for example, 27 percent of Asian, 32 percent of black, and 34 percent of Hispanic children were poor in 1985-86, in contrast to 10 percent of all white children.[8] In

1984, half of the single women with children lived in poverty, compared to 11.4 percent of two-parent families.[9]

While many children fare well in households with low income, studies have shown that these children are more likely to die in infancy and early childhood,[10] suffer serious illness,[11] become pregnant during teen years, or drop out of school,[12] and are less likely to continue education beyond high school.[13] Despite statistical associations of these outcomes with poverty, the direction of causality is less clear.[14] The life chances may be linked to the lack of access to adequate health care and nutrition, the often lower quality of schooling in poorer neighborhoods, the stress of poverty on family relationships, or other elements.

Family structure. Most institutions that serve children and youth are structured on the assumption that children live with two biological parents, one working in the home and the other in the formal labor market. This traditional type now comprises only a small proportion of families—less than a third. Forty-six percent of children live in homes where both parents work or the only parent is working.[15] Because of an increase in divorce and a rise in the number of births to single mothers,[16] about one-half of all children and youth will live in a single-parent family for some period of their lives.[17] However, at any particular time 75 percent live in two-parent families, including stepparents.[18] Nationally, about one-tenth of families have a stepparent present. The proportions living in single-parent families vary substantially by race and ethnic group: in 1985, roughly 10 percent of Asian children, 12 percent of white children, 24 percent of Hispanic children, and 52 percent of black children lived in these family settings.[19]

Family structure, as we have said, is a good predictor of children's economic well-being, with single mothers disproportionately represented in poverty statistics. The hourly wages of single mothers are lower than those of other women (whose wages are generally more than one-third less than men), and although the majority of these women work, many depend on public assistance. Child support payments are notoriously meager or nonexistent for most primary caregivers. In 1985, only half of all custodial mothers had court-ordered support decrees for financial assistance, and most received less than 50 percent of the payments stipulated. For mothers with income below the poverty level, the situation was worse. Only 40 percent obtained support decrees from the courts, and one-third of these actually received nothing.[20]

The way family structures develop has consequences for children. When single-parent families occur as a result of divorce, the consequences, at least in the short term, may be negative for children's emotional well-being. A study of seven- to eleven-year-olds found children of divorce twice as likely to use mental health services as other children the same age. Children of divorce are more likely to become substance abusers, marry as teenagers, become sexually active at an earlier age, and become pregnant more often. Single parenthood, whether as a result of divorce or otherwise, is often a stressful situation for the parent, and one which may have consequences for the child-parent relationship. In addition, children of single mothers who have never been married tend to be even poorer, more dependent on welfare, and living in poor housing.[21]

Work. In recent decades both female and teenage work behavior has changed dramatically. While working mothers from poor families were not uncommon in the past, women from middle- and upper-income families have come to join them. Economic pressures have made the option of becoming a full-time homemaker almost obsolete for the majority of women and men.

As of 1987, over half of all mothers with children under age six and nearly 70 percent of mothers with children aged six to seventeen were seeking employment or worked in the formal labor market outside the home.[22] As with other indicators reported here, this varies by race and ethnic origin. Forty-two percent of white and 51.4 percent of black mothers of children under age six worked.[23] The consequence of changing work patterns is a high (and unmet) demand for affordable quality child care and after-school care.

Teenagers, too, are working in the formal labor market in large numbers. In 1985, almost 62 percent of all sixteen- to nineteen-year-olds worked during some part of the year. At least one-third of all high school students hold part-time jobs in any given week, with 75 percent of seniors working an average of sixteen to twenty hours weekly.[24] The majority of this income is used to buy clothes, food, and personal items. The evidence on the effect of work on teenagers is not definitive. Some studies have found that working detracts from schoolwork and is associated with dropping out. But other research and program evaluations suggest that work can provide positive models and can lead to improved academic performance.[25]

Health. In general terms, progress has been made on a number of fronts concerning children's health. In California, for example, 97 percent of kindergartners have received adequate immunization for measles, rubella, and mumps. Death rates from communicable diseases such as tuberculosis and pneumonia have fallen by a hundredfold in the past fifty years as a result of antibiotics, sanitation, and other advances. Fewer than 10 percent of California's children are considered to have serious health problems or chronic disabilities that limit their activities.

However, the conditions of poverty not surprisingly lead to disproportionate amounts of health problems. As mentioned, the morbidity rates of these children is higher than the rest of the young population, and they are more likely to suffer serious illness. A relative lack of prenatal care for women in poverty leads to children with low birthweights, a condition that often predicts persistent health problems. In California, children in poverty in 1984-85 spent twice as many days in the hospital as other children. The two to one ratio also held true between minority and white children. In addition, blacks, Hispanics, and other minorities are less likely to have health insurance than white non-Hispanics, especially in the "near poor" category where family incomes are too high to qualify for Medicaid benefits but low enough to make private health insurance a serious financial burden.[26]

The major health problems for adolescents result from things they do to themselves or to each other as is revealed by a disturbing trend in deaths from suicide, murder, and preventable accidents. In addition, 5 percent use illicit drugs, 20 percent smoke cigarettes, and 35 percent regularly use alcohol.[27] Physicians estimate that over 15 percent of the children born in big city California public hospitals had drug- or alcohol-addicted mothers.

In sum, the overall condition of children as indicated by income, family structure and background, health, and other measures has changed considerably in the last few years. These changes warrant a reassessment of the delivery of services to children and a reconsideration of the appropriate role of the school.

Problems of Providing Services for Children with Multiple Needs

The condition of the services currently delivered to children and youth are plagued by two broad problems—underservice and service fragmentation. These two problems amplify the issues and challenges confronting children outlined above, issues that have important implications for schooling. In short, given these societal changes business as usual in children's services is not good enough, and may contribute to even greater long-term problems.

Across areas of child abuse, mental health, child care, and other domains of youth policy, the information collected in the report on the *Conditions of Children in California* leads to a clear conclusion: a substantial portion of the nation's needy youth are either unserved or underserved by existing policy arrangements.

At a time when families in poverty are on the increase, funding for supplemental income programs like Aid to Families with Dependent Children (AFDC), for instance, has been diminishing—down $7 billion since 1980. In 1985-86 the parent(s) of less than *half* of all poor children nationwide received income from AFDC. Furthermore, the supplemental income that AFDC does provide falls short of families' minimal needs.

Other evidence also indicates a declining infrastructure of support for children from poor families. Thirty-nine percent of eligible children do not receive free or reduced price lunches; one-fourth are not covered by health insurance; 38 percent do not receive food stamps; public housing accommodates only 21 percent of all families in poverty.[28]

Although California far exceeds other states in providing funding for child care, public programs met only 2.2 percent of the child care needs of children up to two years old in families eligible for subsidy. For children aged three to five, public programs served only 17.9 percent of the eligible population, and 7 percent for children six to ten years old.[29] And the cost of care exceeds the ability of most families to pay. Again using California as an example, the average costs of preschool care for one child in 1986 consumed about 11 percent of the income of a family earning at the median level, and 27 percent of the income of a family of four at the federal poverty level.[30] Also overburdened are facilities for dealing with child abuse; in California, for example, one-fifth of the emergency response calls concerning child abuse went unanswered for a week or more.

The following account illustrates the problem of service fragmentation:

Consider the San Francisco family of six foster children headed by a severely disabled 67 year old woman. The family lives in public housing, receives financial assistance, and receives services from multiple agencies. The broad array and diversity of the agencies is reflected as follows. The Department of Social Services (DSS) is involved with the foster children; the woman has a DSS worker from the Adults Division. San Francisco General Hospital Family Health Center is the health care provider of the woman and many of the children. Staff of the Visiting Nurses Association of San Francisco make regular visits to the patient and a public health nurse visits the fourteen-year-old teen mother. The Teenage Pregnancy Parenting Program (TAPP) and the Unified School District provide special services to this teen. The San Francisco General Hospital Early Parenting Program also provides services to the mother. Some of the older children who have drug problems have been involved with the police and have received drug rehabilitation program services. There have been reports that the younger foster children are having school problems, and one of the foster children has recently been placed in a special education program. All of the foster children have either Big Brothers or Big Sisters.[31]

The lawyers, psychiatrists, physicians, and mental health and education professionals, each from their own perspective and within the context of their particular involvement, try to develop support strategies and services. In California, over 160 programs located in thirty-five agencies and seven departments exist to serve children and youth, an array which certainly is not unique to that state. The tally does not include the many private organizations that also provide important assistance. Existing fragmentation is a monument to the single-issue policies and single-issue solutions that dominate social policy in America. Historically, children's policy has proceeded ad hoc as problems are "discovered," leading to a patchwork of solutions with little consideration of the existing policy configuration. Policies and programs for children are driven largely by political definitions of the problem and administrative definitions of the solution—specific responses to specific problems—rather than a consideration of the aggregate policy environment.

Lost in this fragmented intervention is an opportunity for professionals providing children's services to observe or acknowledge the cumulative impact of their activities on the lives of children and their families. With compartmentalization, children and families continue to fall between the cracks of various administrative definitions of "the problem," bringing costly redundancy at a time of general underservice. This can lead to an absolute loss of resources and support for children who need it most. The isolation of services has particular consequences for schools, the institutions that have the most sustained contact with children and their families. While the manifestations of fragmentation and underservice most often are evident as problems in school, the majority of schools do not have, for example, family counselors or health facilities. Furthermore, they lack much information about or contact with other services that could help address these needs.

CONSEQUENCES OF FRAGMENTATION

In addition to underservice or nonservice, fragmentation has a number of consequences on the conditions of children, consequences which may be especially acute for children with multiple needs.

Isolation of problems and labeling. Public policy responses typically focus on individual pathologies; task forces investigate problems like suicide, substance abuse, or other disturbing conditions. Though important, the method of isolating particular problems for investigation or response leads to a fundamental loss of vision on the often close linkage *between* these various problems for any particular individual. Too often youth with multiple problems receive a programmatic label (substance abuser, delinquent, dropout, teen parent) that misrepresents or oversimplifies the nature of the trouble and obstructs comprehensive assessment or response. No existing mechanisms trigger the comprehensive planning and integrated case management that are particularly important for children and youth with multiple needs.

Discontinuity of care. When children and youth move from one level of care to another (e.g., from home to detention in juvenile hall, from inpatient psychiatric hospitalization to residential treatment, or from dependency to emancipation), they move in and out of different departmental jurisdictions, encountering different groups of service providers who do not follow them to the next level of care. If service systems were better integrated, high-risk families, children, and youth would be part of a system of care that responded to their needs knowledgeably and consistently regardless of their place in the service continuum.

Conflicting goals. Conflicting concepts of purpose or treatment philosophy generate dissension and attenuate service. While the debate in part reflects differences between liberal and conservative political factions, it also reflects important differences in notions of service and standards of effective service or quality. For example, in California there is a longstanding debate in the area of child care between the Department of Social Service and the Department of Education. The former frames the fundamental purpose of child care services as custodial; the latter conceives of child care as a developmental program. This elemental lack of agreement has generated incapacitating suspicion and lack of cooperation between agencies at both state and local levels. Within the juvenile justice system an unresolved disagreement exists between those who believe programs should continue a dominant focus on rehabilitation, and others who believe in deterrence through punishment.

Few services see the child as more than a temporary "recipient" with documented needs to be filled. In all children and youth sectors, there is a crucial imbalance favoring acute care over preventative or developmental services. This de facto definition of the "problem" as short-term and compartmentalized is compounded by the absence of any system of longitudinal record keeping or assessment.

Inability to bring existing resources to bear on problems. Lack of communication among service providers also frustrates service provision. School staff are often unaware of services available through juvenile justice, social service, or mental health agencies. One cannot expect actors at the base of the children's services to have developed broad networks for sharing information when no one at the top of the system knows the extent of services available for children. In California, for example, counties and school districts are the major providers of children's services but no data are available concerning total expenditures on children in the counties. A major study was needed just to compile and analyze children's programs and budgets in one county.[32]

Disempowered youth. Partly as a result of fragmentation and partly as a result of an embedded paternalistic approach toward children and youth, these populations have not been asked to participate in a dialogue to identify problems and possible alternative solutions. By segmenting out the different manifestations into isolated agencies it becomes difficult for the individual to coordinate what he or she wants or needs.

"Who is there for the children?" This question can not be answered if no one is looking at all the elements of children's lives and considering how they fit together. It is the whole environment that creates the conditions for an adult life of satisfaction and productivity. Few teachers, physicians, workers in the juvenile court system, social workers, or others focus on the interactive or interdependent nature of their contribution to the experience of youth. Instead they look only at their own performance as members of particular agencies. Research has barely begun to develop a broader frame of reference that could answer these questions or illuminate the aggregate effects of the totality of policies regarding children on youth and their families. California, for example, simply collects no data on how the recipients or targets of the state's byzantine services for children experience the system.

Rethinking Services to Children: Short-Term and Long-Term

As we have seen, the consequences of a system of children's services that are defined by administrative boundaries and conceptions of "turf" are more than simply exasperating or inefficient. The system, many professionals and analysts agree, is beyond fixing with a bit of this improvement and some of that innovation. It is in need of fundamental rethinking. This is not a new conclusion. Neither is the prescription of "more integration," "more coordination," and "more collaboration."

Yet most analyses stop with this plea. The problems of doing other than continuing current arrangements are admittedly formidable. An institutional structure of childen's services that is built upon political compromise, time-honored professional terrain, and existing administrative arrangements intimidates efforts at reform. Such a structure comprises fundamental obstacles to serious consideration of a different model of children's services. The usual prescription encourages an earnest nod at the need for "more integration" or "new approaches," but quietly counsels a return to existing practices for reasons of political, bureaucratic, and fiscal feasibility. Schools are a major element in this fragmentation since they have been independent from the governing authority of county, city, and other children's agencies, and have their own property tax base. What are some of the obstacles to coordination?

Few earmarked resources for coordination. The monetary incentives for agencies or institutions to do other than move along in single-track service are nonexistent to negative. Few resources are designated by policymakers to encourage cooperation among agencies or agents. When efforts to integrate or coordinate do occur, they generally come "above and beyond" the already crowded scope of professionals' current responsibilities.

Finding mutuality. The *Conditions of Children in California* provides numerous examples of debates among service providers: Who would get the money following the child if services were shared? Whose treatment philosophy would dominate? Who would get to decide about the standards, scope, and nature of programs or services for children in a joint-agency setting? How would instances of misaligned incentives be resolved?

One need only look at programs authorized by different levels of government to see the difficulties of coordination and cooperation. For instance, numerous bureaucratic problems have arisen over efforts to merge federal and state eligibility requirements. Even more problematic from the perspective of the local service provider (and so from the perspective of the intended beneficiary) are the obstacles to effective service delivery created by programs that involve multiple agencies or centers of authority, even within the same service sector such as mental health or juvenile justice.

Training segregation. The isolation of professionals, agencies, and services is the inevitable result of a system that reifies and reinforces conceptions of discrete problem areas and bounded professional turf. The socialization and training of professionals begins at the university where traditional departmental structures stymie interprofessional or coordinated professional programs. Most people who work with children and youth sectors are trained in separate schools within the academy, such as schools of education, social work, public health, and public administration. Nor do they find common ground once they begin practicing since professional meetings and conferences rarely overlap the fields. These professionals thus form separate networks for their entire careers. For example, the San Diego Superintendent of Schools had been in his job over five years before he met the major county-level administrators of children's services.

PROMISING RESPONSES TO TACKLE THE CONCERNS: THE SHORT-TERM

Even in the face of such imposing difficulties, however, a number of promising responses to the problems inherent in present arrangements are appearing in California and other communities around the country. Pushed by a sense of urgency and conviction, practitioners and policymakers in diverse arenas have moved to recast aspects of children's services both structurally and conceptually. While they fall short of addressing dysfunctions in the system and attempt more modest goals of making a particular domain of children's services work better, in the future they can provide valuable and real-life lessons about the problems and the potential benefits of cooperation and coordination. However, our intent here is not to evaluate these projects or describe them in fine detail but merely to point out efforts that move in the right direction.

To deal with the discontinuities of a fragmented service system and isolated professional staff, Ventura and San Bernardino counties in California created coordinating mechanisms to integrate services to clients. Ventura County established an interagency network that includes cooperation at the highest administrative levels. The agency directors of mental health, social services, corrections, and special education formally consented to share responsibility for the system. All services are based on written interagency agreements identifying the full range of problems that place a child at risk and the treatments they will implement. With a specific focus on high-risk children who are either potentially or actually living out of their natural homes, the Ventura program reportedly has been successful in blending services and personnel from agencies participating in the network into a comprehensive and continuing treatment for troubled youth. Services follow the child, thereby establishing new links with private sector providers.

The San Bernardino program is modeled after Ventura's efforts, but has its own distinctive features. All major youth-serving agencies in the county—juvenile justice, the schools, public health, community services, the district attorney, the sheriff, libraries, Head Start, probation, and others participate in the Children's Policy Council. This council in turn is served by a Children's Advocate Council which provides advice and "grassroots" awareness of problems and community-based children's issues. Members include representatives of the PTA, United Way, Foster Parent Advisory Committee, Maternal, Child and Adolescent Health Advisory Board, Drug Advisory Board, ministers, and the Native Americans group. A Children's Services Team provides the vehicle for ongoing monitoring and evaluation of program services. A First Fund of Children's Resources seeks to form a partnership between the public, private-for-profit, and nonprofit sector to provide monetary and in-kind contributions, goods, and services.

In both Ventura and San Bernardino, planning for an integrated service model was facilitated by special funding from state sources, and influential members of the community—a juvenile court judge in both cases—pushed for change. Both efforts had high-level support from key agencies from the beginning, as well as a strong commitment of middle-level professional staff.

Minneapolis also has a structure to coordinate a range of youth services. Unlike the Ventura and San Bernardino efforts, which originated with and are sustained by youth service professionals, the Minneapolis Youth Coordinating Board (MYCB) is a creation of municipal government and the mayor. Created through a joint powers agreement between the City of Minneapolis, the Minneapolis Public Schools, Hennepin County, the Minneapolis Park and Recreation Board, and the Minneapolis Public Library Board, the eleven-member MYCB defines its goals in terms of promoting the integration and quality of services for *all* of the community's young people, not just youth with special needs.

As in Ventura and San Bernardino, funds were made available for planning and operation of the coordinating body. Each of the five sponsoring governmental bodies contractually agreed to provide at least $100,000 per year for five years to support basic staffing and operating costs. The apparent success of the MYCB thus far is to a significant degree a consequence of the vigorous commitment of the mayor to an integrated youth policy for the city and to making its development a top municipal priority. Further, the strategy for getting started and mobilizing broad community support for the effort was important to the MYCB's present level of operation. Plans and activities began with a well-regarded early childhood family education program that did not, in the words of the executive director, "isolate the poor or particular neighborhoods" but served all children from 0-5 years with home visits, child advocates, and other services. MYCB has created its own local property tax base that can provide revenue for continuing its integrated services plan.

The Ounce of Prevention Fund in Illinois, created in 1982 as a partnership between the state child welfare agency and a private, philanthropic institution, serves as a broker and coordinator of services in a number of communities throughout the state. The Ounce of Prevention Fund supports a statewide system of service, research, training, and technical assistance focused on community-based programs for pre-teens, teen parents, and their families. The Fund was launched with matching grants of $400,000 each from the Illinois Department of Children and Family Services and the Pittway Corporation Charitable Foundation. Other funders include an array of state agencies and private foundations as well as the National Center for Child Abuse and Neglect and the U.S. Department of Health and Human Services. The Fund appears to be an effective response to the regulatory tangles that impede interagency coordination because as a third party organization it has more flexibility to blend services and activities. Also, because it is dedicated to brokering services and leveraging community-based support from a variety of sources (e.g., churches, community action groups, corporations, the schools, and so on), it is able to enhance the resources available to the youth it serves. As a third party intermediary, the Fund is free of suspicion of "special pleading," narrow institutional self-interest, and problem definitions rooted in professionally prescribed domains.

While each of these efforts has pursued substantively different programmatic strategies, each also has self-consciously *reconceptualized* the purpose of children's services, moving from the traditional clinical and constricted notions that dominate most practices to a developmentally based view that sees the needs of youth as evolutionary and continuing. These approaches place youth services in the broader context in which children live—family, school, neighborhood. For example, the Ounce of Prevention Fund seeks explicitly to shift services from traditional perspectives based on notions of individual pathology to services that are built on models of individual development. The MYCB also features developmental language. While it is difficult (and perhaps too early) to tell the extent to which these reconceptualizations of the "problem" signal more than superficial or rhetorical change in policy, they nonetheless are prominent in self-reports, in service guidelines, and in goal statements. Only systematic evaluations over several years could tell us whether these approaches have been successful in meeting their objectives. But merely locating many children's services in one place helps clients use the system more easily.

GOALS FOR THE LONG TERM

To make integration work—to create a community of resources responsive to children's needs—children's services will have to be marked by comprehensiveness, competency, and diversity. It will do little good to talk of integrating services for children unless we integrate children as active participants into the community of services and resources. It is not integration if we simply move to integrate services that continue to talk *at* rather than *with* children; or that continue to do *to* and *for* children rather than plan and work *with* them and with their identified needs. Current practices send social workers to observe and to talk with adults for the first and primary sources of information about how children are faring. Comprehensiveness comes in creating channels of communication, using the child as a prime transmitter of information. To be sure, the rearrangements of institutions to facilitate an easy flow of information and a comparison of available resources must come with a reconceptualization of the role of the child. Forging a matrix where individuals from at least one part of the services system are in touch with children on an ongoing basis could facilitate exchanges that begin with the child. As it is, the majority of children's services respond to crises as they emerge and they do not know what has happened in other parts of children's lives or their interactions with other service agencies.

Relatedly, competency is the second feature that must mark long-term solutions. Here we mean creating institutions and institutional tasks that actively engage children in identifying and solving their own problems and that involve them in tasks, group support systems, and long-term commitment. Adults in both schools and service agencies typically talk *at* children, labeling their problems and fixing solutions dictated by administrative fiat or "that's just how it's done" procedures. Children and youths rarely have a chance to enter into the dialogue for problem identification or to consider and evaluate possible alternative solutions, weighing risks and benefits. Youth services personnel, as well as procedures and policies, offer and dictate a paternalistic approach and argue that the "mess of their lives" indicates that they have no such capabilities.

Diversity cuts two ways. At one level, we mean to imply a diverse but coordinated set of agents and organizations available to serve children and youth. At another level, diversity comes from the array of ethnic, linguistic, and socioeconomic groups that respond to these agents and organizations in different ways as a result of cultural values, behavioral norms, language, and available resources. Different families encourage or discourage their children to participate in the array of community resources beyond the primary family unit. For example, urban black families are more inclined to permit their children to find work and leisure resources beyond the family than are recently arrived Mexican families. Single-parent, middle-class families who have chosen "voluntary poverty" are much more likely to enable their children to take advantage of an array of free public services than are single-parent households which did not choose poverty. Services must be aware of and sensitive to this diversity not only as a way of reaching out to those who may need assistance but also to respond with assistance in a meaningful way.

GETTING FROM HERE TO WIDESPREAD INTEGRATION
OF SERVICES FOR YOUTH

The political momentum for a new, more comprehensive policy for children and youth has unusual potential now, in part because of possible intergenerational linkages. For instance, the concerns of the middle class about child care can be fused with the urgent child care needs of disadvantaged groups. People are realizing that security in their older ages rests to some degree on the productive capacity of the young. Building a broader coalition for improvement depends on public support, but another crucial element will be the successful enlistment of professionals and leaders from education, health, protective services, and other sectors, as well as among those across the public and the private sectors. Their support is needed to give a momentum to changes that would bridge the various services, and to give integration a chance for success.

We are skeptical of symbolic reorganization devices like a state department of children's services or a state children's code of law. Surface reorganizations fail to acknowledge that the problems we have analyzed are deeply rooted and can not be solved by superficial changes in organizational structures. Our understanding of the ingredients needed for successful initiation of local service coordination suggests that money from foundations for flexible initiatives has been crucial in generating effective local child resource policies. Other key characteristics are cooperation among mid-level bureaucrats, commitment from top executives, and adaptation to particular local contexts. Consequently, we believe that federal and state government should provide seed money and prescribe a local process for the reconceptualization and planning of integrated children's services.

The longer-range perspective requires support from research and evaluation that presently is missing. One of the chronic problems in attempts to develop complex understandings of the conditions of children's lives is the lack of adequate information about the aggregate effects of the national, state, and local services on individuals and groups. Because children's needs are not neatly compartmentalized, and because a consequential part of the policy debate cuts across categories, labels, and professional domains, it is essential that research on children and children's services also not be bound by existing institutional arrangements or authorization. Information specific to the state and local contexts is a prerequisite for any kind of policy analysis that will successfully lead to change. Policymakers realize that support from the public emerges when they perceive connections to special local issues and problems.

This longer-range perspective will also require that the high boundaries between professions be lowered, beginning with university training and extending through professional practice. Programs to prepare educational administrators should provide more interprofessional experiences and curriculums. The Ohio State University has designed such programs, which bring together nurses, doctors, lawyers, social workers, educators, and others. This early orientation to interprofessional preparation can help break down the barriers that are built into the delivery system and create integrated professional networks.

But most importantly, coordination of youth services must find an organizational and structural center. We suggest that the school would be one logical hub of integration. Other hubs are needed, but that matter is beyond the scope of this chapter.

The Role of Schooling

Schools provide the organizational context for the most sustained and ongoing contact with children outside the family setting. This element facilitates a relatively long-term understanding of the needs and concerns of youth, a perspective often missing from other services. Because of everyday contact, the school can provide a setting for continuing exchanges with children that can better include them in the processes of identifying problems and possible solutions and can more quickly catch new needs as they arise. The developmental approach embedded in much of schooling activities could also provide a much needed perspective to other services that tend to respond to episodic and acute crises as they emerge.

The historic separation of schooling from city or county government, however, mitigates against coordination and against the notion of the school as a center of activity for youth services. In the early part of this century schools developed a separate board and tax base with few formal linkages to other units of local government. However, this separation did not protect schools from politics, as was intended; rather, it created an alternative set of politics. It did succeed in encouraging only sporadic interaction with general government and often adversarial relationships with town and municipal governments.[33] We contend that this metropolitan political separation is dysfunctional with respect to meeting the multiple needs of many students. The political or informal linkages between most cities, counties, and schools are minimal and not oriented around the particular developmental needs of at-risk children. Furthermore, separation has weakened a potential coalition for children since educators rarely coordinate political strategy with other service providers.

Those who advocated the separation of school governance from other local governments accomplished their objectives, as evidenced by a national study of school boards.

Local boards and their members have only sporadic interaction with general government and tend to be isolated from mainstream community political structures.

There is very little systematic communication between school system governance and general government, despite the fact that increasing numbers of students have learning problems associated with nonschool factors. These include poor housing, lack of family support and resources, and limited employment opportunities. In addition, when interaction between the school system and general government does exist, it often is only through the superintendent. Fiscally dependent boards which must interact with town/municipal government bodies frequently are mired in adversarial relationships.[34]

Under a new vision the school could become the site or broker of numerous services such as health clinics, child care, alcohol and drug abuse programs, and organized recreation programs. More child care and preschool programs could be located on or near school grounds to provide a better transition with the regular school program. While the school should not financially underwrite these services, it could provide the facilities and welcome city, county, and private agencies to school grounds. Schools would need additional funds to help provide integrated case management of the student with multiple problems and would not be the only place where interagency collaboration might take place. The familiarity of a case manager with all matters of consequence currently affecting the family would improve assistance to parents and youth and help prevent problems before they emerge or become severe.

The effective case manager knows about the various public or private agencies that can help and attempts to orchestrate the fragmented service delivery systems. In successful examples, the case manager coaches the individual in identifying his or her own problem and course of action. The case manager does not take over for parents or tell them what to do—responses that would serve to reinforce the dependence of the family on outside authorities to solve their own problems. Schools need to create incentives for teachers and administrators to prevent problems through effective collaboration with other agencies. Collaboration needs to penetrate the classroom and help students achieve academic success.

The school as the site of numerous children's services will require a rethinking of the role of the principal. If the principal were designated as chief administrator of the broader array of services for children, time for instructional and other schooling duties might be insufficient. This kind of change would also require drastic alterations in the current scope of principal preparation and programs for staff development. Another strategy would be to locate a children's services coordinator at the school who would be employed by county or city government. This option would relieve the school of stretching its already often burdensome administrative obligations. The services coordinator would report to an interagency council of local children's services. In the California context, county government has the major nonschool responsibility for children with multiple needs and would hire the school site coordinator.

While there are many visions of the next wave of school reform, the school as the hub for comprehensive student services should become more prominent. The bottom third of the achievement band and students who are failing because of numerous interrelated problems are not likely to be helped much by a strategy that focuses *solely* on raising academic standards or providing more teacher decision making. Children's prospects have a good chance of improving only through a broader conception of childhood.

In Conclusion

Today's schools build on yesterday's notion of "family" and on children's environment in both form and function. The social institutions upon which schools build have shifted dramatically, and the problems of family/school relations are too complex, too varied, and too enmeshed with larger social realities to respond to single policy solutions such as parent partnerships, parent involvement mechanisms, and the like.[35] Although school administrators and teachers acknowledge that children and youth arrive not as empty vessels but as complex individuals whose entire experience shapes how well they learn and attain in school, policies and practices generally do not reflect this understanding. Policymakers intermittently demonstrate this view with monies for school counselors, lunch programs, parent involvement mechanisms, and the like. But primarily the school is considered the locus of learning while other bureaucracies—the juvenile courts, health and welfare agencies, drug and substance abuse programs—are conceived to meet separated components of children's lives.

Given the rapidly changing nature of school populations and the persistence of poverty, health, and other problems, policymakers and school practitioners must bridge the connection between the conditions of education and the total conditions of children. Promising responses can be crafted by moving from a focus on component aspects of the problem—teachers, texts, families—to a focus on the functional requirements of a healthy, curious, productive, motivated child. This changed perspective draws attention to the child as an actor in a larger social system and to the institutional networks and resources present in that larger environment. It requires looking beyond family to the primary networks that make up a child's environment, and thinking of the school in a new way, as a nexus of institutions within this environment. Taking this view, the school moves from the role of "deliverer" of educational services to the role of broker of the multiple resources that can be applied to achieve successful, productive, and happy lives for children.[36]

FOOTNOTES

1. We refer here in general to the ages 0 to 18. For the sake of linguistic convenience, we will often use the terms "children" or "youth" but we mean to refer to the entire cluster of legal juveniles.

2. We mean by this term any primary caregiver, who may or may not be biologically related to the child. We lay out other distinctions later in the chapter.

3. The extent to which poverty itself or other characteristics within the context of the environment account for the problems is not clear, although poverty does have a direct impact on goods and services that affect the quality of children's lives.

4. Defined here in terms of money income. Although some studies include other types of income, such as public welfare monies, children in poverty still tend to fare worse on a variety of measures than their peers.

5. Martha S. Hill and Greg J. Duncan, "Parental Family Income and the Socioeconomic Attainment of Children," *Social Science Research* 16 (1987): 39.

6. From Current Population Survey Profile, 1986, California State Census Data Center. Cited in Michael Wald, John Evans, and Marc Ventresca, "The Economic Status of Children in California," in *The Conditions of Children in California*, ed. Michael Kirst (Berkeley: Policy Analysis for California Education [PACE], 1989).

7. In 1986 dollars.

8. Current Population Survey Profile, cited in Wald et al., "The Economic Status of Children."

9. Ibid.

10. Maine Department of Human Services, *Children's Deaths in Maine, 1976-80, Final Report* (Augusta, ME: Department of Human Services, 1983), cited in Wald et al., "The Economic Status of Children."

11. Lisa Egbuonu and Barbara Starfield, "Child Health and Social Status," *Pediatrics* 69 (1982): 550.

12. Andrew Hahn, Jacqueline Danzberger, and Bernard Lefkowitz, *Dropouts in America: Enough Is Known for Action* (Washington, DC: Institute for Educational Leadership, 1987).

13. John C. Flanagan and William W. Cooley, *Project Talent: One-Year Follow-up Studies* (Pittsburgh: School of Education, University of Pittsburgh, 1966) ERIC ED 010 087.

14. Wald et al., "The Economic Status of Children."

15. U.S. Department of Education, Office of Educational Research and Improvement, *Youth Indicators 1988: Trends in the Well-Being of American Youth* (Washington, DC: U.S. Department of Education, 1988), pp. 16-21.

16. A condition that results not from an increase in birthrates to single women, but because of a growth in the number of women in the U.S. population.

17. Larry Bumpass, "Children and Marital Disruption: A Replication and Update," *Demography* 21 (1984): 71.

18. Only 60 to 65 percent of all children presently live with both biological parents.

19. U.S. Department of Health and Human Services, *Social Indicators*, cited in Michael Wald, John Evans, C. Smrekar, and Marc Ventresca, "Children's Family Life," in *The Conditions of Children in California*, ed. Michael Kirst.

20. William T. Grant Foundation Commission on Work, Family, and Citizenship, *The Forgotten Half: Pathways to Success for America's Youth and Young Families* (Washington, DC: William T. Grant Foundation, 1988).

21. See Wald et al., "Children's Family Life."

22. U.S. Department of Education, *Youth Indicators 1988*, as cited in William T. Grant Foundation Commission on Work, Family, and Citizenship, *The Forgotten Half*.

23. Family Service of America, *The State of Families* (Milwaukee, WI: Family Service of America, 1984) as cited in William T. Grant Foundation Commission on Work, Family, and Citizenship, *The Forgotten Half*.

24. William T. Grant Foundation Commission on Work, Family, and Citizenship, *The Forgotten Half*.

25. Ibid.

26. Neal Halfon et al., "Health," in *The Conditions of Children in California*, ed. Michael Kirst.

27. Neal Halfon, Integrated Services Testimony to the California Senate Select Committee on Children and Youth, December 7, 1988.

28. Current Population Survey File, cited in Wald et al., "The Economic Status of Children."

29. Norton Grubb, "Child Care and Early Childhood Programs," in *The Conditions of Children in California*, ed. Michael Kirst.

30. Ibid.

31. Provided by Dr. Laura Grandin, Project Director, County of San Francisco Children, Youth, and Family Service Feasibility Study, 1988.

32. Paul Goren and Michael Kirst, "An Exploration of County Expenditures and Revenues for Children's Services" (Berkeley: Policy Analysis for California Education, February 1989).

33. Lila N. Carol et al., *School Boards: Strengthening Grass Roots Leadership* (Washington, DC: Institute for Educational Leadership, 1986).

34. Ibid.

35. Shirley Heath and Milbrey McLaughlin, "Policies for Children with Multiple Needs," in *The Conditions of Children in California*, ed. Michael Kirst.

36. Ibid.

Section Three
FAMILIES, COMMUNITIES,
AND EDUCATIONAL LEADERSHIP

CHAPTER V

Schools, Families, and Communities: Idealized Images and New Realities

LONNIE H. WAGSTAFF AND KAREN S. GALLAGHER

The question of what is school success and who should define it has dominated the study and practice of administration in education. As the decade of concern for "educational excellence" draws to a close, we chose to ask it again. We posed other questions, as well. In particular, we wondered when those who govern public schools and those who prepare educational leaders will accept the inevitable contradiction and tension between the idealized images and the complicated realities of schools, families, and communities.

In our search for answers we turned to metaphors. Metaphors related to family, community, or school relationships in the 1980s provide some enlightenment. Metaphors are surrogates for our perspective of society's order, an idealized world.[1] When families or homes are described as "broken" or when city governments work like "well-oiled machines," the generative metaphor suggests a parallel between social behavior and another important domain of human experience. The machine metaphor suggests a mechanistic and linear vision of societal institutions. Labeling families or children "at risk" suggests an analogy to the self-regulating characteristics of living organisms. Describing magnet schools or voucher plans in terms of consumer choice and competition fixes educational relationships in the marketplace. Characterizing school-community activities as a "dialogue" implies a human conversation where motive and shared meaning are equally important.

The more we delved into the task of how to describe and understand the relationships among families, communities, and schools, the more frustrated we became. The ill-defined nature of the relationship underscores the current dilemma facing politicians, practitioners, professional organizations, and academic researchers. The home-school relationship is problematic. We believe there are problems in how schools relate to different family structures, in how schools fit into diverse communities, in how schools perform their roles, and in what the proper roles are. Thus this chapter is a critical essay rather than a comprehensive review of research literature on families, communities, and their relationships with schools. Essentially, three questions guide our excursion on the nature and status of school, family, and community relations.

1. Where did our current conceptions of the family and the community originate, and how do these idealized concepts relate to the political, social, and demographic realities of the 1980s and 1990s?

2. What are meaningful indicators of family, community, and school well-being?

3. What is meant by the terms "school-community relations" and "home-school relationships"?

After addressing these three questions, we tried to tease out the critical issues for school practitioners, professors of educational administration, and school reformers.

School, Family, and Community in Sociohistorical Context

Traditionally, parents in the United States have borne the primary responsibility for meeting the needs of their own children. Most parents make an effort to give their children not only food, clothing, and shelter but "intangibles" such as motivation and emotional support. Yet few families have ever shouldered the task of educating their children completely alone. Even in Puritan Massachusetts, there were laws defining the relationship between family needs and school responsibilities.[2] In 1787, the language of the Northwest Ordinance noted the relationship between "religion, morality, and knowledge being necessary to good government and the happiness of mankind."[3] Thomas Jefferson was among the first to propose a system of free public elementary schools. George Washington recommended the establishment of a national university. Lincoln administered the

Morrill Act, granting land and legitimacy for colleges, but he also signed into law the Freedman's Bureau. This agency provided fifteen million food vouchers, clothing income supplements, job training, energy assistance, and housing assistance for 250,000 families and reimbursed medical expenses for a million persons after the Civil War.[4]

In the twentieth century, the federal government enacted several pieces of major legislation affecting the relationship between families and schools. Democratic and Republican presidents alike have signed such bills as the Smith-Hughes Act (for vocational education), National School Lunch Act, National Defense Education Act, Head Start, Elementary and Secondary Education Act, Education for the Handicapped Act, and Juvenile Justice and Delinquency Prevention Act. In addition, most American children are educated in public schools funded by the taxes of parents and nonparents alike. Taxpayers are then allowed to deduct state and local tax payments from their income in figuring federal taxes. In this way, the federal government subsidizes the contributions of high-income taxpayers (as those who itemize usually are) to elementary and secondary education.[5]

Communities also have been shaped by the actions of the federal government. As taxpayers, we have been less bothered by direct public support for decrepit neighborhoods and bankrupt cities than we have for direct public support for families. From the 1930s until the 1970s, the prevailing political debate at the national level was over *how* to alter formal community structures through governmental action.[6] Those who favored direct federal regulation of schools and local governments believed political power must be distributed properly to eliminate social conflict.[7] The national government's system of checks and balances is a reflection of the historical concern over the need to control power. Episodically, calls have been made for radical changes in community power structures. Central to these arguments has been the prominence given to equity as a social value promoted by direct governmental action. Those who favored definitive federal action to define and to articulate public purposes were concerned with empowering social institutions like schools through extensive governmental intervention.[8]

With few exceptions, public school administrators have supported the soundness of the traditional American social order and the belief system supporting it.[9] They have extolled the capacity of the American education system to promote family and community values.

It is a long-recognized bond between schools and parents to turn children into productive citizens.[10] Yet many American families in the 1980s are either unable or unwilling to shape, support, stimulate, or encourage their children in the traditional ways schools expect.

Parental inability or unwillingness to work with school administrators stems from many causes. Perhaps the most often cited reason for the perceived decline in parental support of public schools is the perceived decline in the stability of the American family. Clearly, the family as the basic unit of society has experienced profound pressures and demands over the past quarter century. More and more educators cite family disruption or turmoil as *the* central factor placing students "at risk." On the other hand, many parents blame the schools for not educating their children properly. As the next generation perhaps withers on the vine, neither educator nor parent seems willing to take significant responsibility for the nurturance of children and youth, especially those young souls who inhabit the margins of society.

The Social History of American Families

Historically, idealized images of family life were derived from the prevailing political, economic, social, or religious ethos. In colonial times, most children of white European descent were seen as financial assets who could help work the farm or be apprenticed out of the home at an early age.[11] The Puritans advocated harsh disciplinary measures for children, but the attention they focused on children's upbringing became a standard practice of nineteenth-century wealthy merchant families in the United States and England. In the eighteenth and nineteenth centuries, children of slaves were extreme examples of the "child as financial asset" metaphor. With the industrial revolution, children from immigrant and poor families became a source for cheap factory labor. While the Victorian era vacillated from harsh to permissive treatment of children, the child-centered family began to take form. By the twentieth century, the importance of a child's upbringing was an integral value of the middle-class family.

Family historians have found that the prevailing family mode in the United States today, the small nuclear family, is not new to modern culture.[12] Even in colonial America, the large extended family with seven or eight children and several generations living under one roof was more the exception than the rule. The functions and structure of the American family have changed continuously over the decades and a variety of family types coexisted in each historical era in different regions and among different classes. Yet the nuclear family is the dominant idealized image of family life in America. Indeed, the nuclear family definition served as the normative measurement standard for the United States Census until 1980. Sociologists have defined the nuclear family as, "two adults of opposite sex, living in a socially approved sexual relationship with their own or adopted children."[13] This definition has been a popular conception of family in books, films, television shows, and art. Norman Rockwell's paintings provide the idealized portrayal of nuclear family life in twentieth-century America.

Although industrialization began in the United States in the early nineteenth century, the farm family as the image of self-sufficiency remained an ideal model for city-dwelling families. In reality, families in cities ceased to be units of production, becoming transformed by the successes of the industrial revolution into consumption units.[14] Factory employment freed young adults from direct dependency upon their families and weakened the authority of the father, the traditional head of the family. Urbanization brought the development of such establishments as hotels, rooming houses, grocery stores, and laundries, making it possible for people to live apart from families. Women no longer had to marry or had to stay married to have a place to live.[15]

Yet despite sometimes rapid and often dramatic changes in the family, schools held tight to the classic image of the self-sufficient family as the standard for home behavior. Families from racial, ethnic, and religious subgroups in American society who did not fit the dominant image often were ignored, considered to be pathological, or excluded from participation in social institutions like schools.[16]

Since World War II, the idealized image of the family has undergone some revisions. Like previous eras, this image has been affected not by changes necessarily experienced by real families but by the collective imaginations and inventions of the popular media and public policymakers.[17] Unlike previous eras, the age of television allowed nearly all Americans access to packaged portraits of the all-American family.

A review of highly rated television programs from the 1950s to the present reflects the mainstream media family.[18] The first family show to win consistently top ratings was "Mama," an account of a Norwegian-American family of five in turn-of-the-century San Francisco. "I Love Lucy" provided another version of the nuclear family. For six years, beginning in 1951, it never ranked lower than third in popularity. The comedy plots centered on the relationship between a stay-at-home wife and her hardworking husband, for whom she made life interesting. Lucy did not work because Desi wanted a "loving housewife" to welcome him home every night. This became the plot device for most of Lucy's exploits into the world outside their apartment.

From the early 1950s until 1968, many top-rated television shows featuring families shared the following characteristics: white and middle-class characters, housewife-mother, working father, bratty but competent children, and suburban or small-town setting. Even the genre of male head-of-household shows like "My Three Sons," "The Andy Griffith Show," and "Family Affair," kept the nuclear family image intact by replacing the deceased mother/wife with a surrogate mother/wife role. In 1968, "Julia" broke new ground in television programming. The black female lead was a single working parent, a widow whose husband had been killed in Vietnam. Situations were integrated but middle-class, including the presence of a kind and fatherly figure. The crank but lovable boss of Julia, Dr. Morton Chegley, substituted for the missing father.

In 1971, "All in the Family" touched off a series of shows about atypical (at least for television) families. There were ethnic families, black families, bi-racial families, families headed by divorced working mothers with teenage children, and families at the bottom of the economic ladder. All these shows dealt with relevant issues to the viewers: divorce, drugs, generation gaps, antiestablishment rebellion, feminism, homosexuality. But also popular in the 1970s were "throwback" programs like "The Waltons," "Little House on the Prairie," and "Happy Days." The uncertainty and diversity within and among families was reflected in television programming, although attention to the twelve- to eighteen-year-old market prevailed.

In the early 1980s, popular shows like "Dallas" featured extended families whose primary purpose was the greedy and self-indulgent accumulation of wealth and power. After 1985, three shows resurrected the traditional middle-class, nuclear family. "The Cosby Show," "Family Ties," and "Growing Pains," feature two parents, competent children with solvable problems, and secure homes. Although the specifics of each family reflect the late 1980s (black husbands and wives holding professional jobs; 1960s hippies having conservative children; fathers working at home), the situations still center on a stable nuclear family.

Theory can imitate television. Mainstream social theories explaining and predicting family behavior assume order is generated through shared values and a common belief in the sacredness of a hierarchical structure that places some individuals like working parents in positions of authority over others, namely children and stay-at-home parents.[19] Such assumptions often are bedrock principles of television family lives. Many of these theories concentrate on the quality of the family's performance of its functions, while other theories focus on quality of family life issues. Nonetheless, television and the traditional paradigm in the social sciences have shaped our view of the American family and the children and youth who come to our schools.

Modern American culture, however, still does not seem to have a clear fix on the notion of family. The various media inundate us with idealized images of family, but they do not help us explain or predict the future. Programs like "Divorce Court," "People's Court," "America's Most Wanted," and "A Current Affair" are as popular as most conventional family shows. Perhaps "family" has lost any sociocultural meaning. James Comer's *Maggie's American Dream*[20] reminds us of the important historical role black mothers played in transmitting the cultural importance of education for the next generation's future well-being. Maggie's dream was attainable as long as Maggie's children accepted the power and influence of family to explain the past and promote a sense of security for the future. Such dreaming has been the lifeblood for the hope and the promise in public education. The legitimacy of the American system of education fundamentally has depended upon parental and family belief in the power of education to change lives and to change destinies. Maggie's dream is still viable, but the reality of family crisis threatens to undermine the school's capacity to transform the future.

Images of American Community

Like the image of the strong nuclear family, the concept of the frontier town, farm community, and New England village pervades our collective psyche of the places American families reside. Towns, cities, and neighborhoods exist not only as real social and physical entities but also as inventions of people's minds. In fact, these terms exist as ways of thinking about the various realities they are meant to define. For some people, *town* is synonymous with a sense of a communal and pastoral life, while *city* often engenders the antithesis of such feelings. We tend to believe it is important to identify the differences between the concept of community and the physical places people inhabit. Community is often characterized as self-sufficiency, a common life, shared ends or norms, a collection of institutions, an emphasis on features of localism, and group uniqueness.[21] A community exists not only if all these characteristics are present, but social interaction and a specific geographic area are needed before a social collective is considered a community. This definition ties together the emotional attachment experienced by those within a community and the reality of a physical place.

The classic social science definition of community is "a social unit which consists of persons who share a common geographic area interacting in terms of a common culture and which incorporates a range of social structures which function to meet a relatively broad range of needs of all persons who make up the social unit."[22] This traditional interpretation views the community as a place, as the focal point of virtually all meaningful social activity. One of the century's greatest social scientists, Talcott Parsons, expressed the notion of community in the phrase "concrete collectivity."[23] Sociologists, urban planners, and city officials often follow Parsons' lead as they demarcate the specific geographic and sociological borders of neighborhoods, specifying who is a member and who is not, seeking a set of values and norms shared by all members as distinguished from every other one, and dealing with such concepts as community interest, community goals, community values, and community decision making. Essentially, this view of community rests on the assumption that community is a concrete place inhabited by individuals and institutions in search of common ground.

Another conceptualization of community suggests that a community is less a social group acting on its own behalf than "an arena or field of interaction manifesting certain systemic tendencies."[24] Taken to its extreme, this meaning of community becomes mass society, utterly independent of geographic location. This concept of community sees social action as more like the richly textured spontaneity of human conversations. The community is an aggregate of clustered interactions of people and associations who may or may not occupy a restricted geographic area. These connecting patterns, incidentally, show remarkable similarity as one goes from one place to another. Shared values and norms are seldom specific to a particular site but rather are part of a larger macrosystem. From this angle, community transcends time and space. It is a condition where people come together over values, needs, and demands.

Besides having cognitive and instrumental implications, these two concepts of community have important normative implications for schools.[25] The "concrete collectivity" model legitimizes community decision-making organizations, such as school boards, assuming there is a single community interest that school boards and other community organizations determine through a rational manner. This view of cooperative community decision making tends to exclude controversial issues and dissenters from the decision agenda. The concrete collectivity model of community demands more highly managed coordination. The assumption of a single set of community priorities fits well with a centralized and hierarchical governance structure administered by professionals who possess a sense of formality. Individuals and groups who do not agree with the dominant community interests are assumed to be acting from selfish interests. The second view of community does not promote conflict nor deny the value of cooperation in matters where all parties benefit. It does, however, challenge the notion of universal and rational community interest brought about by consensus of powerful individuals and institutions. *245541*

There are many metaphors for communities, especially cities, that offer meaningful insights about the relationship between concept and place. There is city as sandbox,[26] metropolis, and a transaction-maximizing system,[27] city as reservation or as unwalled,[28] and city as growth machine.[29] Other metaphors include the secular city[30] and the good city.[31] Descriptions of neighborhoods are less adjectival. Downs described neighborhoods by their stages of deterioration.[32] Schoenberg and Rosenbaum proposed elements of viability as a framework to classify and to understand neighborhoods.[33] Williams used the concept of development of political organizations as a meaningful description of neighborhoods.[34] Frankly, as in many areas of social science, scholars show little agreement on how to define and understand notions of community, city, and neighborhood.

The force pulling people to the city has prevailed for a hundred years. By the twentieth century, cities reached a new peak in immigration and industrial energy with clusters of interlacing neighborhoods.[35] As cities grew in size and racial, ethnic, and class diversity, social science theories shifted from city as community to city as place.[36]

From 1900 to 1940, several generations of reformers, politicians, social scientists, and concerned citizens identified and prescribed cures for a long list of urban ills: corrupt political bosses in the 1910s, mass transportation needs in the 1920s, and economic depression and poverty in the 1930s.[37] Although World War II momentarily diverted attention from domestic problems of the city, new concerns erupted after 1945. Urban blight became pervasive. Central cities were decaying, shoppers were avoiding central business districts, and slums were spreading. Even smaller cities, which had previously not experienced "urban" problems, faced extinction as shopping malls stripped Main Street of its businesses. High-rise public housing for the poor, urban renewal projects for Main Street, and the exodus of the white middle class to suburban America rocked traditional notions of community in the 1950s and early 1960s. Solutions to urban ills quickly became problems themselves.

During the postwar era, new migrants from the southern states and Latin America congregated in the largest cities in the United States—Puerto Ricans in New York City, blacks in Chicago, white Appalachians in Cincinnati.[38] Like previous newcomers, they adjusted gradually to the urban environment. Assimilation was slow and unsteady, civil unrest grew, crime rates increased. The theme of most social and political commentary and research of the 1960s was urban crisis and decay. Although racism and poverty were as prevalent in rural as in urban America, the city encapsulated the nation's tensions and problems. Like the battles in Vietnam, the problems of the city were viewed nightly on television newscasts. In the 1970s, urban problems grew in another dimension. New York City virtually went bankrupt, as did Cleveland. Detroit and Boston nearly reached insolvency. The focus of the 1980s has centered on problems common to frostbelt cities of the northeast and midwest and sunbelt cities of the west and south: illegal drugs and related crime, runaway youth and abused children, and the homeless.

Urban decline has two meanings.[39] One meaning is descriptive and refers to loss of jobs and people. The second meaning is functional and refers to quality of life indicators and to the viability of social institutions. Both relate to racial and ethnic prejudice and to economic prosperity. Over the last decade, at least, the central cores of cities did not receive adequate supplies of capital investment from the private sector and the federal government.[40] The federal government began diverting capital from cities in the northeast and midwest to the southwest and the sunbelt in the 1970s. By 1980, 300,000 federal government jobs had been relocated there as well, a disproportionate share of defense contracts went to companies in the sunbelt, and entitlement programs did not differentiate for the higher cost of living in the northern cities. The public hears little of these economic-based, public policy decisions. Instead, federal grants to cities received public attention. Since 1980, most frostbelt cities have used block grant funds to supplement their insufficient city budgets. As federal funds were redirected toward military expenditures, the fiscal discrepancy between regions and cities grew.

The cycle of urban decline goes on. Jobs and people leave the city. Those who remain are less able to support city budgets and city services. So taxes must be increased and further urban exodus occurs. In addition, the cycle is fed by lowered expectations in schools, in safety and security, and in other social and human services, leading quickly to the perception that decline is inevitable. The loss of civic confidence leads to behaviors that hasten deterioration.[41]

In the social science literature of the 1980s, the term *neighborhood* became popular again.[42] Neighborhood seems to imply both a social and a political sense of community. Neighborhoods and neighboring allow for informal interactions and influence, make provisions for help when there is need or emergency, and promote local pride and status giving. Neighborhoods, also, are places for political organization and action rooted in concerns about local conditions, feelings of threat, a sense of identification with the area, and the degree of optimism about residents' ability to discover and maintain collective well-being.

Common perceptions of public school ills have tended to parrot criticisms on the status of the American community. Currently the needs and wants for both school and community are great. The steady erosion of the sense of community in cities, as in schools, has preoccupied us in recent years. Attempts to "rebuild" school and community seem to crop up every few years. For many people, "family" and "community" used to be common, powerful concepts. They described individual and group experiences and real and idealized connections to places and people. The nuclear family with middle-class values prevailed as the normative image in both popular culture and public policymaking for several generations. But the family and the community as transmitters of culture now are considered dysfunctional. Many assume that neither family nor community is needed for survival anymore. Divorce, occupational transfers, surburban isolationism, and blended families suggest that family and community do not automatically mean security, permanence, or attachment. Our individual and collective sense of belonging may no longer be enhanced by our perception of the power and security of family and community.

Demographic Indicators of Family
and Community Status

Modern technology, especially in the form of television and information processing, shapes our perceptions of the problems families, communities, and schools face. Norman Rockwell's tranquil family scenes lose out to evening news dramatizations about child abuse, youth gangs, teenage crime and pregnancy, and battered teachers. New forms of information processing, such as the computer, provide a more comprehensive view of the stresses and dysfunctions of family and community life. Much of the information used in the formation of family and community development policy comes from the federal government, namely the Census Bureau. Private and public consultants take government databases like the census and "add value" for their clients by stripping irrelevant data, updating useful data, and adding data from other, often proprietary, sources. Identifying and comparing relevant statistical indicators of families, communities, and schools means contending with literally billions of pieces of data, unequal access to electronic technology, and blurred distinctions between publications and records and between data producers and data suppliers. Given the demands for information from businesses, advocacy groups, political parties, governmental bodies, and academic researchers, however, it is unlikely that in the future we shall have less information on schools, communities, and families or a solution to this problem of data overload.

INDICATORS OF FAMILY WELL-BEING

With all the data available for reporting on the status of families, communities, and schools, we decided to explore family and community well-being in a statistical fashion. First, we chose statistics that allowed us to examine how families and communities of the 1980s fit idealized images of the past. Second, we looked for information about families and communities that helped to clarify political, economic, and social relationships with public schools. Third, we chose social indicators that most likely will capture the attention of governmental and educational policymakers now and in the next decade. Our overall goal is to present data as continuous information rather than as discrete bits.[43] In other words, we wanted to provide a comprehensive and understandable picture of how school, family, and community relationships are evolving.

We selected indicators on the current status of families in the

United States that have immediate relevance to parent-school relationships, especially expectations parents and school administrators bring to their interactions.

1. Married couples have slipped from a 61 percent share of all households[44] in 1980 to 57 percent in 1988; married couples with children have fallen from 31 percent of households in 1980 to 27 percent in 1988; nonfamily households (people who live alone or with unrelated people) account for 28.5 percent of all households.[45]

2. Between 1960 and 1987, the number of families[46] grew by 43 percent, while the number of families headed by females grew by 232 percent.[47]

3. Between 1960 and 1987, the number of families headed by females with children under 18 tripled.[48]

4. The percentage of children under 18 involved in divorce doubled between 1950 and 1970, tripled between 1950 and 1980, but has declined slightly since 1980.[49]

5. The number of children under 18 involved in divorce increased 3.6 times between 1950 and 1984.[50]

6. The median income of all households in 1987 was 0.9 percent greater than in 1979; but the median income of households headed by people 34 years old or younger decreased 10 percent, while the median income of households headed by 65+ year-olds increased 17 percent.[51]

7. The proportion of children living in poverty declined significantly during the 1960s, but has risen since 1970; in 1985, 20 percent of *all* children, 54 percent of children in female-headed families and 78 percent of black children in female-headed families lived in poverty.[52]

8. In 1987, both parents worked in 55 percent of married-couple families with children under 18.[53]

9. Between 1970 and 1987, the labor force participation rate for married women with children under six years old rose from 30 percent to 57 percent.[54]

10. Living in a mother-only family increased the odds of dropping out of school by more than 122 percent among whites and by 30 to 55 percent among blacks and Hispanics.[55]

11. Most black families who have reached the middle-class standard of living have managed to do so because both husband and wife work.[56]

12. In 1987, those making $10,000 to $19,000 annually paid 34 percent of their income in taxes; those making between $20,000 to

$59,000 and $70,000 to $89,000 paid 31 percent in taxes; and those making between $60,000 to $69,000 paid 35 percent in taxes.[57]

13. People over 65 comprise 12 percent of the population but receive 22 percent of all federal spending; if expenditures for national defense, interest on the national debt, and spending abroad are excluded, the elderly receive 48 percent of domestic dollars.[58]

The most obvious generalization from these indicators is that pluralistic America possesses no dominant form of family. Another harsh statistical conclusion is that poverty has increasingly become a black, female, and youthful condition. Third, the nature and degree of parental engagement with their children has been altered through divorce, dual-income families, and erosion of financial conditions. Fourth, there is a widening gap between the economic, social, and political well-being of children and the aged. Essentially, people over 65 are winning the battle of reduced governmental funds designated for support systems and services. Fifth, more and more families who fit the idealized image of the nuclear family have uncertain economic and educational futures, a condition nontraditional families have experienced consistently in the past. Sixth, the growth in Hispanic families is particularly important to the future operation of many public schools. Unlike black families, Hispanic families often do not speak English as a primary language.

Each of these "new realities" affects the home-school relationship. The participation of parents in school activities has changed dramatically over the last two decades. Yet, the activities of the PTA still are based largely on the idealized image and the expectation that "mothers" are available during school hours to participate. Traditional modes of parental involvement such as volunteer programs, advisory committees, teacher-parent communication structures, and student activities like athletics assume an understanding and acceptance of the importance of home-school contacts as well as parental competence to manage increasing demands on their time.[59]

Parents with school-aged children account for a little more than a quarter of the population. Those families are increasingly at risk of school failure. Middle-class families too find themselves balancing time demands on two working parents with time required to meet the emotional needs of their children as well as their needs for assistance with homework. The expectation that parents will ask if there is homework, let alone supervise the homework, are unrealistic for many families. In addition, the decreasing percentage of families with children forces the schools to compete for financial support to address the needs of families and children who are poor or disenfranchised. While not a new situation, the fact that the most affluent demographic age group in the United States in 1989 is 65 years and older, white, and politically well-connected means that competition centers on whose interests dominate the domestic policy agenda. Money spent on the elderly is basically a debt come due whereas money spent on children is a personal and national investment for the future.[60] Schools hold a vital stake in the political resolution of the demands of the elderly and the young.

INDICATORS OF COMMUNITY WELL-BEING

The indicators of community status reflect pernicious conditions, particularly for urban and rural areas. The popular image of the city in crisis is pervasive. Rural communities are battling for survival as well. Nearly 60 percent of all schools in the United States are in rural communities.[61] Although urban schools have received the majority of media attention about school reform, rural communities struggle to keep their schools open and to maintain a "way of life." Suburban communities are not without problems, although they have a much greater capacity to solve them.

1. Between 1970 and 1980, in the five largest cities in the United States, the number of poor people living in poverty areas increased by 58 percent and the number living in areas of extreme poverty went up by 182 percent.[62]

2. In 1980, 2.5 million people (labeled the underclass) or 3.1 percent of all households lived in 880 urban census-tract neighborhoods where more than half of the men had worked less than 26 weeks, 35 percent of the sixteen- to nineteen-year-olds had dropped out of high school, more than a third of the households received welfare assistance, and 57 percent of the families were headed by women.[63]

3. Six cities have the highest concentration of the underclass: New York, Chicago, Detroit, Newark, Philadelphia, and Baltimore.[64]

4. In the 880 census tracts labeled as underclass areas, 58 percent of the population are black, 11 percent are Hispanic, 28 percent are white; and 36 percent are children.[65]

5. In 1988, the majority of American households in rural poverty areas were white and located in Appalachia, the farmlands of the south or along the Mexican border; 59 percent dropped out of high school and over 60 percent earned less than $15,000 annually.[66]

6. One in five communities in the United States has 40 percent or

more households with children under eighteen; these communities are generally middle- to upper-middle-class in income, suburban, and predominantly white with high levels of home ownership and dual incomes.[67]

7. In 1985, 77 percent of the population lived in a metropolitan area; 84 percent of the black population lived inside metropolitan areas, with 59 percent in the central core; and 91 percent of the Hispanic population lived inside metropolitan boundaries.[68]

8. Almost 90 percent of the immigrants to the United States live in a metropolitan area.[69]

9. In 1985, about 62 percent of the serious crimes were committed by those twenty-four years old or younger. The number of arrests per 1000 young adults eighteen to twenty-four years old more than doubled between 1965 and 1985. There were particularly large increases in arrests for drunk driving, drug abuse, and larceny/theft.[70]

Like the family well-being indicators, statistics on communities reflect the pluralistic nature of the United States. The distinctions among places based on population, geographic, and economic factors are clear. Cities in the northeast and midwest are predominantly poor, black, and unable to offer many economic opportunities for their inhabitants to improve their lives. Rural poverty looks much the same, except the residents are predominantly white and they are not so densely concentrated. Suburban communities, particularly in the west and south, continue to be middle class in income, predominantly white, and often populated with growing families with school-aged children.

Urban school districts have different racial and ethnic populations to serve as compared to suburban and rural schools. When poverty and single-parenting are not only family facts but community facts, the effect can be highly disruptive to child and community development. When whole neighborhoods are made up of families without a consistent male presence, not only the income but the role models that fathers provide are missing. In one block in Harlem, 454 families live with 600 children and ten to fifteen men.[71] Urban schools with high concentrations of poverty face cost constraints, bureaucratic rigidities, loss of tax base, and political pressures hampering their effectiveness with "at-risk" students.

Suburban schools with growing numbers of children under eighteen face traditional administrative problems: where to find space for all the students, how to recruit and hire enough good teachers. Those suburban school districts with high percentages of retired folks need to redefine school-community relations to include significant nonfamily involvement. Rural schools must create and maintain programs that offer skills and opportunities for students to improve their future economic chances.

All these social indicators have implications for all Americans irrespective of race or ethnicity. For example, although the proportion of the non-Hispanic white population younger than twenty-five years of age is shrinking, that proportion among Asian families and most Hispanic groups (except Cubans) is growing.[72] If the economic disparities between those who fail in school and those who succeed continue, not only our ability to act as a democratic society is threatened but our current standard of living is at risk as well. Our economic viability and our means to cooperate with other countries are endangered. It is not only a compassionate choice, but a prudent and self-serving one as well, to support the kind of education that offers all children and youth an opportunity to learn and to act and to feel part of a democratic community. A primary link between the economic well-being of individuals and their sense of what is the "good life" within a community has been, and most likely will continue to be, the public school.

INDICATORS OF SCHOOL, COMMUNITY, AND
FAMILY RELATIONSHIPS

Dissatisfaction with public schools in the United States is not a new phenomenon.[73] Americans began to voice doubts about the graduates of their schools shortly after World War II, when the curriculum seemed unable to meet challenges of global citizenship and when images of the school moved away from the rural or small-town model. While there are many indicators of diminished links between families, communities, and their schools, the few noted here reflect the status of more traditional ties of the home-school relationship.

1. Membership in the PTA dropped from 12 million in 1962 to 5 million in 1982, but has steadily increased every year since 1982 with increased membership reported in 43 states and the District of Columbia. Today, the PTA has 6.64 million members.[74]

2. More than nine out of ten members of the high school class of 1985 had used alcohol, more than half had tried marijuana, one in six had used cocaine, and one in eight had used hallucinogens like LSD. The majority of students made the decision to use drugs between the seventh and tenth grades.[75]

3. In 1985, students spent more time watching television than

doing homework; these patterns varied across race and age, with elementary students in general and black students specifically watching the most television.[76]

4. The job outlook for high school dropouts[77] is dismal; of the 562,000 dropouts in 1985, 54 percent were unemployed and likely to remain so.[78]

5. Scout membership for boys and girls dropped between 1960 and 1985; about one in seven eligible boys was a Boy Scout and one in ten girls was a Girl Scout.[79]

6. The percentage of ethnic and racial minority students in Catholic elementary and secondary schools has increased from 10.8 percent in 1970-71 to 22.4 percent in 1987-88.[80]

7. About half of the teenagers in the United States are sexually active by the time they leave school; only half of the school districts that offer sex education cite reduction of teen pregnancy as a major goal.[81]

8. One in four teenagers has experienced a pregnancy; 70 percent of the large urban school districts have at least one program for pregnant teenagers.[82]

9. A majority of the American public believes that people have a legal right to educate their children at home, although the number of students being schooled at home is not significant.[83]

However compelling the arguments may be about the roles of parents and families in their children's educational experience, the desire for a tight fit between the two ignores current social and communal realities. This expectation is based on a narrow view of the outcomes of schooling, namely academic achievement. Although it has traditionally been defined as the measure of school success, academic achievement does not mean that students automatically will be effective citizens and adults.

Demographic and cultural indicators show the altered functions families and schools play in the nurturance of children and youth. Today's policies are no more likely to "fix" the problems of American youth than the social policies of the past. Remedies focused on the improvement of home-school relationships are unlikely to succeed because they ignore the structural realities of today's families, the resources available to the schools and to families, and the family's ability to interact with the school. Taken as a whole, indicators of school, community, and family relationships present strong evidence that schools cannot overcome demographic, economic, social, and political realities simply by expanding the curriculum, adopting a parent education program, or changing programs for preparing teachers and administrators.

New Perspectives

We began this chapter by discussing the problematic nature of relationships across schools, families, and their communities. One of the major reasons for these troubled ties is the discrepancy between idealized images of families and communities and recent realities. Central to a new perspective on these problems are two questions: (a) What is school success? and (b) Who is responsible for ensuring that children and youth find success in school?

As mentioned earlier, since the end of World War II the prevailing definition of school success has been academic achievement and competency.[84] Periodic educational reform debates have focused on assigning the responsibility for successful student achievement and competency and on fixing the blame for failure. In the 1950s, when the Soviet Union challenged the educational system to the "space race" by launching Sputnik, school systems were blamed for academic and technological failure. In the 1960s, critics and policymakers from inside and outside education blamed the victims—the students—and their environments for the failure to maintain the nation's competitive edge. We tried to "fix" society and its institutions under the hunch that such solutions would improve the educational environment for children. In the 1970s, we focused on single issues, such as functional literacy and lack of basic skills. Teachers were blamed for student failure. It was widely assumed that teacher incompetence caused poor student performance on nationwide and state tests. Reform shifted away from institutional fixes, as many states prescribed performance measures as remedies. In the 1980s, reports like *A Nation at Risk* shifted the blame once again. Although the report cautioned against focusing on one group or one aspect of the reform, parents and families came under fire for student mediocrity.[85]

Finding ways for schools to establish family support for education is a salient focus of many groups today. The relationship between family and school has been compared to that of the right and left hemispheres of the brain; both are necessary to each other— complementary, nonduplicative, and vital.[86] Increased student achievement and improved student behavior are typical outcomes of programs emphasizing closer home-school relationships. Yet, for such programs to fulfill the ideal image of being complementary, nonduplicative, and vital to school success, the dissonant realities of families and communities must be understood and confronted by school officials and policymakers.

Parent involvement programs are based on one of four models: parent as receiver of information about the school; parent as volunteer; parent as advisor; and parent as educator in the home.[87] The first model assigns a passive role to the parents. The information flow is one-way, with the school reporting on student achievement and educational programs. The second model also assigns a passive role to parents. As volunteers, parents perform duties that relieve teachers of noninstructional tasks, or business and community agencies provide resources to solve problems identified by the school. Volunteers, in whatever capacity, extend services to students to solve manageable problems. The third model, parent as advisor, is less passive; parents are involved in specific programs because their children are receiving the services of such programs. The impetus for this model was the requirement of parental involvement found in most federal education legislation of the 1960s and 1970s.[88] Unfortunately, many non-English-speaking families, single parents, and working parents cannot or do not participate in parent advisory committees. The fourth model, parent as educator in the home, encourages active involvement by parents and targets specific educational needs of individual families and their children. Evidence supports the effectiveness of the last model in improving student performance and in sustaining parental participation.[89]

However, regardless of which model for parent involvement is chosen, conflict will exist. The stress between defining school success and assigning blame for failure is inherent in the politics of educational decision making. The basic tension between school administrators and their constituencies underlies the conflict between the community's need for school leadership that can lead and be trusted and the desire to have lay control of public education. With a certain repetition, the last forty years of public school history can be characterized as the ongoing search for methods to ensure "controlled" public participation in schools.[90]

Each community group creates special tensions for a school's leadership because each core constituency challenges the leadership on resource allocation issues. These core groups and their issues include parents who want shared or community control, advisory input, and decentralization; students who want civil rights, freedom of expression, dress, and behavior; teachers who want job security and collective representation; taxpayers who want local finance reform that places larger cost burdens on the state; minorities who want resolution of enduring issues related to desegregation and integration; business leaders who want cheap, well-trained, obedient workers; and federal and state authorities who perpetuate guidelines, mandates, and court orders on matters of discrimination, personnel, curriculum, and finances. Although the specifics of any controversy among these groups over such issues vary by location, the important point is that they do move in response to certain forces. Local school conflict is shaped by forces both outside and inside an individual district.[91]

Between 1920 and the late 1960s, the leadership in public schools prevented organized opposition from affecting internal school operations by stressing consensus, by claiming schools were "above partisan politics," or by absorbing, co-opting, or deflecting outside forces. They were able to channel external demands for change because they were steadily expanding and could reform by accretion. In the 1970s and 1980s other strategies were needed. Schools were no longer expanding in terms of student enrollments. The addition of state and federal mandates caused divisions as priorities for scarce resources were debated.[92] Such debates will continue well into the next century as the demographic, social, and political indicators of families and communities continue to present a picture of increasing diversity and complexity.

Much of the conflict between schools and their communities arises from the purposes of schools as institutions in a democratic society. Three paradoxes underlie the conflict.[93] First, schools must teach not only support of the state but also the virtues of the individual. Individualism can result in opposition to the state. How far can the state go in commanding the obedience of the individual (or the family)? The second paradox is the disparity between the belief held about school by many minority and poor parents and communities and the school reality they encounter. These parents and communities believe that school is the source for the realization of their hopes and dreams for a brighter future for their children; education is the passport to that future. However, too often they find school to be a place where the dispiriting tradition of racism, sexism, and ethnocentrism grind away their children's enthusiasm for learning, lower their expectations for achievement, and dim their hopes and dreams for a successful future. A third paradox results when the range of pluralistic values meets the institutional demands of both state and school for social control and order. The potential for conflict over which value receives greater attention exists because of our pluralistic population and because of the selective emphasis on values by those in authority. It is this very conflict over the virtues of individualism and the virtues of pluralism that places heavy burdens on schools and school leadership.

How can the school socialize students to the norms of the American society when there is a lack of consensus about such norms? The traditional response is that the school does not act alone in the cultivation of civic virtues, nor does it act at all in some cases.[94] Another response is that schooling alone cannot change the economic and social forces of inequality, poverty, racism, sexism, and ignorance. A third response looks at the cultural ecology of the family. Ogbu[95] argues that families need to be understood within their context rather than being compared with other groups. Childrearing practices in families are geared toward the development of instrumental competencies required for adult political, economic, and social roles. Many socializing behaviors reinforced by school policies assume that childrearing strategies cause adult behaviors. The cultural-ecology model assumes that roles allowed for adults determine the strategies parents use to prepare their children for adulthood.

Current Practices and Future Directions

There are successful schools that have accepted the reality of families and students who by traditional standards are at risk of achieving any measure of school success. There are successful schools that have overcome dismal economic and social conditions within their communities and provided meaningful experiences for students and their families. There are successful schools that have transformed the lives of students, families, and other community members.

Successful schools do not buy the myth that nothing works. Rather than blaming teachers, parents, students, or society in general, school administrators and teachers in these successful schools are involved in the lives of children and their families. They attack the problems affecting their students and families with comprehensive plans and intensive strategies. They develop a sense of constancy between home and school that cultivates shared visions.

Schools such as those operating under the leadership of James Comer in New Haven, Connecticut, and Prince Georges County, Maryland, and Deborah Meier in New York City's Harlem[96] have accepted the challenge of creating school environments where families play critical roles in the education of their children and where school climate promotes learning in a consistent manner. Students learn and exhibit behaviors that are effective in nonschool contexts. These schools are models of how the inherent tensions and conflicts can be recognized as essential to success rather than as overwhelming obstacles. They are effective in their particular contexts.

Successful programs share several common assumptions about home-school and school-community relationships. The assumptions are important to designing schools that recognize and address specific family and community needs. The resulting programs and practices differ because the families and communities differ. The assumptions about the home-school relationship are based on mutual respect and collaboration. First, successful schools expect and support parental responsibility for their children's education. Second, they provide families with information addressing the specific needs of their children. Third, they respond to family diversity and diverse parental needs. For example, schools for four-year-olds may be good for some, while daycare centers and health promotion programs may be needed by others. These concerns are not in conflict with successful school goals; school personnel work closely with families and community agencies to identify and ameliorate family problems. Fourth, successful schools encourage all members of the extended family to take an active role. Last, they provide ways for families to help one another become self-sufficient and resourceful. Parent-to-parent support restores the sense of community and strengthens home-school relationships.

Assumptions underlying successful school-community relationships include the provision of meaningful roles for the private sector, the connection of community agencies with school-based efforts, and the involvement of citizens who are not directly involved in schools. These assumptions reflect local attention to local problems, mutual respect, and recognition of diversity as a positive force for school improvement.

These assumptions also have relevance to two other groups involved in shaping school success: professors who prepare future school administrators, and researchers who try to understand schooling and its effects on students. No one group can or should control the debate over definitions of school success and school outcomes. When groups collaborate to resolve common problems, it is assumed that conflict and tension are beneficial to the change process. Professors and researchers can provide information and knowledge about what works and why. They can assist in helping schools, parents, and communities realize new horizons of well-being.

Rather than searching for one model of effective practice or working to eliminate or control conflict, the focus of school administration, whether in practice, in preparation programs, or in research, should be on developing consistent, intensive, comprehensive, and personalized programs aimed at the needs of students, their families, and their communities. Of course, this always has been a mission of public education and educators. The difference for twenty-first century America is that school, family, and community relations *must* be at the epicenter of the teaching-learning process. The demands of an information age for an educated and educative society place renewed importance on school, family, and community ties. The central question remains whether or not we search for community using idealized images of the past or new inventions based on current realities.

FOOTNOTES

1. Joe Kelly, *Organizational Behavior* (Homewood, IL: Irwin, 1974); Douglas E. Mitchell, "Educational Policy Analysis: The State of the Art," *Educational Administration Quarterly* 20, no. 3 (1984): 129-160; D. A. Schon, *Educating the Reflective Practitioner* (San Francisco: Jossey-Bass, 1987).

2. Peter Benson, "New Pictures of Families Emerge from Research," *Common Focus* 6, no. 1 (1985): 3; Roald Campbell, Luvern Cunningham, Raphael Nystrand, and Michael Usdan, *The Organization and Control of American Schools* (Columbus, OH: Charles E. Merrill, 1985); Marian W. Edelman, *Families in Peril: An Agenda for Social Change* (Cambridge, MA: Harvard University Press, 1987).

3. *Public Education* (Columbus, OH: Ohio Department of Education, 1983), p. 9.

4. Edelman, *Families in Peril*, pp. 23-49.

5. Ibid.

6. Norman J. Boyan, "Administration of Educational Institutions," in *Encyclopedia of Educational Research*, Vol. 1 (New York: Free Press, 1982), pp. 22-49; Mitchell, "Educational Policy Analysis"; Lisbeth B. Schorr and Daniel Schorr, *Within Our Reach: Breaking the Cycle of Disadvantage and Despair* (New York: Anchor Press, 1988); Frederick M. Wirt and Michael Kirst, *Schools in Conflict* (Berkeley, CA: McCutchan, 1982).

7. See especially the five chapters in "Part IV, Politics and Policy" in *Handbook of Research on Educational Administration*, ed. Norman J. Boyan (New York: Longman, 1988).

8. William L. Boyd, "Policy Analysis, Educational Policy and Management: Through a Glass Darkly?" in *Handbook of Research in Educational Administration*, ed. Boyan, pp. 501-522.

9. David Tyack and Elisabeth Hansot, *Managers of Virtue: Public School Leadership in America 1820-1980* (New York: Basic Books, 1982).

10. Ibid.

11. David Elkind, "The Child, Yesterday, Today, and Tomorrow," *Young Children* 42 (May 1987): 6-11; Elin McCoy, "*Childhood through the Ages*," in *Early Childhood Education 89-90*, ed. J. S. McKee and K. M. Paciorek (Guilford, CT: Dushkin Publishing Group, 1989).

12. G. R. Leslie, *The Family in Social Context* (New York: Oxford University Press, 1976); McCoy, "Childhood through the Ages."

13. Leslie, *The Family in Social Context*, p. 15.

14. Ibid.

15. Ibid.

16. Michael B. Katz, *Reconstructing American Education* (Cambridge, MA: Harvard University Press, 1987).

17. Judith Waldrop, "The Fashionable Family," *American Demographer* 10 (March 1988): 23-26.

18. The following discussion of television programs and ratings comes from Tim Brooks and Earle March, *The Complete Directory to Prime Time Network TV Shows* (New York: Ballantine Books, 1988).

19. Leslie, *The Family in Social Context*.

20. James Comer, *Maggie's American Dream: The Life and Times of a Black Family* (New York: New American Library, 1988).

21. Jon C. Teaford, *The Twentieth-Century American City* (Baltimore: Johns Hopkins University Press, 1986).

22. Roland L. Warren, *The Community in America* (Chicago: Rand McNally, 1978), p. 2.

23. Ibid.

24. Ibid., p. 409.

25. Ibid.

26. George Sternlieb, "The City as Sandbox," *Public Interest*, no. 25 (Fall 1971): 14-21.

27. R. L. Meier, "The Metropolis as a Transaction-Maximizing System," *Daedalus* 97, no. 4 (1968): 1292-1313.

28. Norton E. Long, "The City as Reservation," *Public Interest*, no. 25 (Fall 1971): 22-38.

29. Harvey Molotch, "The City as a Growth Machine: Toward a Political Economy of Place," *American Journal of Sociology* 82, no. 2 (1976): 309-332, 352-355.

30. Harvey Cox, *The Secular City: Secularization and Urbanization in Theological Perspective* (New York: Macmillan, 1965).

31. Lawrence Haworth, *The Good City* (Bloomington, IN: Indiana University Press, 1963.

32. Anthony Downs, *Neighborhoods and Urban Development* (Washington, DC: Brookings Institution, 1981).

33. Sandra P. Schoenberg and Patricia L. Rosenbaum, *Neighborhoods That Work: Sources for Viability in the Inner City* (New Brunswick, NJ: Rutgers University Press, 1980).

34. Michael F. Williams, *Neighborhood Organizing for Urban School Reform* (New York: Teachers College Press, 1989).

35. Maurice H. Yeates and Barry J. Garner, *The North American City* (New York: Harper and Row, 1971).

36. Ibid.

37. Teaford, *The Twentieth-Century American City*.

38. Ibid.

39. Williams, *Neighborhood Organizing for Urban School Reform.*

40. Ibid.

41. Ibid.

42. Ibid.

43. Anthony Wilden, *Man and Woman, War and Peace: The Strategist's Companion* (London: Routledge, 1987).

44. The definition of household is the same as the U.S. Census Bureau uses: all persons who occupy a housing unit.

45. Waldrop, "The Fashionable Family," p. 24.

46. The definition of family is the same as the U.S. Census Bureau uses: a group of two or more persons (one of whom is the householder) related by birth, marriage, or adoption and residing together.

47. U.S. Department of Commerce, Bureau of the Census, *Household and Family Characteristics*, Current Population Reports, Series P-20 (Washington, DC: Bureau of the Census, 1960, 1970, 1988).

48. Ibid.

49. U. S. Department of Education, *Youth Indicators 1988: Trends in the Well-Being of American Youth* (Washington, DC: U. S. Department of Education, 1988), p. 21.

50. Ibid.

51. U. S. Department of Commerce, Bureau of the Census, *Money Income of Families and Persons in the U.S.*, Current Population Reports, Series P-20, nos. 105, 107 (Washington, DC: Bureau of the Census, 1988).

52. Edelman, *Families in Peril*, p. 25.

53. *Youth Indicators 1988*, p. 38.

54. Ibid., p. 41.

55. Gordon Berlin and Andrew Sum, *Toward a More Perfect Union: Basic Skills, Poor Families, and Our Economic Future*, Occasional paper no. 3, Ford Foundation Project on Social Welfare and the American Future (New York: Ford Foundation, 1988), p. 36.

56. Bart Landry, *The New Black Middle Class* (Berkeley and Los Angeles: University of California Press, 1987), p. 138.

57. D. R. Francis, "U. S. Taxes Hit Poorest Hardest," *Christian Science Monitor*, 18 April 1989.

58. S. N. Charavarty, with K. Weisman, "Consuming Our Children?" *Forbes* 142, no. 11 (1988): 225.

59. Wirt and Kirst, *Schools in Conflict.*

60. Charavarty, "Consuming Our Children?"

61. Bob Cole, "Teaching in a Time Machine: The 'Make-Do' Mentality in Small-Town Schools," *Phi Delta Kappan* 70, no. 2 (1988): 139-144.

62. Schorr and Schorr, *Within Our Reach*, p. 17.

63. Michael J. Weiss, *The Clustering of America* (New York: Harper and Row, 1988).

64. Schorr and Schorr, *Within Our Reach*, p. 17.

65. Ibid.

66. Weiss, *The Clustering of America*, p. 386.

67. Ibid.

68. Ibid.

69. Ibid.

70. *Youth Indicators 1988*, p. 117.

71. Schorr and Schorr, *Within Our Reach*, p. 21.

72. H. L. Hodgkinson, "Facing the Future," *School Administrator* 45 (1988), Special Pullout Section, unpaged.

73. James P. Comer, "Home-School Relationships as They Affect the Academic Success of Children," *Education and Urban Society* 16 (1984): 323-337; Shirley Brice Heath and Milbrey W. McLaughlin, "A Child Resource Policy: Moving beyond Dependence on School and Family," *Phi Delta Kappan* 68, no. 8 (1987): 576-580.

74. "PTA Sees Popularity Rise Again," *Cincinnati Enquirer*, 16 June 1989.

75. *Youth Indicators 1988*, p. 98.

76. Ibid., p. 70.

77. The definition of dropouts is the same as the U.S. Census Bureau uses: persons 16 to 24 years old who are not enrolled in school and who are not high school graduates; those who have received their high school equivalency credentials are counted as graduates.

78. *Youth Indicators 1988*, p. 54.

79. Ibid., p. 106.

80. National Catholic Education Association, *Catholic Schools in America* (Montrose, CO: Fisher, 1988), p. 728.

81. Asta M. Kenney, "Teen Pregnancy: An Issue for Schools," *Phi Delta Kappan* 68, no. 10 (1987): 728.

82. Ibid., p. 729.

83. Alec M. Gallup and Stanley M. Elam, "The 20th Annual Gallup Poll of the Public's Attitudes toward the Public Schools," *Phi Delta Kappan* 70, no. 1 (1988): 33-46.

84. Heath and McLaughlin, "A Child Resource Policy."

85. Ibid.

86. Dorothy Rich, *Schools and Families: Issues and Actions* (Washington, DC: National Education Association, 1987).

87. Ibid.

88. J. Burns, *The Study of Parental Involvement in Four Federal Education Programs: Executive Summary* (Washington, DC: U. S. Department of Education, 1982).

89. Rich, *Schools and Families*.

90. Wirt and Kirst, *Schools in Conflict*.

91. Ibid.

92. Tyack and Hansot, *Managers of Virtue*.

93. Wirt and Kirst, *Schools in Conflict*.

94. Ira Shor, *Culture Wars: School and Society in the Conservative Restoration 1969-1984* (Boston: Routledge Chapman and Hall, 1986).

95. John U. Ogbu, "Origins of Human Competence: A Cultural-Ecological Perspective," *Child Development* 52 (1981): 413-429.

96. In *Within Our Reach*, the Schorrs describe in detail the elementary schools that James Comer and Deborah Meier have established; their programs have combined the deliberate attention to families as educator and to climate that promotes learning.

CHAPTER VI

Changing Families and Communities: Implications for Schools

THOMAS B. HOFFER AND JAMES S. COLEMAN

The growth of systematic data collection on American education over the past few decades has allowed researchers to articulate a sounder conception of both the directions of change and the factors involved in the observed trends. The educational outcomes most closely watched and analyzed are students' levels of cognitive achievement and the duration of their formal education. Recent trends for both outcomes have not been encouraging. Average achievement levels measured by standardized tests showed sharp declines in reading comprehension, vocabulary knowledge, science, and mathematics through the 1970s. Over the last decade some gains have been apparent, although the pre-1970 levels have not been regained. The trends in formal educational attainment have been less dramatic but also give cause for concern. The high school graduation rate increased at a rapid rate for several decades but quite abruptly leveled off at about 75 percent of the eighteen-year-old population in the early 1970s. Among high school graduates, the rate of college attendance has shown a similar leveling trend since the great gains of the 1950s and 1960s. In recent years, moreover, there has been considerable concern over the number of dropouts among urban youth.

The collection and dissemination of systematic trend data has coincided with growing concerns over the viability of the United States economy and the quality of the public school system. Since education policy is the most readily altered variable available to social reformers, responses to many of these trends have targeted the school. Less attention has been given to a long line of research demonstrating the importance of students' family environments for their educational success. There is reason to believe, in fact, that many of the deficiencies in student outcomes are at least as much attributable to difficulties faced by the American family as to the school. Such research calls into question the feasibility of some school reform efforts. In this chapter, we will review some of the major trends in American family and local community life and attempt to relate the implications of these changes to school organization and educational administration. While recognizing the importance of other outcomes, we have restricted our current focus to achievement and attainment because of their centrality to the educational enterprise and because much more is known about their determinants and consequences.

Changes in the Structure and Function of the Family

Educational research has clearly demonstrated the importance of family background for student success in school. Family background is usually conceptualized as a combination of parental resources and family functioning, where resources include such variables as parental education and income, and functioning includes the emotional stability of the home as well as socialization practices (e.g., the extent and nature of active interaction with the child, the scope and nature of communication, and the standards of behavior set forth and enforced by the parents). One would expect that historical changes in the key dimensions of family resources and functioning should have consequences for children's educational development.

PARENTAL EDUCATION

According to an extensive body of child and family development research, families increasingly possess more of the resources considered important to children's development. Most significant in this regard has been the steadily rising levels of parental educational attainment over the past several decades. Current national surveys indicate that about 15 percent of elementary and secondary students have a parent with a four-year college degree or higher, and about 60 percent have at least one parent with a high school diploma or better. A majority of parents have attended some kind of postsecondary educational institution.[1]

One likely consequence of the trend toward higher educational attainment is that parents will have a better idea of what is taught in school and should be better able to help their childen academically. It also is likely that as longer periods of formal education become necessary for attaining more desirable employment, parents are more likely to stress its importance to their children.

HOUSEHOLD INCOME

A second family resource with consequences for children's educational development is household income. The estimated effect of income on academic achievement is usually found to be lower than that of parents' education, probably because the income effects are mediated not only by the goods and services purchased but also by the ways the purchases are actually used. The effect of income on educational attainment is substantially larger than the effect on achievement, reflecting the direct expenses and foregone income that higher education necessitates.[2]

The most significant recent trend in household income appears to be the growing number of impoverished families with school-age children. While median family income has grown at a fairly steady rate, the proportion of school-age children growing up in families with incomes below the official poverty level increased from 14 to 19 percent between 1969 and 1985.[3] Part of this increase is attributable to the growth of female-headed households, which disproportionately tend to suffer economic deprivation, and part is due to the higher birth rates of lower-income families. In any case, the demographic prognosis for American schools is that a larger proportion of their students will be subject to the stresses associated with poverty and the difficulties they pose for academic success.

FAMILY SIZE

National surveys have consistently shown a negative relationship between the number of siblings and students' school achievement. The usual explanation for this pattern is that larger numbers of children result in less parental time and attention for each child. Over the past quarter century, the trend in families has been markedly toward fewer offspring. The overall age-specific birth rates of American women have shown steady declines.[4] While birth rates have declined among all subpopulations, the decline has been greater among women in higher-income households.

Other things equal, the general decline in family size may translate into an exchange of "quantity" for "quality."[5] That is, parents should be able to devote more time, attention, and money to the smaller number of children they are now bearing, and the children should be able to do better in school as a result. Alternatively, the decline may reflect other factors quite independent of parental concerns for children—women may reduce childbearing in favor of employment or parents may opt for smaller families in order to have more time and money to pursue their own interests.

LABOR FORCE PARTICIPATION OF MOTHERS

The most pervasive and perhaps most important change in family life over the past several decades has been the extensive movement of adults, first of fathers and then of mothers, out of the household and into employment settings. The consequences of maternal employment have been the subject of much recent controversy, with critics claiming negative effects on children's development and supporters arguing for benefits or at least no harm. The grounds of the controversy are indeed impressive. In 1900, less than half of the working adult males were employed outside the household in nonagricultural occupations and a mere 20 percent of adult women were in the paid labor force. As recently as 1940, the comparable figures stood at 80 percent of males and 25 percent of females. Today the rates are 95 percent for men and 55 percent for women.[6] For married women with children under eighteen years old, the labor force participation rate grew from 45 percent in 1975 to 61 percent in 1986.[7]

The effects of maternal labor force participation on children's educational development cannot be simply identified. Negative effects on cognitive achievement appear to be confined to sons whose mothers worked full-time during preschool years. Daughters, in contrast, realize advantages from having a working mother. While the reasons for this mixed pattern are not entirely clear, researchers speculate that the explanation may be tied to gender differences in personality development. Young girls tend to be somewhat more independent and self-controlled than their male counterparts at a comparable age. Girls are thus able to find a more achievement-oriented role model in their working mothers (who are likely to respond in a positive way to the admiration they receive), while young boys tend to suffer (and thus become more difficult to manage) from the decreased time and attention associated with the mother's hours away from the home.[8]

Whatever the balance of positive and negative consequences, the trend toward increasing labor force participation of mothers with children at all ages is likely to continue. The issue of negative consequences of working parents is rapidly being superceded by concerns over the feasibility and consequences of alternative forms of day care and work scheduling.

HOUSEHOLD DISRUPTIONS

Another trend widely believed to have adverse consequences for children's development has been the increasing incidence of single-parent households. Census data show the percentage of school-age children living in such households rose from 9 percent in 1960 to 19 percent in 1980. The chance of growing up in a family where the original parents have divorced is much higher and has grown from 29 percent in 1960 to 43 percent in 1980.[9] While many children in single-parent households remain in contact with the parent who has left the home (normally the father), the extent of engagement usually decreases and the material resources of the household are often substantially diminished. The most important effects of marital disruptions, however, appear to lie with the emotional difficulties that the parents and the children typically experience. The evidence indicates that the effects on children are strongest on outcomes measured soon after the parental breakup.[10] This suggests special difficulties for the children of recently separated families in coping with school, and evidence of substantial effects of single-parent households on the probability of dropping out of high school appears to support this hypothesis.[11]

FAMILY FUNCTIONING

Sociological research on the effect of family background on student outcomes has shown a marked tendency to emphasize parental resource factors often to the exclusion of the family functioning variables which translate those resources into outcomes. Insofar as family functioning variables have been studied, it has been primarily in the context of seeking to clarify the effects of resource or family structure variables. It is important to note that family socioeconomic status and family structure variables are not the sole determinants of either family functioning or student outcomes. Many students from families with few material or formal educational resources manage to succeed in school while many students with great advantages fail. However, systematic research has had little success in identifying or measuring the key dimensions of family functioning. Since the relevant variables have not been firmly identified, it is not possible at this point to develop a picture of how family functioning has changed over time. This situation is likely to change in the near future with the analysis of detailed data on family socialization values and practices from successive national surveys (most prominently, High School and Beyond of 1980 and the National Educational Longitudinal Survey and the Longitudinal Study of American Youth which started in 1988).

To summarize, the trends reviewed here indicate that the resources of American adults have increased while the resources of American families have decreased. The points of greatest concern appear to be the increasing fragility of marital arrangements and the increasing risk of growing up in a family facing severe economic deprivation. It would appear that children who are fortunate enough to avoid these hazards stand in a very good position with respect to many historically important correlates of academic success: their parents have more education, make more money, and have fewer other children among whom to divide their resources and attention.

These trends suggest a pattern of growing inequality in family background which one would expect to find reflected in measures of educational outcomes. While some measures of educational outcomes bear this out (for example, recently declining rates of minority enrollment in higher education), other important indicators do not. The trends in cognitive achievement, for instance, show that the pattern of test score declines is a general phenomenon, affecting all strata of the student population. Insofar as differences are found, they seem to indicate that the declines have been lower for some groups at greater risk, particularly blacks and Hispanics.[12]

One possible explanation of this apparent paradox is that parent-child relations have generally changed in ways which adversely affect school performance. Some observers argue, for example, that parents are devoting less time and attention to their children, either because of increasing work demands or because parents have become more devoted to personal or adult-peer leisure pursuits. Others claim that parents have progressively adopted less authoritarian styles of child-raising, and that the emergent egalitarian style is less conducive to successful performance in school. Evidence in support of either perspective is at best circumstantial and at worse anecdotal, and more work is needed to determine the actual extent and consequences of these reputed trends in parental behavior.

Resources and Social Relations
outside the Family

Social relations and resources within the home are not the only influences on children's educational development. Most children establish and maintain a set of relationships with a number of their peers and with a (usually smaller) number of adults, and these relationships can have a strong influence on how the child perceives and functions within his or her role as a student. Taken together, these various relationships constitute the community to which the student essentially belongs.

The impact of community variables on student outcomes has been the subject of a large number of studies over the past few decades. One line of inquiry that has attracted attention concerns the effect of the local community on student outcomes. Two types of variables have been identified through the research: *global* variables, which characterize the community as a whole, such as whether the community is a small town, a suburb, or a city; and *aggregate* variables, which summarize characteristics of individuals within a local area. The most commonly used indicators for aggregate community variables include median income, average parental education, and racial or ethnic demographics. The research problem is one of determining the extent to which these variables affect student outcomes, controlling for the effects of individual student characteristics. Material resources and social relationships seem to be the most studied community variables related to student achievement. A student attending a school serving higher socioeconomic status communities, for example, might realize advantages from the better teachers or laboratory equipment that a higher tax base allows the school to purchase and maintain. Alternatively or in conjunction with such advantages, the same student could benefit if a larger proportion of high socioeconomic status parents results in the school maintaining higher academic standards for all students, irrespective of the student's own family background. Research conducted in this vein has generally found that global and aggregate measures of school communities are much less important than the characteristics of individual students and their families.[13]

One explanation for the relatively weak effects of aggregate measures of community is that schools exercise a certain autonomy in relation to the communities they serve. As a consequence, the effective community for students is best measured at the level of the school rather than the larger residential area. McDill and Rigsby developed a number of measures of school climate based on aggregations of student responses to questions about the importance of academic achievement in the school, academic standards, intellectual interests, and curricular emphases.[14] These measures were found to exert a stronger influence on student achievement than the aggregate socioeconomic status of the student body. Moreover, the climate measures continued to show positive, although relatively weak, effects on individual student achievement when measures of the individuals' family and academic backgrounds were controlled. Such research suggests that schools can develop a culture that exerts an influence over student behavior independently of the individual's own predispositions.

Since school climate measures have been developed quite recently, there are no systematic data on historical trends along these dimensions. The idea that school climate is important has probably gained broad dissemination via the "effective schools" movement of the 1980s, but the extent to which schools have actually changed in such directions is not yet known.

In any case, the normative context of the school as a whole is still located at some distance from the individual student. Research on the effects of school climate generally fails to take into account the more proximate social relations of individual students with their peers and school officials. Other studies have focused on these relations and found more substantial consequences for individual achievement and attainment. The extensive analysis of Wisconsin high school students carried out by Sewell and his colleagues estimated the effects of friends' educational plans and teachers' expectations on individual aspirations and eventual educational attainment. Their findings show a significantly greater impact of these variables than the effects normally found for aggregate measures of school climate.[15]

While these results emphasize the importance of the social relations that students maintain, they do not tell much about how they are formed. This issue is particularly salient in regard to the student peer group because of its manifestly great importance in the life of children and adolescents. Under what conditions do peer groups support academic success, and under what conditions do they discourage it? Have the strength and direction of peer group norms generally shifted over time and, if so, in which directions and for what reasons?

Unfortunately, we have no systematic evidence on these points at present and cannot give specific answers. However, adolescent peer groups do define themselves largely in relation to the adult authorities in their lives. If those adults offer incentives for the pursuit of educational goals and sanctions for spurning them, then the peer group is likely to have a reinforcing effect on the aims of the school.

Some studies of adolescent peer groups have argued that the historical trend is toward a reduction of adolescent-adult contact and a strengthening of the peer group. Coleman notes that industrialization and the concomitant shift of work to corporate settings has reduced the power of the family to socialize children. The corporate economy fills positions on the basis of achieved competence, whereas children from households engaged in agriculture or trades would merely follow their parents in these pursuits. The responsibility for educating children for the new economic order has been largely removed from the family and given to the school. The relatively impersonal relations between teachers and students, however, lacks the strength once held by the family to develop close attachments and loyalties. As a result, adolescents find themselves increasingly in the company of their peers. It is here they seek guidance and support.[16]

The separation of youth from the family has been countered to some extent by the growth of organized activities supervised by adults. Most prominent in this regard are athletic teams and religion-based youth groups. While there is some evidence that participation in these groups has a positive influence (particularly as a deterrent to dropping out of high school and to juvenile delinquency), the benefits may be limited by a lack of connections between the activities and the individual child's family life. Parents frequently do not have ongoing relations with the adults who supervise the youth groups and often get little indication of how their child is faring beyond what the child himself reveals.

Some of the more striking illustrations of how groups of inter-related families can collectively affect the socialization experiences of children are found in the early community studies conducted by sociologists. In *Elmtown's Youth*, for example, Hollingshead described a small town in the 1940s where each family was at least roughly attached to other families in terms of socioeconomic status and moral reputation. Parents in higher status families went to considerable lengths to ensure that their children did not develop close attachments to children from lower status families and that their children received preferential treatment in the public schools. This effort was greatly facilitated by the close-knit nature of the small-town life where parents obtained information on their children's activities quite easily.[17]

The social structure of this type of functional community represents what we have referred to as "intergenerational closure."[18] The parents of one child maintain relationships with the parents of their child's associates. While Hollingshead was critical of the inegalitarian consequences of the small-town community organization, intergenerational closure does not necessarily bring social inequity. Nor is inequality the only consequence of interest. For example, the connection of youth to the adult community offers protection against peer environments that encourage delinquency. A social structure with intergenerational closure seems to characterize the religious communities that maintain private schools for their children and that may also still survive in smaller communities across the country served by public schools. But there are several reasons to believe that it is in decline for most communities.

A number of factors make it less likely that parents of school-age children living in a common residential neighborhood will maintain regular contact with one another. Perhaps most important has been the growing rate of geographical mobility in the United States. As firms and labor markets have become increasingly national in scope, career advancement has demanded changing residence from one locality or region to another. The High School and Beyond national survey of 1980 sophomores shows that 36 percent of the students reported changing schools at least once since the end of elementary school because of a family residential move. Over 11 percent moved three times or more in the same time span.[19] Analysis of survey data shows that a higher frequency of moving increases the probability that a student will drop out of high school, controlling for other aspects of family background.[20]

Within local areas, advances in transportation technology have also had the effect of dispersing employment relative to place of residence. The near universality of automobile ownership, and in large urban areas, the availability of public transportation, allow people to live at considerable distances from their workplaces, and make it less likely they will live next to people whom they see in the ordinary course of the day. The same tendency toward local anonymity and isolation is further strengthened by the centralization of retail sales organizations. Until quite recently, residents of a local neighborhood would be in regular contact with each other when shopping. Such contacts facilitated exchanges of information about the activities of each other's children.

While changes of residence often result from economic gains of the individual family, they can also hold negative effects for the community. Families that live near each other form a functioning community, that is, a community wherein information is exchanged, standards are defined, and action is taken to uphold the standards through the expenditure of a considerable amount of time and effort. When the odds are good that a new family in the neighborhood will stay in the area for several years, then both the new family and the established families will consider the time and effort to be a "good risk" investment. But when the odds shift, as they have over the last few decades for much of the population, the investment is likely to be considered a risky one.

These trends do not imply that community has been lost in American life. Sociologists studying urban life have demonstrated that people living in the "anonymous" central cities and bedroom suburbs maintain as many close contacts as people living in stable small towns.[21] The central point is that the circle of adult relationships is now less likely to include parents of their children's associates, thus reducing the availability of knowledge about what their child is doing, and the opportunity to influence the child's actions through norms and sanctions.

Intergenerational Closure and Schools

Relationships among parents are not the only source of intergenerational closure, however. Children spend much of their days in school, and the adults who work there as teachers, administrators, and support staff are often the adults who have the most contact with them. Educators often take a strong interest in the welfare of their students and establish and maintain relationships with individual students. The recent literature on effective schools frequently notes the beneficial influence of principals and teachers who seek to build rapport with students, and there is no shortage of biographical and journalistic accounts of outstanding educators who have made real differences in the lives of their students.

As schools are currently structured, however, a number of factors work against the development and maintenance of strong student-adult relationships in the school. In the first place, the school has always stood as a relatively impersonal, goal-directed institution as compared to the family. The role of the school traditionally has been to mediate between the personal affiliations of the family and local community and the impersonal order of the economy and the state. To expect schools to integrate more of the socialization functions traditionally assumed by the family and community would entail far-reaching changes in administrator and teacher training, as well as internal organization. Schools have assumed more responsibility in this regard, but this has been handled largely by means of diversification and specialization rather than by integration. Sex education and personal counseling, for example, have rapidly grown as new responsibilities of the school, but they are part of specialized programs rather than new dimensions of the student-teacher relationship.

One of the more important trends in school organization over the past several decades, school consolidation, likely has had the effect of increasing the impersonality of the school. Consolidation has been pursued as a means of realizing economies of scale and as a way to increase the range of course offerings in the curriculum. As a consequence, however, students spend less time with any given teacher, and teachers and other school officials are less likely to have ties outside school with the parents of their students. These factors work against the development of both intensity and scope in the student-teacher relationship, with the likely parallel enhancement of the strength of the student peer group.

The reduction of intergenerational closure has not been the only factor reducing the importance of parents and responsible adults in the lives of children and youth. The growth of a youth-oriented commercial culture, particularly linked to rock music, has drawn the attention of youth away from parental influence. The American child has become a major target for many commercial markets. It often is difficult for parents to compete with the slick images of peer association generated out of Madison Avenue.

Policy Implications of Changing Families and Communities

The problems discussed in this chapter have their roots in larger social and economic trends in the United States. Clearly, policies designed to address the challenges must be framed in a comprehensive fashion and some of the problems are outside the purview of educational policy at any level. Nonetheless, there are a number of steps state and local educational authorities can take to confront the consequences if not the causes of the changing conditions of families and communities.

If our analysis is correct, the single most important problem that American society faces in its effort to educate children is that young people have become segregated from the structure of responsibilities and rewards of the productive adult society. As a result, children and adolescents face historically unprecedented challenges in finding a sense of purpose in their schooling tasks and a sense of connection with adult roles of authority and responsibility. The problem for policymakers is to find ways of overcoming the obstacles presented by the forces that have generated this segregation.

The solutions we propose represent a two-sided effort to bridge the gaps between schools and their constituencies. On the one hand, schools can be reorganized in ways that could bring them closer to currently existing functional communities. The most common form by which schools are currently tied to functional communities is the private school serving a religious community. Evidence indicates that this form has clear benefits for students,[22] but it is also clear that relatively few families are interested in a religion-based schooling experience for their children. Another type of functional community, however, could also serve as a basis for providing educational services: the employment-based community. Schools could be organized in conjunction with private firms and government agencies in much the same way that universities maintain laboratory schools that mainly serve the offspring of their employees. Such an arrangement offers the advantages of greater adult contact with children, and parents would be able to monitor their children's progress better due to the increased information they would receive from the network of "similarly situated" adults. A few firms apparently have adopted this model with some success for the primary grades, and it would be worthwhile to see if success can generalize to the secondary level grades as well.

One obvious problem with schools tied to workplaces is that most adults do not work for firms that are large enough to support a school. Labor force data from 1980 show that only about 31 percent of the private-sector workforce is employed in business establishments with 250 or more employees on the payroll.[23] In some cases, schools could probably be successfully established to serve the employees of a number of geographically proximate firms, but the model is clearly best suited to the large corporation or office complex where the employees are in some sort of regular contact with one another.

Linking schools with adult workplaces is a policy that state and local school district authorities can consider as either an alternative for or a supplement to the currently popular magnet school concept. Magnet schools are usually designed to serve a population defined by interest or skill in particular subjects and bounded by a school district organization. While magnet schools focus on excellence, two problems are worth noting. First, the magnet school has developed essentially as an elite or exceptional institution and as such may not provide a general model for educational reform. It is conceivable that the idea could be generalized so a system consists entirely of magnet schools, each specializing in a different aspect of the curriculum and each recruiting students from a broad geographical area. The problem here is the potential for greater fragmentation in the secondary curriculum. The competitive pressures of the system could drive schools to define unique niches of dubious long-range value to students rather than to risk failure in head-to-head competition in appropriate subjects.

A second problem with the magnet school is more fundamental. As the discussion of different types of communities implies, the magnet school seeks to serve a value- or interest-based community. While this arrangement may hold certain advantages over the residence-based community, it still has the problem of intergenerational segregation. Since school and home are likely to be even more distant than in the residential community structure, the magnet school may indeed exacerbate the problem.

Schools linked to places of employment could, in a manner similar to magnet schools, develop specialized problems in conjunction with the standard curriculum. The most obvious way to develop such specialties would be to draw upon the knowledge and skill base of the work organization itself. Members of the organization could teach classes or give demonstrations and students working part-time could be involved in various capacities in the organization itself. In either case, students would gain exposure to careers and their actual knowledge bases in a context where the adults have ongoing relationships with the students.

Despite its attractiveness, the option of linking schools to workplaces is limited by the relatively small size of most employing organizations. For the most part, efforts to develop closer ties between adults and students will have to be initiated within the currently existing framework of schools serving residential communities. A number of recent initiatives appear promising in this respect. Recognizing the importance of parental guidance and support for student success, many schools are looking for ways to increase parental awareness and participation in their children's education. In some localities, school systems have recruited private business enterprises and other institutions to "adopt" students or whole schools in an effort to give students more guidance and a greater sense of purpose in their schoolwork.

Another approach, one which has attracted more research and experimentation, is to restructure schools internally in ways that could strengthen the relationships between teachers and students, or reshape the content of relations among students. As noted earlier, a major constraint on the development of more influential teacher-student relationships is the short periods of time the two groups typically spend together. If this analysis is correct, the effect of this structural arrangement is that the student peer group becomes the primary normative reference for most students, a normative reference often indifferent or even antithetical to school achievement. One challenge to school officials, then, is to find ways to redirect the peer group so its goals are consistent with those of the school.

The work of Slavin and his associates on cooperative learning provides one attractive alternative.[24] Cooperative learning methods generally divide classrooms into small groups of four to six students, each given learning tasks related to an initial whole-class presentation by the teacher. Students are directed to work with each other on the materials in preparation for individual tests that are scored to reward both individual and group gains. The experimental evidence shows such methods tend to result in greater student engagement and higher levels of academic performance.

Choices and Challenges

We have identified two major constraints faced by contemporary families in their efforts to support and guide their children's educational experience: a lack of time and a lack of social support. The constraint on time results mainly from the separation of employment and the household, such that virtually all fathers and an increasing majority of mothers now participate in the labor force. The problem is exacerbated in a growing number of households by marital disruptions. The lack of social support parents receive is attributable in large part to the loss of intergenerational closure in communities such that contemporary parents are less likely to know other adults who also know and are in regular contact with their children. The increasing absence of intergenerational ties in contemporary functional communities has created the further problem that children are now less likely to maintain ongoing relationships with adults and thus have lost the opportunity to learn firsthand about the structure of roles and responsibilities that constitute adulthood. Schools traditionally have assumed that the family and community will establish the foundation for good work habits and a sense of duty to complete assigned tasks, both basic necessities if education is to proceed. As parental and adult community influence over children has waned, schools have lost considerable efficacy for many children and youth.

It is not clear that schools possess the necessary resources to meet these challenges. In the 1970s, many secondary schools diversified course offerings and programs in an effort to be more relevant and more attractive to students. The recent study by Powell, Farrar, and Cohen argues that high schools have come to resemble the modern shopping mall, providing a great array of curricular and extracurricular options.[25] Comparisons of the 1972 and 1980 national surveys of high school seniors, NLS72 and High School and Beyond, document a substantial movement of students away from the academic curricular program and toward vocational studies and relatively amorphous general programs of course taking.[26] Whether the current wave of legislation requiring students to complete more coursework in academic areas will reverse the tendency toward curriculum diversification and toward lower academic standards remains to be seen. We can speculate, however, that these reforms will not attain the desired results unless complementary measures addressing the problems of student interest and study habits and their roots in the family and community are also adopted.

Footnotes

1. Calvin Jones, Penny Sebring, Joanna Crawford, Bruce Spencer, Brenda Spencer and Marjorie Butz, *High School and Beyond 1980, Sophomore Cohort, Second Follow-up (1984)* (Washington, DC: U.S. Department of Education, Center for Statistics, 1986).

2. Christopher Jencks, Marshall Smith, Henry Acland, Mary Jo Bane, David Cohen, Herbert Gintis, Barbara Heyns, and Stephan Michelson, *Inequality: A Reassessment of the Effect of Family and Schooling in America* (New York: Harper Colophon, 1972), pp. 138-142.

3. U.S. Bureau of the Census, *Statistical Abstract of the United States: 1987* (Washington, DC: U.S. Government Printing Office, 1987), Table 746.

4. Ibid., Table 82.

5. Gary S. Becker, *A Treatise on the Family* (Cambridge, MA: Harvard University Press, 1981), pp. 103-112.

6. U.S. Bureau of the Census data cited in James S. Coleman and Thomas Hoffer, *Public and Private High Schools: The Impact of Communities* (New York: Basic Books, 1987), pp. 229-230.

7. U.S. Bureau of the Census, *Statistical Abstract of the United States: 1987*, Table 655.

8. Urie Bronfenbrenner and Ann C. Crouter, "Work and Family through Time and Space," in *Families That Work: Children in a Changing World*, ed. Sheila B. Kamerman and Cheryl D. Hayes (Washington, DC: National Academy Press, 1982).

9. James A. Sweet and Larry L. Bumpass, *American Families and Households* (New York: Russell Sage Foundation, 1987), p. 264.

10. E. Mavis Hetherington, Kathleen Camara, and David L. Featherman, "Achievement and Intellectual Functioning of Children in One-Parent Households," in *Achievement and Achievement Motives: Psychological and Sociological Approaches*, ed. Janet T. Spence (San Francisco: W. H. Freeman, 1983).

11. Sara McLanahan, "Family Structure and the Reproduction of Poverty," *American Journal of Sociology* 90 (1985): 873-901.

12. Donald A. Rock, Ruth B. Ekstrom, Margaret E. Goertz, Thomas L. Hilton, and Judith Pollack, *Factors Associated with Decline of Test Scores of High School Seniors, 1972 to 1980* (Washington, DC: U.S. Department of Education, Center for Statistics, 1985).

13. Susan E. Mayer and Christopher Jencks, "Growing Up in Poor Neighborhoods: How Much Does It Matter?" *Science* 243 (March 17, 1989): 1441-1445.

14. Edward L. McDill and Leo C. Rigsby, *Structure and Process in Secondary Schools: The Academic Impact of Educational Climates* (Baltimore: Johns Hopkins University Press, 1973).

15. Robert M. Hauser, William H. Sewell, and Duane F. Alwin, "High School Effects on Achievement," in *Schooling and Achievement in American Society*, ed. William H. Sewell, Robert M. Hauser, and David L. Featherman (New York: Academic Press, 1976), pp. 309-341.

16. James S. Coleman, *The Adolescent Society: The Social Life of the Teenager and Its Impact on Education* (New York: Free Press, 1961).

17. August B. Hollingshead, *Elmstown's Youth* (New York: John Wiley, 1949).

18. Coleman and Hoffer, *Public and Private High Schools*.

19. Jones et al., *High School and Beyond*.

20. Thomas B. Hoffer, "Educational Outcomes in Public and Private High Schools" (Ph.D. dissertation, University of Chicago, 1986).

21. Claude Fischer, *To Dwell among Friends: Personal Networks in Town and City* (Chicago: University of Chicago Press, 1982).

22. Coleman and Hoffer, *Public and Private High Schools*.

23. U.S. Bureau of the Census, *County Business Patterns, 1980* (Washington, DC: U.S. Government Printing Office, 1981), Table 1B.

24. Robert E. Slavin, "Cooperative Learning," *Review of Educational Research* 50 (1980): 315-342.

25. Arthur G. Powell, Elizabeth Farrar, and David K. Cohen, *The Shopping Mall High School: Winners and Losers in the Educational Marketplace* (Boston: Houghton Mifflin, 1985).

26. Rock et al., *Factors Associated with Decline of Test Scores of High School Seniors, 1972 to 1980*.

CHAPTER VII

Reconstituting Local Government for Well-Being and Education

LUVERN L. CUNNINGHAM

In this chapter I argue for substantial change in the structure and management of local governments, including school districts. I also call for reconsideration of the philosophy, leadership, and management of local-level institutions that affect the lives of children and youth in particular. I propose that the focus of local government be fixed on well-being, acknowledging education as primary to the quality of life for Americans of all ages. Over the next generation or two, communities need to phase out local school districts, local school boards, and local school superintendents in favor of new jurisdictions and authorities through a carefully developed and statutorily approved reconstituting process centered on the notion of well-being.

A reconstituted local government for well-being would govern such areas as mental health, physical health, public safety, preschool and nursery school education, adult education, libraries, museums, child day care, adult day care, K-12 schooling, job retraining, employment counseling and placement, literacy, community development, and provisions for the homeless. Today these public services are the responsibility of a melange of agencies with little or no policy coordination or continuity of service for individuals over time.

Note the language here. The process is reconstituting, not reorganizing. New jurisdictions will be governed by elected commissions. A broad range of new, as well as traditional, professions and professionals would provide public service. Federal and state policy eventually would be adjusted to correspond to reconstituted local well-being governance systems.

The call for reconstituting local government around well-being and education rests on several arguments:

- the "general welfare" provision of the Preamble to the U.S. Constitution has never been fully achieved nor addressed at the local level;

135

- the general responsibilities for well-being at the local government or community level are essentially unspecified;
- recent federal and state governmental policy has redirected the burden of social responsibility to the grass roots level;
- the mission and goals of local governments (townships, municipalities, counties, school districts, special districts) have remained constant, for the most part, since their establishment;
- state constitutional conventions, infrequent in recent times, leave local governments untouched;
- many current problems of well-being (poverty, homelessness, AIDS, substance abuse, teen-age pregnancy, family violence) dot local landscapes and present a clear delineation of public responsibility;
- attempts at interagency cooperation, important as they are, often are incremental and lack support;
- new imperatives such as lifelong learning and national public service are currently without clearly defined institutional and administrative homes and should be included in reconstituting formulations; and
- leaders across the public service professions are excellent sources of insight about the reconceptualization of local governments and can play central roles in their reconstitution.

The mission, philosophy, broad goals, and features of governance and management might best be worked out through local constitutional conventions convened for reconstituting purposes. Such local constitutional conventions would be authorized by state legislatures through enabling legislation. Again note the emphasis on local constitutional conventions, not state constitutional conventions. Thinking must be concentrated on local vision and responsibility and not be allowed to escape or drift toward state and federal levels, as so often happens when local citizens find it difficult to face choice and accountability.

Culbertson has compared today's challenges confronting educational leaders with those of a century ago. Late nineteenth-century school superintendents such as William Torrey Harris in St. Louis and William Payne in Adrian, Michigan were incredible leaders.[1] They found themselves in a period of large-scale change where a nation was moving from a rural agrarian society to an industrial society. They were exemplary leaders because they charted a vision for education commensurate with the rapidly changing needs of the society they served. Harris and Payne were not satisfied to be buffeted by the stiff winds and choppy seas of their time; they ranged far beyond the boundaries of their school districts, exerting leadership on many community fronts beyond education.

Culbertson believes the same broad leadership and the same willingness to capture an educational vision is needed in the 1990s to carry the nation through the transition between the industrial society and the information age.[2] I am, in some respects, making the same appeal. Educational and lay leaders must support what appears to be, on first blush, a radical structural reform in local government including the elevation of individual and social well-being as the primary goal of reconstituted local government. Schooling is to be a subsidiary but instrumental goal in the achievement of well-being.

Some Historical and Philosophical Notes

Well-being is an important concept at a time when the personal welfare of so many citizens seems to be in jeopardy. In its simplest meaning, well-being refers to fundamental matters of health, safety, even comfort. It is the condition of being well—happy, free of fear and unusual anxiety; it is the ability to survive. Welfare, at a very general level of meaning, is a synonym, but well-being should not be confused with a "welfare state" or being "on welfare." Well-being does not have the same political connotation as welfare often does in American history and modern society.

The nation seems to be searching for a clearer vision of how human beings can move through life shaped and hopefully enhanced by institutions. Many institutions, public and private, have been constructed to address critical aspects of well-being, e.g., families, churches, and schools. Now we are in need of a fresh tapestry of individual and institutional interdependence designed to promote community strength and general well-being. To contribute to well-being is to assist others in feeling secure, confident, competent, even comfortable with themselves, their friends, their coworkers and, most important, their families. Interdependency and respect are essential. As Heclo has noted, "the chains of mutual obligation across generations and in other areas" have become more visible and problematic, raising public and private questions about matters that seemed more settled in earlier times.[3] Heclo asks:

What is it that the younger generation owes to its elders and what can they in turn expect in terms of support from the next generation of workers? What do the childless owe to those with children, if anything, and what support should aged parents expect from their children? What do regions favored by economic change owe to other regions bearing the attendant dislocations of such change?[4]

I would add two more to Heclo's list of questions: (1) What do rich communities owe to poor communities? (2) What do poor communities have the right to expect from their affluent neighbors in a truly democratic society?

Such questions were not alien to the founding fathers as they struggled to frame a constitution for a government mindful of public-private tensions present then and so abundant now. The stress between "self-sufficiency" and "mutual dependence" is very real in our time as it has been historically.[5] Each is anchored in values that are deeply held and widely shared. "Self-sufficiency" translates into "rugged individualism" and "private enterprise"; "mutual dependence" connotes proverbs such as "love thy neighbor" and "my brother's keeper." Over our national history we have witnessed expressions of these sentiments in national behavior. Mutual dependence has been in evidence often in the form of patriotism, our bonding together to address common enemies, as we did in World Wars I and II. The Civil War, on the other hand, was fought in part as an imposition of northern states to expand individual freedom. The Homestead Act was another example of invoking the public will to enhance individual economic freedom and security. Again, as Heclo has noted, "Americans as a people were *born* imprinted with the polarity between welfare (well-being) as self-sufficiency and welfare (well-being) as mutual dependence."[6]

The authors of the United States Constitution signaled the importance of our collective or general welfare in the Preamble:

We, the people of the United States, in order to form a more perfect union, establish justice, insure domestic tranquility, provide for the common defense, promote the general welfare, and secure the blessings of liberty to ourselves and our posterity, do ordain and establish this constitution for the United States of America.

Note the phrases "we, the people," "a more perfect union," "common defense," "general welfare," and "for the United States." These are far from hollow, meaningless diatribes; they are expressions of conviction and collective belief, honored and protected for more than 200 years. They are values extended and sustained through a complicated, intricate, often cumbersome set of federal, state, and local governments, including local school districts.

The local school district, as a governmental form, predates the Constitution by more than a hundred years. From its humble beginnings in the New England colonies, it spread across the country by imitation, acquiring some distinctive characteristics here and there, but never departing far from the form or philosophy its New England architects gave it.[7] In form, it was marked by geography, a territory, a physical area to be served. In philosophy, it was single purpose, to support and provide public schooling under local control. Over more than three centuries, little has been done to disturb either form or philosophy. The U.S. Constitution, when it arrived, was silent on matters of education, thus leaving those responsibilities to the states. State or commonwealth constitutions, as they appeared, essentially respected the sanctity of local school districts, embedding them, however, in the concept of state responsibility for education, imposing state will on them as local jurisdictions, even calling local school board members "agents of the state," subject to constitutional and statutory boundaries of state authority.[8]

It is quite remarkable to realize that there are more than 14,000 local school districts in this country. Notable too, is the historical adjustment in their number, which at one time was over 100,000. We have legislated ways to consolidate and reorganize them, even change the scope of their service. From time to time, and place to place, we have created districts to serve special needs such as special education or vocational education plus those that serve as regional service units.[9] Form and philosophy remain, as noted before, essentially untouched. Why should local school districts, the lay persons who control them (school board members) and the persons who manage and supervise them (superintendents) be the object of intense concern now? Why should the viability of school districts as well as counties, cities, and townships suddenly become suspect?

Most state constitutions contain a framing statement for the state's responsibility for education. Often it is as simple as "to provide a uniform and common system of schools." Subsequent statutes, rules, and regulations have added definition and specificity, but the principal provision remains—i.e., to provide a uniform and common system of schools.

Prior to the professionalization of school teaching and school administration, the content of schooling was essentially determined by citizens serving as local board members. These early school administrators, as Tyack and Hansot have noted, were overwhelmingly white, Anglo-Saxon, Protestant, and male.[10] They were stewards of resources as well as of what was to be learned. The purposes to be served through schooling were simple, paralleling Protestant values and Anglo-Saxon, white, and male traditions.

In the late 1800s and the first half of the 1900s, the professionalization of school teaching and school administration was developing. Occasionally, there was collaboration between leaders from colleges and universities and those from public schools, often involving leading superintendents such as William Torrey Harris of St. Louis and Ella Flagg Young of Chicago. Collaboration was aimed at several targets, including the depoliticizing of schools, establishing standards, incorporating business principles and practices, framing curriculum parameters, and clarifying the purposes of schooling.[11] The Committee of Ten and the Committee of Fifteen, comprised of University presidents, professors, and public school leaders, are examples of the influence early twentieth-century leaders had on American education through focused and well publicized commentary on the aims and purposes of education.[12]

In 1938, the National Education Association's potent Educational Policies Commission published a widely quoted report entitled *The Purposes of Education in American Democracy*.[13] This was the last NEA comprehensive statement on the aims of education. It appeared twenty years after World War I, in the twilight of the Great Depression and three years before the United States entered World War II. It was a time of struggle. Enormous economic upheaval remained—large-scale unemployment, bankruptcies, hunger, suffering, homeless families, and endless trains heading west to the land of golden opportunity. Thus, the Educational Policies Commission's goals of education emerged from, as well as reflected, turbulent economic, social, and political conditions.

There were four general goals. Many teachers and administrators memorized them. The first was *self-realization* and included such objectives as the appetite for learning, mastery of oral and written communication, reading, writing, numbers, aesthetic interests, and character. There were thirteen objectives in all. The second goal was *human relationships*, incorporating the objectives of respect for humanity, friendships, cooperation, courtesy, appreciation and conservation of the home, homemaking, and democracy in the home.

Economic efficiency was the third goal, comprised of objectives like good workmanship, occupational choice, appreciation, and adjustment, personal economics, consumer judgment and protection, and efficiency in buying. And the fourth goal, *civic responsibility*, was made up of objectives such as social justice, social understanding, critical judgment, tolerance, conservation, social applications of science, world citizenship, observance of law, economic literacy, political citizenship, and devotion to democracy.[14]

These four goals were widely endorsed a half-century ago. They remain today the last national statement of educational goals in the United States. The transformation of the NEA in the 1950s and 1960s to a teacher's association interested in issues of compensation and working conditions spelled the end of the Educational Policies Commission as well as a national professional capacity to define and endorse broad national educational directions. Since then, we have been, as a nation, essentially aimless and adrift educationally, vulnerable in the extreme to short-term political and economic expediency. The rash of local, state, and national reform reports in the 1980s, the emergence of "education" governors and "education" presidential candidates, and pressure from corporate executives try to fill the void. Local districts are awash in a sea of prescriptions, often cosmetic, absent even a general set of purposes to provide direction and stability.

The 1938 Educational Policies Commission goals are broad and comprehensive. Although formulated fifty years ago and largely forgotten, they remain contemporary. They address *issues of well-being* beyond intellectual development: health, recreation, appreciation of the family as a social institution, the conservation of family ideals, understanding of work, maintaining a job, planning the economics of one's own life, sensitivity to the disparities of human circumstances, regard for the nation's resources, respect for measures of scientific advance and their contribution to the general welfare, respect for the law, economic literacy, and civic duty.

Current Threats to Well-Being

Many can identify disturbing conditions in our midst that affect our lives and our institutions: the AIDS tragedy, transformations within families, the unfriendly corporate takeover, the abuse syndromes, escalating costs of health services, teenage parents, teenage suicide, unemployment, underemployment, dropouts, and the deterioration of ethical behavior. Slightly more remote but still germane are international terrorism, acid rain, nuclear waste disposal, soil loss, despoliation of rain forests, ground water contamination, and infrastructure disintegration. Obviously, other ages and other generations confronted their own psychological, social, political, and economic dislocation and turbulence. But ours is distinctive in terms of the sources of change and the intensity of change that impact on our selves and our institutions.[15] The sources of change may be far removed from our neighborhoods. Terrorism, for example, has occupied our psyches since World War II, and as Lasswell noted, provoked a worldwide response in the form of expensive and unending surveillance. The intensity of change is most evident in computer technology, which in less than fifty years has affected and metamorphosed many aspects of our lives. To repeat, the distinction between us and our predecessors lies in how we perceive the incredible diversity of sources of change and the intensity of change within those sources, as well as the interactions among them. And within these sources of change and rates of change and the interaction among them, reside the threats to our well-being.[16]

Institutional Contributors to Well-Being

There are many notable contributors to individual and collective well-being. Families, schools, churches, hospitals, clinics, police and fire departments, libraries, museums, and parks come readily to mind. They are traditional and enduring. Hospices, halfway houses, alcohol and drug treatment centers, shelters for the homeless are more recent cultural innovations. The Salvation Army, the American Red Cross, Alcoholics Anonymous, the American Cancer Society, the Muscular Dystrophy Association, the United Negro College Fund are examples of national organizations dedicated to problems of well-being. And all of these are joined by hundreds of thousands of formal and informal networks and support groups put in place to meet human need.

Two respected traditional contributors to well-being are the nation's numerous public and private museums and libraries. Aided initially by the philanthropy of Andrew Carnegie, most communities in the United States have a public library. These are remarkable institutions in their own right, yet they, like public and private education, are undergoing revolution and reform. Public and private museums are experiencing similar transformations. The future of museums, including threats to their existence, was highlighted in a recent issue of the *New York Times*. The impact of technology on museums and libraries as institutions is much like that undergone by hospitals and other health-serving institutions. It is jarring, unrelenting, and, in the short run, disorienting.

Schools, libraries, and museums have coexisted historically under an aura of independence rather than interdependence. Despite examples of cooperation in some communities, their missions have not been examined in common, nor have efforts been made to reduce overlap of programs, repetition, and competition, in order to achieve an integrated set of purposes. Each is in the business of education and enlightenment. Technology is likely to force a reexamination of mission and commonality involving these three institutions and may be a factor in speeding up public attention to reconstituting local governments.

In the early 1980s, the California Commission on Technology was formed. Its purpose was to appraise the need for a new governing system for all educational institutions. The work of the Commission was based upon the recognition of California's rich educational resources but the limited ability to access information and provide methods for handling costs associated with knowledge dissemination across institutional boundaries. As is recognized, it is technically possible to move large amounts of information from one place to another instantaneously. Capacity is almost unlimited. A group of public school sixth-grade students in San Francisco, for example, may wish to use art information located in the J. Paul Getty Museum, a private institution in Los Angeles. The information in the Getty Museum could be transmitted to the sixth graders in a matter of seconds, but as of now, that cannot be done. The question is one of politics, cost, and information control. How would the transmission of data be priced if it could be accessed? Who makes decisions in respect to control of such data? The California Commission explored information sharing between public and private educative and enlightening institutions at all levels to determine whether a new system of governance for education and enlightenment would be necessary soon. Parenthetically, the same questions of information ownership, accessing, pricing, and sharing exist at the community level. Answers to such questions would fall to new governing boards established for local jurisdictions to address well-being.

Although the nation's commitment to general well-being is anchored in the Constitution, we have treated it casually, almost with indifference. We have created units of local government, such as school districts, and charged them with part of the responsibility for well-being, but not the whole of it. Public schooling may well be the flagship of a flotilla of approaches to well-being but it is not the exclusive provider. Physical and mental health, employment counseling, infant education, preschooling, day care, extended day care, criminal justice, libraries, museums, community cable television, foster care, churches, and synagogues are other partners that must be integrated if local communities are to address issues of well-being in a just and proactive fashion. These contributors to well-being are reasonably well known. Some are public, some private, but each addresses a part, not the whole. Each is noble and defensible in its own right and historically significant, but as isolated parts they all fall short.

Program extensions and expansions, in the name of well-being, have occurred in many public school districts over the last twenty years. Examples are suicide prevention, employee assistance, parent education, alcohol abuse, drug abuse, preschool services, day care and latch key programs, and intergovernmental and business partnerships. These expansions and extensions of the work of the school occur during the normal school day, summer vacation periods, and weekends. Some schools open earlier in the morning and remain open late into the night to accommodate populations with special needs.

Interest in community service for children of school age exploded in the 1980s, stimulated in part by the National Society for Internships and Experiential Education. Literally hundreds of local, state, and national associations, alliances, compacts, and other forms of interagency and interinstitutional cooperation sought to have community service become an integral part of formal education. Today, there is the prospect of some form of compulsory or mandated community service to be administered by local school districts.[17] New federal community service legislation was introduced in the U.S. Senate by Senators Sam Nunn of Georgia and Charles Robb of Virginia in 1989. Early passage seemed unlikely, but given President Bush's interest in public service, the nation appeared to be more aware of the need to rebuild community service.

As noted earlier, public schools have been unusually receptive and accommodating to a wide range of human needs, many of them extending beyond the ordinary school populations and parent groups. Some critics suggest that schools have been forced to use their scarce resources for ancillary and nonacademic purposes. School officials are sometimes chastized for going outside the defined mission of public education and assuming accountability for a multitude of functions. On the other hand, some critics believe schools have not gone far enough to satisfy the many unmet needs of citizens in modern America.

Interagency Cooperation and Collaboration

Interest in how schools relate to their communities is not new. Some school superintendents and other school officials, especially principals, have worked conscientiously with other public and private community agencies for years. In fact, there is a strong philosophical commitment in some districts to community education, which has emerged as a strong curriculum emphasis over the past thirty years. Many community educators were prepared in Michigan universities through curricula designed to further community education objectives across the country. The Charles W. Mott Foundation in Flint, Michigan, invested millions of dollars in an effort to disseminate the concept and prepare superintendents and other educators to lead in community education. Courses in school-community relations become a requirement for administrative certification in most states.

Interagency collaboration has, however, become a new theme at the local level. Experience with collaboration between and among public and private agencies has shown that new skills are required on the part of administrative leaders. Likewise, altered personnel policies and procedures are needed to support collaboration. Time must be set aside and resources reallocated to make interagency collaboration happen. In the case of school districts, school boards must endorse it and superintendents support it through tenacious leadership.

Almost daily some districts confront in some form the needs of other populations and other age groups that are not currently within the scope of their legal responsibilities. The AIDS babies, the chronically unemployed, the recently deinstitutionalized, the homeless, the abused, the morally bankrupt, the abandoned come to mind. Something has to be done; these problems spill over the boundaries of individual institutions. They are natural candidates for interinstitutional and interagency collaboration.

The rapid expansion of interagency and interinstitutional collaboration in the 1980s and 1990s, however, is likely to be a way station on the road to reconstitution. Human problems often outstrip the capacities of single service providers. Consortia or institutional alliances formed to support children born with AIDS are examples of cooperative effort that is well-intended and useful in the short term. It is doubtful, however, that such alliances can be sustained through the years. As schools, hospitals, nursing homes, clinics, half-way houses, juvenile authorities, employment services, cooperative extension, and family service agencies build increasing numbers of cooperative arrangements, more and more energy and resources are invested. Eventually, the drain on resources erodes the capacity of each partner to achieve its primary mission. As the primary missions of a number of institutions begin to crumble, community leaders are likely to seek ways to reconstitute institutions, public and private. At some point in the near future communities must be ready to engage in institutional analysis and assessment leading to substantial redrafting of institutional missions and organizational forms.

Local Districts for Well-Being

What would local entities for well-being be like? Having raised the question, I am tempted to say that no one knows. Most efforts at reform, including education, have left the structures and missions of local governments untouched. There has been little intellectual investment in developing new theories of local government. Political scientists, with a few exceptions, have avoided theorizing about local jurisdictions, in lieu of describing them as chaotic, fragmented, marble-cake, proliferated, ineffective, duplicative, and wasteful.

Venturesome political scientists such as Vincent and Elinor Ostrom at Indiana University, who have generated new theories and fresh language to use in thinking about local government, especially in metropolitan areas, have felt the sting of collegial rebuke.[18] An initiative in New York sounds promising. A project sponsored jointly by the State Academy for Public Administration and the Nelson Rockefeller Institute of Government in Albany is addressing the critical issues of policy, structure, and governance confronting state and local governments. The project involves the participation of elected and appointed persons from the public and private sectors and higher education. The premise undergirding the work is that the profound changes extant in the world will have a cataclysmic effect upon the demand for community services including education.[19]

There are no models, no real guidelines to follow in the invention of a new jurisdiction devoted to well-being. James S. Coleman argues persuasively for the invention of new institutions to form "social capital" to augment and, in many instances, replace the social capital formation previously provided by families and other community institutions such as scouting and nonschool related clubs.[20] Coleman describes how, in sequence, fathers, followed by mothers, exited the home to become wage earners. Fathers, lunch buckets in hand, left home first in massive numbers, abandoning their responsibilities for social capital formation at the turn of the century. Mothers followed, entering the labor force in the mid- to late 1900s, severely lessening opportunities for close, enduring social relationships with children.[21]

Consequently, the range of exchange has been so narrowed between parents and children that millions of children enter the classroom bereft of human belonging so essential to self-esteem and personal confidence about their emerging roles and to the meanings formal education can have in their lives. Coleman urges the creation of new institutions designed expressly for child rearing that can serve as surrogates for parental associations not likely to be reclaimed on a large scale by contemporary families.[22] Coleman goes on to assert:

The general shape of the demand for a new institution is clear: It is a demand not for further classroom indoctrination, not for any particular content, but a demand for child care: *all day; from birth to school age; after school, every day, till parents return from work; and all summer.*[23]

Coleman argues that these new institutions must be able to induce the kinds of attitudes, effort, and conception of self that children and youth need to succeed in school and as adults.

It is premature to describe definitive functions, roles, and responsibilities for new local governments. There are, however, some premises on which new units might be constructed, as well as notions about how to move from where we are to where we must be.

The *first premise* is that a new jurisdiction must reflect in philosophy and structure a total commitment to well-being, both individual and collective. Its leaders must construct and be guided by a vision of community grounded in a philosophy that supports the general welfare provisions of the U.S. Constitution encompassing the paradoxical values of individual self-sufficiency and mutual dependence.

The *second premise* is that a local government devoted to well-being must be locally controlled, much in the fashion school districts are governed by school boards. The problems of human living, including those of intellectual development, are across the street, next door, and down the road. They are not elsewhere, in state and federal places. This is not to dismiss basic federal and state roles in achieving well-being but to recognize that those closest to human need on a day-to-day basis must measure up and address such needs head on.

The *third premise* is that local control can fix responsibility for monitoring major threats to well-being such as hazardous waste disposal, for example, and other problems related to environmental protection. Citizens would have an outlet for their concerns at the local level rather than carry their causes to remote state and federal agencies. The threats to well-being at the Love Canal, so widely publicized in the 1980s, were local. The threats were not national, although they were observed nationally. Remedial actions had to happen there, on site, not elsewhere. Thus, the monitoring needed to be there, in the hands of local officials at the place where lives were in jeopardy.

The *fourth premise* is that such an entity is not a "welfare state" devoted to providing solutions to problems people have, but rather to an enabling capacity, leading to self-sufficiency and civic responsibility.

The *fifth premise* is that education is now, and likely forever will be, the central factor in achieving well-being and may become the rod around which service providers will gather. Learning must be lifelong and compulsory. Mandated data-gathering for each individual might begin at birth or as soon after conception as possible, continuing through the life span. Edward Zigler of Yale University suggests that when pregnancy is known, the prospective mother should register the unborn child at the local public school.[24] The purpose of such an action would not be to increase public sector regulation over private lives. Rather, Zigler's notion is based on the belief that child service providers need a much more comprehensive view about the cognitive, physical, and psychological development of all children if effective problem prevention and early intervention services are to be provided.[25]

The *sixth premise* is that new concepts of resource support must be developed to break away from traditional patterns of finance, many of which are marked by inequity and unintended negative consequences. A fresh concept of entitlement may be in order—entitlement that is lifelong and available to every citizen. It would include support for lifelong continuing education encompassing career retraining and help with adaptation to rapid change. It would include support for physical and mental health needs, rehabilitation, employment counseling, social capital formation in Coleman's terms, information accessing and utilization, a range of diagnostic services, even personal financial planning.

The road to reconstituted local governments may well be a long one. Moreover, there are no maps or reliable human experience, short of violent revolution, to take us there. John Dewey, in his remarkable book *The Public and Its Problems*, observed that:

The belief in political fixity, of the sanctity of some form of state consecrated by the efforts of our fathers and hallowed by tradition, is one of the stumbling blocks in the way of orderly and directed change; it is an invitation to revolt and revolution.[26]

An early task, therefore, is to forgo our attachment to the school district and its mission of schooling and bond with the larger and, in the long run, more important public value of well-being.

The prospect of remaking local government and reconfiguring the scope and content of local control generates a host of problems. Simple cosmetic reforms even now produce difficulties of consequence, since basic structural transformations toss so many things up in the air. Two major scholars of this century had something to say about accomplishing large-scale change, either structural or social in content. John Dewey maintained that an essential civic need is the improvement of the methods and conditions of debate, discussion, and persuasion about public problems.[27] Harold D. Lasswell proposed community-based decision seminars as the means to public learning essential to fundamental change.[28] Lasswell advocated social planetaria as permanent locations for community problem solving, financed and managed much in the fashion of public libraries and museums. Dewey contended citizens have the capacity to pass judgment on new ideas when thoroughly informed about them. Lasswell added a structure and process for the public to learn about its problems and take part in the formulation of solutions in an essentially quasi-political environment. The need for reconstituting local government would be an ideal issue to be addressed through Lasswell's decision seminar process located in a social planetarium and invoking widespread public participation along the way.

The public and private institutions of a democracy, including the government itself, are subject to adjustments at any time according to the wisdom, tolerance, and enlightenment of the individuals who function in them.[29] Private institutions are changing all about us—

financial organizations, hospitals, museums, businesses, media, agriculture, and transportation. Only governments seem to remain unaltered, albeit there are ebbs and flows depending on the presence or absence of strong executives, strong legislatures, and the continued power struggles between them. Unchanged are our constitutional and statutory expectations for them. Reports from prestigious sources flow endlessly, many with promising ideas, but none suggests we modify, even slightly, local governments so that there is an improved capacity to achieve a general well-being so desperately needed.

In November of 1988, the final report of the William T. Grant Foundation Commission on Work, Family and Citizenship was published. It is entitled *The Forgotten Half: Pathways to Success for America's Youth and Young Families*.[30] Chapter 3, "Toward More Responsive Communities," contains ten solid recommendations, none of which is fanciful or cosmetic.[31] Each recommendation, however, is jeopardized because the authors of the report assume jurisdictional status quo. No reconfigurations of local governments are proposed.

Are current public officials, both elected and appointed, so deeply entrenched that there are no prospects for taking a fresh look at local jurisdictions? Lawrence A. Cremin, Harold D. Lasswell, John Dewey, Yehezkel Dror, and others believe we can and should have a new look. Cremin has signaled the need for widespread public discussions about our institutions, informally in small groups and formally in organizations.[32] Dror argues for promoting citizen policy enlightenment and periodic constitutional revisions.[33] Ostrom believes Americans will be forced to draw back from nationalization and explore ways to free society from central government and to return to local self-government for well-being.[34]

New Public Officials for Well-Being

The leaders of emerging units of local government devoted to well-being will need a much broader view of the human condition than most possess today. Essential to the performance of the leader/administrator/facilitator function will be a commitment to a philosophy of well-being, including a grasp of the myriad ways the well-being of each person can be enhanced. Central to well-being will be skill development and enlightenment as addressed now by a broad range of public and private agencies. But philosophy will be basic, a philosophy of well-being. From philosophy, visions of how to achieve general well-being will emerge. Tenets of that philosophy will be anchored in our federal and state constitutions in respect to general welfare. At bedrock will be an administrative understanding and commitment to local direction and control—a premise on which education of children and youth between the ages of five and sixteen is currently based.

The philosophy of local control of and responsibility for well-being will likely be extended and expanded over time to include citizens of all ages. The burden of governance and management will be more severe in some respects than what is experienced now by local township trustees, commissioners, council members, and school board members. The heavier burden will be reflected in the scope of responsibility and the oversight knowledge required of stewards of a radically expanded and more complex enterprise.

A Time for Patience and Hope

Obviously, the proposed changes in local government are broad in concept and narrow in detail. The focus has been limited to local jurisdictions omitting the self-evident need to achieve parallel accommodations in state and federal policy. The proposal is based on a tacit assumption that the continued extension of burden and responsibility on school districts for meeting human need is nearing the breaking point. Omitted also is citation in detail to the impact the reconstitution of local government would have on local private agencies currently devoted to individual and collective well-being.

Basic too is the belief that the education of individuals can be enhanced through infant and early childhood education and the use of sophisticated diagnostic data to help produce better educational judgments. Data about a person's physical and mental health acquired from birth and aggregated throughout the life span can be related to compulsory lifelong learning as a matter of policy. Implications abound for the education professions, at the prepractice and practice levels. The need for interprofessional education and practice are clearly in evidence.[35] New professions are likely to emerge as better estimates of need and opportunity are clarified through experience.

As Jack Culbertson and others have noted, we are living in a parenthesis. A century ago, an era marked by large-scale social, economic, and political transformations, educational leaders, many of them superintendents, joined in envisioning what education would have to become to meet the new realities and requirements. The kindergarten, vocational education, the junior college, health and physical education were among the social inventions advanced. Now the need is even more severe with the threat of a permanent underclass and of an ever-increasing number of social pathologies invading our communities.

The story of Tom, a boy of eighteen who took his own life, is illustrative.[36] His biography is sobering, first for the tragedy itself, and second for the trail of inadequate institutional and individual professional judgments Tom encountered. Eleven professional decisions can be identified in Tom's life any one of which, if made on the basis of adequate professional knowledge, might have altered the outcome. Some of those decisions were made by teachers, a school nurse, and two principals; others were made by medical personnel, two military chaplains, a local minister, and a clinical psychologist. The case illustrates how the well-being of Tom's parents, and eventually Tom, was placed in jeopardy by institutional and individual professional incompetence and the absence of a trail of diagnostic information beginning in infancy that could have made a difference. There are many Toms in our communities today and there will be many more in the future. Better ways must be found to ensure their well-being. We talk of new technologies and new reforms. Perhaps we need to return to basic questions such as what kind of life is worth living and how might our social institutions be reconstituted to enhance the prospects of a just and moral life for all? Educational leaders are in a unique position to ask these questions. I am not entirely confident they will but I know they must.

FOOTNOTES

1. Jack A. Culbertson, "Tomorrow's Challenges to Today's Professors of Educational Administration" (Paper presented at the meeting of the National Conference of Professors of Educational Administration, Western Michigan University, Kalamazoo, August, 1988), pp. 4-8.

2. Ibid., p. 9.

3. Hugh Heclo, "General Welfare and Two American Political Traditions," *Political Science Quarterly* 101, no. 2 (1986): 179-196.

4. Ibid., p. 194.

5. Ibid., pp. 182-186.

6. Ibid., p. 185.

7. Roald F. Campbell, Luvern L. Cunningham, Raphael O. Nystrand, and Michael D. Usdan, *The Organization and Control of American Schools* (Columbus, OH: Charles E. Merrill, 1985), chap. 4.

8. Ibid., chap. 8.

9. Ibid., chap. 5.

10. David B. Tyack and Elisabeth Hansot, *Managers of Virtue* (New York: Basic Books, 1982).

11. David B. Tyack, *The One Best System* (Cambridge, MA: Harvard University Press, 1974), pp. 129-147.

12. Campbell et al., *The Organization and Control of American Schools*, pp. 366-368.

13. Educational Policies Commission, *The Purposes of Education in American Democracy* (Washington, DC: National Education Association, 1938), as summarized in J. Galen Saylor and William M. Alexander, *Curriculum Planning* (New York: Rinehart and Company, 1956), pp. 220-223.

14. Ibid.

15. Stephen R. Graubard et al., "Some Issues of Technology," a symposium, in *Modern Technology: Problem or Opportunity?*, *Daedalus* 109 (Winter 1980): 3-24.

16. It should be noted that these threats to well-being are worldwide. See Soedjatmoko, "Education Relevant to People's Needs," *Daedalus* 118 (Winter 1989): 211-218.

17. Anne C. Lewis, *Facts and Faith: A Status Report on Youth Service* (Washington, DC: William T. Grant Foundation Commission on Work, Family, and Citizenship, 1988), p. 32.

18. Vincent Ostrom and Elinor Ostrom, "Public Goods and Public Choices," in *Alternatives for Delivering Public Services: Toward Improved Performance*, ed. E. S. Savas (Boulder, CO: Westview Press, 1977), pp. 7-49. See also, Robert T. Golembiewski, "A Critique of Democratic Administration and Its Supporting Ideation," *American Political Science Review* 71 (December 1977): 1488-1507, 1526-1531.

19. Nelson A. Rockefeller Institute of Government, *New York Governance in the 21st Century* (Albany, NY: Nelson A. Rockefeller Institute of Government, 1987).

20. James S. Coleman, "Families and Schools," *Educational Researcher* 16, no. 6 (August-September 1987): 32-38.

21. Ibid., p. 32.

22. Ibid., p. 37.

23. Ibid., p. 38. Italics in original.

24. This assertion was made by Edward F. Zigler in an address to the Ohio Commission on Interprofessional Education and Practice, Columbus, April, 1980.

25. Additional support for gathering data early in the life span appears in Thomas T. Kochanek, "Conceptualizing Screening Models for Developmentally Disabled and High Risk Children and Their Families," *Zero to Three* 9 (December 1988): 16-20.

26. John Dewey, *The Public and Its Problems* (Denver: Alan Swallow, 1927), p. 35.

27. Ibid., p. 208.

28. Harold D. Lasswell, *A Preview of the Policy Sciences* (New York: American Elsevier Publishing Co., 1971), pp. 142-157.

29. Educational Policies Commission, *The Purposes of Education in a Democracy*, p. 17.

30. Commission on Work, Family, and Citizenship, *The Forgotten Half: Pathways to Success for America's Youth and Young Families* (Washington, DC: William T. Grant Foundation Commission on Work, Family, and Citizenship, November 1988), p. 203.

31. Ibid., chap. 3. See also, the summation and commentary on the report that appeared in *Phi Delta Kappan* 70 (December 1988): 281-289.

32. Lawrence A. Cremin, *Public Education* (New York: Basic Books, 1976), p. 74.

33. Yehezkel Dror, *Policymaking under Diversity* (New Brunswick, NJ: Transaction Books, 1986), pp. 295-99.

34. Vincent Ostrom, *The Political Theory of a Compound Republic* (Lincoln: University of Nebraska Press, 1987), p. 232.

35. Frederick R. Cyphert and Luvern L. Cunningham, "Interprofessional Education and Practice: A Future Agenda," *Theory Into Practice* 26 (Spring 1987): 153-156.

36. Henry P. Coppolillo, "The Seeds of Suicide" (Unpublished paper prepared in October 1988 and available through the Ohio Commission on Interprofessional Education and Practice, 1712 Neil Avenue, Columbus, Ohio).

Section Four
TEACHERS, PRINCIPALS, AND EDUCATIONAL LEADERSHIP

CHAPTER VIII

Effective Schools, Teachers, and Principals: Today's Evidence, Tomorrow's Prospects

BARNETT BERRY AND RICK GINSBERG

Over the last decade there has been a plethora of research and rhetoric on effective schools, teachers, and, to some extent, principals. For the most part, there has been a refocus on improving school success, typically gauged by student test scores. The research on effective schools points to strong instructional leadership by principals, high student expectations, clear goals, an emphasis on basic skills, an orderly and structured environment, and frequent evaluation of student performance. This formula has been widely adopted and translated into programs for school improvement as well as into checklists for the assessment of school improvement.[1] During the early 1980s, highly publicized national reports, such as *A Nation at Risk*, criticized schools, teachers, and principals for a lack of productivity. Given the widespread criticism, the effective schools research was a readily available reform blueprint for state policymakers and educational decision makers.

State educational policy reforms of the early 1980s have been noted for their frequency and their influence on school systems across the nation (but most notably in southern and rural systems).[2] With significant increases in public resources, early reform initiatives included:

1. state-developed curricula, coupled with new student testing programs that primarily tested basic skills,

2. requirements for school and district planning and expanded state monitoring, and

3. new programs for certification, evaluation, and compensation of teachers.[3]

These reforms focused mainly on problems with assessment and accountability. As a result, many policy initiatives attempted to tighten standards for both students and teachers. To some extent, school leadership was questioned in the form of new processes and standards for the selection and evaluation of principals.

By most accounts, the first round of school reform played to "mixed reviews."[4] While some consider these policies to be "the most sustained and far-reaching reform effort in modern times,"[5] others suggest many of these promulgated policies have been more symbolic than substantive[6] and have not altered significantly the structure and functioning of the nation's public schools.[7] Some even argued that the effects of reform may be somewhat more insidious. These critics lament that state government has become more involved in the details of teaching, testing, and curriculum than ever before.[8] In particular, Ernest Boyer, president of the Carnegie Foundation for the Advancement of Teaching, argues that about 90 percent of recent legislative acts labeled educational reform have in fact been increased regulations. Mary Futrell, a past president of the National Education Association, maintains these regulations severely restrict teachers' rights to use their own judgment and dwell on the quantitative, on what is easily countable, easily measured, and reducible to checklists.[9] Consequently, these state initiatives have "legislated learning." In doing so, these critics believe that state policies of the early 1980s reduced the discretion of teachers and principals and enhanced the bureaucratic conception of schooling with what Arthur Wise has called its "rigid rules" and "pseudoscientific processes."[10]

In the late 1980s, a second round of reform reports began to emerge, with a language calling for the restructuring of schooling, the "de-isolation" of teachers, the deregulation of teaching, and the creation of a new breed of school principal. Major reports released by the Carnegie Forum, the National Governors' Association, and the National Commission on Excellence in Educational Administration spoke of the need for site-based school management, the professionalization of teachers, and the development and deployment of principal leaders. Simply stated, these reports were conceptual templates intended to focus on the professionalization of teachers and principals and the transformation of school practices. Interestingly, the key spokespersons for these heralded reforms were once again highly visible political and business leaders.

All the demands for school restructuring have emerged primarily because of economic imperatives. Asserting that our schools are inadequately preparing students for an increasingly technological labor market, educational reform leaders have called for teachers and principals who will facilitate a new form of education for a new form of worker. They also want school personnel to convey highly technical knowledge and stimulate students to think critically about the widening range of complex issues they will face in their lives and careers. This requires not only significant curricular changes but new approaches to attracting and retaining bright educators who themselves possess the capacities desired for students.[11]

However, problems arise in the transition from the desire for change to classroom reality. Despite the best of intentions, policymakers are discovering that the effectiveness research and calls for school restructuring do not easily lend themselves to changes that will dramatically alter output measures.

In this chapter, we will assess the prospects for school reform by examining the evidence on the nature of effective schools and their relationship to teachers and school leaders. We will argue that the effectiveness research, although a sound beginning for understanding successful school practices, moved from the laboratory to the real world before research elucidated more precise yet context-driven procedures of effective practices. School culture, history, and environment have been shown to be critical determinants of the activities and behavior of teachers and principals. It is widely held that school context has a major effect on student outcomes and school effectiveness.[12] However, the realities of school life and the work of teachers and principals severely limit the likelihood of significant changes using the effectiveness antidote. Education reform will work only when responsive to the demanding realities of teacher and principal work. Sadly, the realities of being an educator in modern-day America are unsettling. Data suggest that today's educators (especially teachers) are frustrated and exhausted from their work, and without their energy and vision school *reform* will go wanting. Without more specific signals from research, which can be easily translated into policy and practice, the prospects of reform do *not* appear to be very positive. However, the aging of the teacher and principal work forces (and concomitantly, the need for "new blood"), the current fervor for school reform, and the involvement of leaders outside the educational community provide a window of opportunity for the substantive restructuring of schools and classrooms.

Recent Efforts to Reform Policies Concerning Teachers

Perceiving that the national and their own state economies were at risk, governors, state legislators, and business leaders in the early 1980s led the charge to reform the public schools. The reported decline in educational standards and outcomes, as elucidated by *A Nation at Risk*, was often linked to the quality of the teacher workforce. A number of studies in the early 1980s indicated the supply of college students preparing to teach had decreased precipitously since 1970. Moreover, prospective teachers were scoring lower on tests of academic ability than their counterparts across the undergraduate disciplines, and more academically able teachers were likely to leave teaching earlier and in greater proportions than their colleagues.[13]

These insights were troublesome particularly in light of increasing demand for new teachers caused by growth in enrollments and in teacher retirements. Nearly 200,000 teaching vacancies are projected over each of the next five years.[14] The supply of newly graduated teacher candidates is expected to satisfy only about 60 percent of this demand.[15] Fortunately, in recent years there has been a slight increase in the number of college freshmen reporting an interest in teaching. In 1988, 8.8 percent of college freshmen planned to teach, compared to 1985, when only 6.2 indicated a desire to teach. However, the percentage of college students choosing teaching would have to double the present rate in order to satisfy the anticipated demand for new teachers.[16]

Over the last decade, virtually every state enacted legislation to reform teacher education, licensing, and compensation. Over 1000 pieces of legislation were developed to upgrade teachers through new certification requirements, competency tests, and tougher evaluations as well as to attract teachers through alternative certification routes, salary increases, and merit pay programs.[17]

Recent reforms of policies concerning teachers essentially were extensions of a growing state influence over education that began in the early 1970s. At that time, state policy focused more on school accountability (budgeting and planning) measures, as well as on curriculum development and evaluation procedures.[18] These policies led to the creation of standardized curriculum and teacher evaluation systems that were to ensure uniformity in what teachers taught and how they would teach it. As a result, school districts mandated that schools and teachers adhere to a curriculum with detailed specifics such as standardized lesson plans, i.e., how much time teachers were to spend teaching each topic as well as how each topic was to be taught.

In particular, Darling-Hammond and Berry found that over the last several years:

1. Virtually all states changed requirements for teacher licensure, including changes in coursework for certification and standards for approval of teacher education programs.
2. Forty-one states mandated tests for initial certification, while three imposed tests for continuing licensure.
3. Twenty-five states mandated programs for the supervision of beginning teachers with some programs linked to initial certification.
4. Several states have allowed new provisions for the emergency certification of teachers, and in only two years (from 1984 to 1986) the number of states with alternative certification programs jumped from eight to twenty-three.
5. Between 1981 and 1986, average teacher salaries increased approximately 40 percent and by the end of 1986 more than half the states had taken some action to implement differentiated pay systems in the form of career ladders or merit pay.[19]

The sheer volume of legislation suggests teaching and teachers were "reformed." However, legislative tallies do not tell the whole story about the status of the teaching profession. In her assessment of recent changes in policies regarding teachers, Darling-Hammond noted the following developments:

1. In their attempts to make teacher certification requirements more rigorous, several states have limited the number of education courses (related to pedagogy and learning theory) prospective teachers may take.
2. In their attempts to assess teacher competency, most states only test basic skills, drawing on *little* of what might be called the rich knowledge base for teaching.
3. In their attempts to supervise and evaluate teachers, many states assess teachers with procedures that posit simplistic, overly standardized, unidimensional indicators of teacher quality.

4. In their attempts to open routes to teaching, some states allow teachers to be certified with only a four- to six-week course in teaching methods prior to entering the classroom.
5. While average teachers' salaries have recently increased, teachers have only regained the purchasing power they possessed in 1972.
6. Performance-based compensation experiments have suffered from both technical and political problems, particularly neglecting to create "legitimate" means of identifying the "best" teachers.[20]

In sum, recent policies concerning teachers serve the dual purpose of both "screens" and "magnets" for the teaching profession.[21] On the one hand, as screens, teacher certification, testing, and evaluation policies attempted to limit access to teaching as well as ensured, to a certain degree, that teaching became "teacherproof." On the other hand, as magnets, teacher compensation and other incentive-based policies attempted to draw talented people into teaching and keep them there. The short-term goals of policymakers appeared to be met: entry into the profession is more difficult and compensation policies are now at least not a blatant disincentive to enter the occupation. However, it is not known whether or not those who have cleared the hurdles actually know more about teaching and whether or not incentive policies are actually attracting and retaining the best teachers. Thus, a new set of policies concerning teachers has emerged around issues of school-based management, teacher assessment, development, and leadership.

By the mid-1980s, influential foundations, politicians, and prestigious universities argued that lasting improvements in education and in the teaching occupation would occur only if teachers were empowered to make the best professional judgments on behalf of their students. Today, reform proposals such as extended teacher education, supervised internships, "holistic" assessments, lead teacher career structures, and school-based management are being debated. Many reformers are unified in their conception of empowered teachers and in the trade-off of greater regulation of teachers for the deregulation of teaching.

The Carnegie Foundation recommended, and the National Governors' Association endorsed, the creation of a National Board of Professional Teaching Standards (NBPTS) to certify teachers who demonstrate high levels of knowledge in their fields and to articulate professional standards of practice. The board's test would be the first teacher examination in the United States developed and controlled by members of the profession rather than governmental agencies. The research undergirding this new genre of teacher assessment is theoretically grounded in content-specific pedagogy. Consequently, this new form of teacher testing requires assessment that includes: (a) understanding the content to be taught, (b) identifying the critical aspects of the content likely to facilitate student learning, and (c) gauging teachers' ability to connect pedagogically to students.[22]

It is anticipated the NBPTS will prompt analogous state boards, comprised of outstanding teachers and education professionals. The state boards would be charged with identifying critical knowledge and skills, constructing evaluation mechanisms, and restricting entry to the qualified and the competent.[23] Recently, Nevada, Michigan, Montana, and West Virginia joined Minnesota and Oregon in the creation of teacher-led professional standards boards.

A consortium of education deans in research universities, organized under the name "The Holmes Group," proposed changes to strengthen and increase the duration of teacher training including a "fifth year" and a supervised internship. The supervised internship is expected to take on the role played by clinical training programs found in other established professions. The structure would provide senior members of the teaching profession the opportunity to assist novices in a meaningful way as well as to assess the novices' skills. The supervised internship, as a part of the licensure process, could encourage confidence in the profession, policymakers, and the public at large.

New career structures, such as those being tried in Rochester, New York, provide "expert" teachers the opportunity to serve as mentors, consultants, staff developers, and curriculum designers and earn upwards of $65,000 per year. Additionally, in Rochester, even though teachers may choose not to become "lead teachers," they may earn, on the average, between $40,000 and $45,000 per year.[24]

Experimentation with school restructuring may best be exemplified by the reforms advocated by Theodore Sizer through the Coalition of Essential Schools. Coalition experiments are being played out somewhat differently in forty schools, each developing a school structure that matches local needs. However, at the heart of the coalition are several key concepts: principal as exemplar teacher-leader, teacher collaborators, teacher leaders as architects of school plans and programs, student assessment through exhibition, and trained parents who serve in leadership capacities.[25]

For these proposals to develop and take firm root in the practice of schooling, the tensions between standardization and professionalization must be resolved. The growing trends of state-level centralization and increasing standardization of the schooling process are running head-on into new demands for decentralization and opportunities for school professionals to exercise professional judgment.

Current Critiques of Policy
Influencing Administrative Work

Reform on any aspect of schooling should not be considered in isolation. Specifically, changes in policies affecting teachers must consider the impact on principals and others who supervise and lead teachers. As previously discussed, much of the school reform movement has focused on teachers and teaching. Most analysts have devoted considerable attention to the effects of policies concerning teachers without examining the effects of reform on administrative work and the school principal.

An exception occurred, however, in 1987 when the National Commission on Excellence in Educational Administration (NCEEA) called attention to policies affecting the preparation, certification, development, and assessment of school leaders (primarily superintendents and principals). The NCEEA leveled harsh criticism against current policies concerning administrators, particularly with regard to the lack of:

1. a definition of good educational leadership,
2. a leader recruitment program in the schools,
3. collaboration between school districts and universities,
4. minorities and women in the field of educational administration,
5. systematic professional development for school administrators,
6. quality candidates for preparation programs,
7. programs relevant to job demands of school administrators,
8. sequence, modern content, and clinical experience in preparation programs,
9. licensure systems that promote excellence, and
10. a national sense of cooperation in preparing school leaders.[26]

While there has not been much systematic study of the impact of policies across these substantive areas, significant research has been conducted. We will briefly review some of the research related to principals in terms of their: (a) preparation and certification; (b) identification; (c) development, and (d) assessment.

The preparation of principals has been characterized as an "unintegrated collection of content-oriented courses, with requirements for performance focused almost exclusively on the principal's acquisition of skills (only) at the level of familiarity."[27] Complaints about graduate studies in educational administration are legion among school administrators.[28] Many of the complaints are lodged because of the emphasis on physical plant management at the expense of problem-solving and conflict management. Course content and instructional techniques generally are irrelevant for students, and when practicums (or internships) are included they are generally inadequate in length and quality.[29]

In a recent review of policies for certification of administrators, it was found that most states require separate certification procedures for different school administrators. Most states require classroom teaching experience as a criterion for certification. Additionally, more states are specifying definitive administrative competencies, while still less than half require an examination, such as the National Teacher Examination, as a certification requirement.[30]

However, while most analysts have called for more quality control in the identification of talented prospective principals, some see the push for behavior competencies for principal certification as having a "chilling effect on innovation and experimentation in administrator preparation programs."[31]

Assessment centers have begun to play a greater role in the identification of principals. In-basket assignments, simulations, individual and group interviews all are used to gauge the leadership capacities of prospective principals. Utilized widely in the private sector, assessment centers are catching on around the country for school administrators. Despite the current fervor for the use of assessment centers, there is limited information on the predictive validity as well as some debate concerning the content validity of the methods employed.[32]

In the past, there was considerable criticism of the process of recruiting and selecting principals. Miklos revealed common problems found in the research on principal selection: (a) the lack of written selection policies, (b) the limited resources devoted to recruitment and selection, (c) a tendency to select local and internal candidates, and (d) "old boy networks" that present barriers for minorities and women.[33] Principal selection is generally controlled by the superintendent, with very limited input from key constituencies such as teachers and parents.[34]

To address adequately the development of effective principals requires a focus on the values, norms, and rules that undergird the study and practice of educational administration. The literature suggests that preparation programs have little impact on a principal's socialization, and the opportunities for socialization are generally informal and unplanned.[35] Induction has been characterized as a process in which principals are given (a) a map to find the building, (b) keys to the school, and (c) several wishes of good luck.[36] Additionally, because assistant principal roles are generally quite different from principal roles, the assistant principalship is not necessarily an appropriate developmental stage to be completed prior to becoming a principal. The development of school principals will continue to be haphazard without focused staff development and meaningful internship opportunities for novices to observe expert mentors.

The assessment of principals is perhaps the least studied aspect of the role. Natriello and others have referred to principal evaluation as being in the "stone age," while Ginsberg's recent review of the literature argued that no research base exists, and all one can rely on is a "folklore" to drive the field.[37] Still, the evaluation of principals usually takes place on a yearly basis, and as Peters and Bagenstos report, about 80 percent of the states now require principal evaluation.[38] Thus, in the area of evaluation, as with preparation, certification, identification, and induction, the field of educational administration is in the process of developing effective practices. Yet, policymakers are altering requirements for administrators without the benefit of clear signals and solid evidence to follow.

Research on Effective Schools

Effective schools research is so widely disseminated that the formula practically achieves "common-sense" status. Edmonds and others popularized a blueprint consisting of clear goals and high expectations (especially related to students), strong instructional leadership of the principal, an emphasis on basic skills, an orderly school environment, increased time on task, positive home-school relations, and frequent monitoring of students.[39]

Some of the effective schools research has been criticized for its methodological pitfalls. Critics point to research problems such as the overreliance on case studies, the comparison of only extremely unique schools, the overuse of correlational instead of causal designs, the lack of longitudinal design, and the sole use of elementary schools as the sampling unit.[40] Despite these methodological flaws, effective schools research does point to several general organizational factors that substantially decrease (but do not eliminate) the differences in basic skills achievement between socioeconomic groups in problematic— primarily inner-city—schools.[41] Susan Rosenholtz, in her review of the "best" of the research evidence, concludes the following about "instructionally effective" urban schools:

1. The psychic rewards for teaching are prevalent, are used to mobilize teacher commitment, and consequently, teacher turnover and absenteeism are low.
2. Unlike the loosely coupled nature of most schools, managerial and technical activities are closely aligned and there is a tighter congruence among the norms, values, and behaviors of principals and teachers.
3. Principals and teachers clearly define goals related to student learning; and these goals become the basis for directing, motivating, justifying, and evaluating organizational behavior.
4. Administrative leaders communicate goals of student achievement and organize action that links teacher and student effort.
5. Teacher selection is elevated as the most critical organizational activity and the process and outcome are used as bases for developing a shared vision in the school.
6. Teachers are less likely to work in isolated settings and new forms of peer socialization and collegial norms emerge that tend to drive improvement in instructional practices.
7. Principals, as school leaders, engineer opportunities for teacher collaboration, buffer teachers from external pressures, and reduce uncertainty about teachers' success with students.
8. Teacher evaluation is ongoing, takes on several informal forms, and is used as another mechanism to subvert teacher uncertainty about goals and standards for the students' academic progress.
9. Joint administrator-teacher decision making in instructional matters is prevalent and is used to enhance the articulation of each classroom with a coherent school program.
10. Collegial interaction is used "synergistically"—fostering new solutions to problems.[42]

In her interpretation of the effective schools research, Rosenholtz emphasizes the primacy of certainty about organizational goals as well as the need for principals to mobilize teachers to work together to combat low student achievement.

Interestingly, some of the more sophisticated effective schools research points to contextual variables that influence school success, implying that no single set of prescriptions will cure all school ailments.[43] Instead, effective schools practices are as much means as ends. In turn, the process of creating effective schools should be viewed as a continuous cycle of improvement and renewal. In essence, effective schools can be seen as moving toward the concept of praxis, whereby teachers and principals work together to understand their practices while at the same time changing and improving them.

Thus, effective schools do not consist of static qualities, nor do they necessarily require instructional leadership by the principal. The importance of the teacher-principal collaborative relationship suggests strongly that teachers, who know best the pedagogical needs of their students, could become instructional leaders, and principals, who understand and can respond to internal and external demands placed on the school, could become leaders of leaders. While this notion is soundly rooted in effective school literature, it is rarely espoused by those who have prescribed the effective schools formula in solving the ills of the public schools.

In sum, while the literature on school effectiveness has pointed to correlates of school success, much more work needs to be done to put these findings appropriately in place. The research is still in its infancy and many effective schools appear to display characteristics that contradict the widely disseminated effective schools findings. Thus, the importance of recognizing the context-specific nature of success is beginning to take hold as researchers explore the variability in factors related to school success. Problems may occur, however, as policymakers are pressed to move to prescriptions prematurely.

The Research on Effective Teachers and Principals

The research on effectiveness goes beyond the school as the unit of analysis. Schools all contain principals and teachers and students, and a growing body of literature has explored the effectiveness correlates of those who function in schools.

The literature on effective teacher characteristics suggests a context-specific view of teaching. For example, the research points to no single set of skills, attitudes, interests, or abilities that consistently discriminates between effective and ineffective teachers.[44] While intelligence and academic ability measures have correlated with teaching effectiveness, the correlations have rarely been significant. Indeed, both intelligence and academic ability have correlated both negatively and positively with teaching effectiveness.[45] Other research has suggested effective teachers must possess general characteristics such as flexibility, creativity, and adaptability[46] and must be placed in the type of classroom situation most suited to their personal attributes.[47]

Research that has sought to identify specific teaching behaviors linked to teaching effectiveness has produced promising results.[48] However, these behaviors are more likely to be high-inference variables representative of teaching patterns—such as clarity and variability—rather than discrete, easily measurable actions that can be readily assessed in short-term situations. The most extensive process-product study of teacher effectiveness found little evidence that discrete teaching behaviors can be linked to student learning.[49]

Other researchers have found that effective teaching behaviors vary for students of different socioeconomic, mental, and psychological characteristics[50] and for different grade levels and subject areas.[51] Additionally, effective teaching behaviors often bear a curvilinear relationship to student achievement, i.e., *overutilized* effective teaching behaviors can produce significantly negative results.[52]

Thus, while researchers on teaching effectiveness are able to point out broad patterns associated with classroom success, clear directions for success remain to be devised. Nevertheless, policymakers often have dictated a host of mandates for teachers despite research conclusions pointing out that precise teaching prescriptions may be an antidote for some students, but a lethal injection for others.

Other research indicates that the success of schools is usually traced to the quality of the building principal.[53] Researchers have identified a wide variety of characteristics and behaviors of effective principals, including:

1. possessing a vision which focuses on students' achievement, and ensuring that this vision is well understood by students and teachers;[54]
2. seizing initiative, actively exploiting resources, supporting teacher projects, spreading good news about the school, and short-cutting the bureaucracy;[55]
3. articulating a vision, possessing coping skills for decisive and quick action, and managing the external environment;[56] and

4. being goal oriented, having a high degree of personal security, having a high degree of tolerance, being able to approach problems analytically, and willing to include others in problem solving.[57]

Without question, effective principals need a wide assortment of skills, including analytic, intellectual, political, and managerial.[58] But as with the research on teachers, these patterns for principal effectiveness are broad, nonspecific, and situational, implying no set pattern for success.

Much of the effective school literature points to the principal as instructional leader who takes personal responsibility in managing *directly* the school's teaching activities. But no single definition of what this means has yet emerged in the literature. Given that instructional leadership is poorly defined and rarely well studied, the activities related to the concept have not been a major thrust in the training, selection, evaluation, and remuneration of principals.[59] More importantly, this conception of instructional leadership, which is widely used as *the* key component of success, presents a very narrow view of the work of effective principals. As we will discuss in the subsequent section on the realities of being a principal, the literature is very clear about the limited amount of time principals can spend directly supervising teachers.[60]

The Realities of Schools, Teaching, and Administrative Work

THE REALITIES OF SCHOOLS

Scholars tend to agree that no understanding of what makes for success is complete without knowledge of what really happens in schools. The pattern of schooling has been remarkably stable since the onset of the common school about 100 years ago.[61] Devaney and Sykes have argued that schooling endlessly "rests on concepts of learning as consumption and teaching as delivery of packaged knowledge, which in turn have formed a set of sociological features for schools that are as pervasive as chalk dust."[62] These pervasive, enduring sociological features, which seemingly have been reemphasized during the first round of reform, include:

1. one teacher confronting large numbers of students in standardized (usually fifty-minute) blocks of time;
2. the imperative of order in the classroom, which results in students spending 60 to 70 percent of their time listening to teachers and

doing seatwork, and another 20 percent of their time in transition between activities;

3. a dependence on textbooks, which in many cases students find "insipid" or "irrelevant";

4. accountability systems that encourage students to exchange performance for grades and subsequently discourage the assignment of tasks that are complex and difficult to assess;

5. standardized tests, which drive the attention of both teachers and students toward low-level skills and facts, so that students subsequently "develop little capacity or inclination . . . to engage in tasks requiring real reasoning."[63]

Throughout this century, schools have been organized to maximize efficiency. The role of the teacher has remained pretty much the same for the last sixty or seventy years. And there is broad professional consensus that the U.S. system of public education, for the most part, has left higher-order learning undeveloped and wanting. In fact, scholars recently have painted "vivid and painful" pictures depicting the learning process as "ritualized hoop jumping" and "educational passivity and disengagement."[64] Such critiques point to several dysfunctional factors in the traditional schooling process. Lanier and Sedlak note that one finds evidence in schools of:

- the erroneous assumption that learning is linear and that basic skill acquisition must come before higher-order skill acquisition,
- students who are likely to be asked to solve "well-structured" problems as opposed to more realistic ill-structured problems, and
- the valuing of "memorizing strategies" to accomplish school tasks and providing the one "right answer" to demonstrate competence.[65]

The challenge for the future, according to some scholars, is to transform the *typical* classroom, with a single teacher lecturing to large numbers of students who are required to do seatwork and use "dumbed-down" textbooks, to *new* classrooms, with teams of teachers helping students make complex constructions of knowledge. In these new classrooms, students would be expected to organize and monitor their own learning and engage in collaborative and situation-specific learning activities.[66]

However, the present reality of schools, consisting of rote-learning, seatwork, lecturing, and testing, is intensified by the current excellence movement (e.g., emphasis on improving test scores). Present modes of accountability exacerbate the long-standing tension between the contradictory goals of educating students and controlling them. McNeil has found that school resources, personnel, and policies focus on controlling student behavior and that "many teachers lapse into a pattern of boring, mechanical teaching that shows little evidence of their full knowledge of a subject or of their ideas of what students need to know."[67] Unfortunately, the current effective schools movement appears to reinforce this pattern of teaching and thus maximizes rather than alters the present realities of schools.

THE REALITIES OF TEACHING

Teachers work on the average forty-nine hours per week, spend approximately ten hours per week on noncompensated school-related activities and have, on the average, thirty-two minutes to eat lunch. Almost half of the nation's teachers are required to eat lunch with their students.[68] Once teachers sign in at the principal's office in the early morning, their world is generally unique and separate from the work world of other adults. Teachers live and work in a controlled environment, attempting to manage the academic, psychological, and social lives of many diverse children.

Yet, when one glimpses inside statutes and regulations, what is most evident is the acute ambivalence many policymakers feel about the nature of teaching and the roles of teachers. There is an apparent tension between the view of teachers as semiskilled laborers who must follow cookbooks for practice and the view of teachers as professionals who must rely on a complex knowledge base to serve the diverse needs of students. As semiskilled laborers, teachers are viewed by policymakers as needing only basic skills and rudimentary abilities to manage a classroom. As professionals, teachers are viewed by policymakers as requiring an understanding of learning theory and pedagogy as the bases for informed educational decision making.[69] Unfortunately, given the negative reaction of today's teachers to the reforms of the 1980s, the "semiskilled laborer" conception of teaching seems to be more prevalent.

By drawing on recent national surveys of teachers and studies of teachers' working conditions in the reform-minded South, we find that the problems and concerns related to overly prescriptive, labor-oriented reforms become clearer.

The 1988 Carnegie study, a survey of 13,500 teachers nationwide, revealed that teachers have a paradoxical view of their profession. On the one hand, teachers noted that since 1983 there have been improvements in principal leadership, technology for teaching, instructional materials, and school discipline. On the other hand, teachers lamented the deterioration of critical working conditions related to classroom interruptions, fiscal resources, noninstructional duties, increases in class size, limited time for preparation and collaboration, teaching load, and overall morale, as well as significant increases in political interference, state regulation, and burdensome paperwork (see table 1).[70]

TABLE 1

PERCENT OF U.S. TEACHERS REPORTING NATURE OF
CHANGE IN WORKING CONDITIONS SINCE 1983

WORKING CONDITIONS	NATURE OF CHANGE		
	BETTER	NO CHANGE	WORSE
Leadership of principal	56	24	20
Use of technology for teachers	74	21	5
Textbooks and instructional materials	61	29	10
Orderliness of classrooms	42	42	16
Classroom interruptions	27	51	22
Fiscal resources available to school	34	28	38
Freedom from nonteaching duties	21	48	31
Typical class size	21	42	37
Time to meet with other teachers	20	49	31
Daily preparation time	16	57	27
Daily teaching load	15	53	32
Teacher morale	23	28	49
	INCREASED	NO CHANGE	DECREASED
Political interference in education	59	37	4
State regulation of local school	57	38	5
Burden of bureaucratic paperwork	52	40	8

Source: Carnegie Foundation for the Advancement of Teaching, *Report Card on School Reform: The Teachers Speak* (1988).

Similarly, in a study conducted by the Institute for Educational Leadership, researchers found, for the most part, working conditions that could best be described as "bleak," "substandard," and "intolerable."[71] Case studies of thirty-one elementary, middle, and high schools revealed working conditions that would not be tolerated in other professions. The researchers pointed out that many teachers were working in dilapidated buildings (dirty and in very poor repair), without classrooms of their own, and without basic instructional materials (like textbooks and paper). These teachers had little confidence in district-level leadership and complained of the lack of respect they received from district officials. Even in those districts that had recently allowed more school-based decision making, teachers perceived these "reforms" to be top-down, ambiguous, and inadequate for their efforts to reach students.[72]

Researchers with the South Carolina Educational Policy Center (SCEPC) surveyed over 4,000 South Carolina teachers (and interviewed an additional 108) about their working conditions, burnout, and the impact of reform (i.e., the highly touted omnibus Education Improvement Act passed in 1984). The findings revealed that while certain aspects of reform were well received (including improvements in in-service training, leadership of principals, and clarity of goals and expectations) teachers reported extraordinarily high levels of emotional exhaustion.[73] The researchers found that the teachers' high levels of emotional exhaustion were linked to several internal aspects of teaching including excessive paperwork, lack of time to prepare for classes and to meet with other teachers, lack of opportunity for creativity in the classroom, excessive nonteaching duties, and role conflict in terms of having to do unnecessary tasks. Interview data disclosed teachers' concerns about overly prescriptive and rigid state and district mandates, especially related to standardized curriculum and testing. One teacher summed up the problem in the following manner:

I am being made into a machine and my students are being made into machines. . . . I am a factory worker, that is what I feel like here. . . . I guess I went to college to become a file clerk [referring to the required documentation related to the curriculum and testing]. . . . Each day I have to come in with the objectives and the skills I must teach. . . . Sometimes I know I am pushing it down their throat—just like pumping gasoline.[74]

Finally, SCEPC researchers studied teacher leadership in a medium-sized southeastern school district (with approximately 375 teachers in 11 schools) that was involved in the planning stages of the lead teacher concept. Surveys of all teachers and interviews with over 100 teachers uncovered "frustrating" working conditions character-ized by a prescriptive curriculum, little instructional support, rigid testing mandates, and burdensome paperwork. In some schools, problematic principal leadership exacerbated these poor working conditions. Many teachers, because of the mundane and frustrating exigencies of their everyday work life, did not see much value in the lead teacher concept. Instead, teachers argued that resources allocated for lead teachers would be better spent on instructional aides and clerical support. Given teacher isolation and their lack of experience in collaborative teaching, the teachers had difficulty envisioning the power of the lead teacher concept. Without training (and socialization) in working with their peers, teachers in the planning district would have problems adjusting to school restructuring and to the role of lead teachers.

In sum, studies of teaching work reveal an unsettling reality about today's classrooms. Teachers see their discretion (in allocating time and in decision making) decreasing while they see their workload increasing. Sadly, reforms that have uplifted the importance of teaching in the eyes of the public have done little to uplift teachers. Instead, teachers are stifled and burdened with pressures and demands, all of which inhibit their vision and zeal for further reform.

THE REALITIES OF ADMINISTRATIVE WORK

On the average, principals work between fifty and sixty hours per week. Over the last decade or so, researchers began to study seriously what principals do during their long work week.[75] What we have learned is that the principal's work is unlike other managerial occupations, as the day is strewn with unexpected interruptions, noninstructional needs of teachers, and problems of student discipline.[76] The daily routine is characterized by variety, brevity, and fragmentation,[77] and by frenetic verbal interactions.[78] More often than not, the politics of dealing with competing constituencies—expressed through state regulations, federal guidelines, school board policies, central office mandates, teacher concerns, parental demands, and student problems—account for a plethora of personal interactions in the typical workday of a school principal. Principals must spend most of their day responding to what might be called "situational imperatives"—nonplanned events that demand their immediate attention.[79]

Drawing on a 1988 study of secondary school principals, we can conclude that most principals face major job-related roadblocks, specifically with respect to the time spent on administrative detail, a general lack of time to do their jobs, an inability to obtain necessary fiscal resources for both operations and school improvement, apathetic or irresponsible parents, new state guidelines and regulations, and too much time supervising student activities.[80] Thus, it is not surprising to hear principals typically describe their work as more challenging, more difficult, more routine, and more boring than they had imagined it would be.[81]

Interestingly, principals in the late 1980s appear to be more satisfied with their jobs than their counterparts in the 1970s and 1960s. In particular, secondary principals point to more job security, greater prestige, more opportunities for independent action, and greater self-fulfillment. These perceptions of job satisfaction occur at a time when, over the last decade, principals' salaries (when adjusted for inflation) have been held constant and discretion in budget allocations and staff selection has been reduced.[82] Of course, these principals who are satisfied with their relatively low pay and reduced autonomy are the same ones who have been harshly criticized by the public and policymakers.

In sum, the realities of teaching and administrative work suggest that the work lives of these educators are characterized by varied, situational, and emotionally charged encounters with diverse groups of children and adults. As the gap between policy and reality widens, the task of truly reforming schooling becomes ever more difficult given the qualities, commitment, vision, and energy of principals and teachers.

The Changing Characteristics of Teacher and Principal Workforces

Current data on the characteristics of teacher and principal workforces present a diverse picture. Teacher supply and demand data suggest continuing shortages—especially in the South and West, in many urban and rural districts, and in subject areas such as mathematics, sciences, foreign languages, and special education.[83] Presently, researchers are developing more sophisticated measures to estimate supply of and demand for teachers.[84] However, there is a dearth of solid, reliable data on the supply of and demand for school principals. In fact, in a recent study, only 63 percent of the state certification directors were able to estimate the number of persons certified as public school administrators. These limited data suggest that there are approximately 2.5 "certified" administrators for each available position. Unfortunately, this does not mean there are "enough" principals to go around. In most states, there are incentives for teachers to receive their administrator certificates (through graduate coursework) even though they may never intend actually to become a school principal.[85]

The following brief demographic descriptions of current teachers suggest that teachers are older, more experienced, and thus closer to retirement than were their counterparts in 1971. Drawing on data collected by the National Education Association, we find that in 1986 the median age of the U.S. teacher was forty-one years, and the median for years of experience was fifteen years, with 28 percent of the nation's teachers having over twenty years of experience. These figures compare starkly to the 1971 composite picture of the U.S. teacher—when the median age was thirty-five years and the median for years of experience was only eight years. Additionally, today's teacher is more educated, with over 51 percent having attained at least a Master's degree. This figure is contrasted to 1971 data indicating only 27.5 percent had attained a Master's degree.[86]

The percent of black teachers in elementary and secondary education is abysmal. Throughout the 1970s and into the 1980s, blacks constituted approximately 8 percent of the nation's teachers. They now constitute less than 7 percent, and it is projected that by the early 1990s the number will decrease to 5 percent of all teachers. The low percentage of black teachers comes at a time of increasing numbers of minority students enrolled in the public schools. By the early 1990s, it is projected that one out of every three public school students will be a minority.[87]

Principals also are older, more experienced, and seemingly closer to retirement age. Recent surveys have indicated the average principal is forty-seven years old and has been in education for twenty-two years. Additionally, 24 percent of the nation's principals expect to retire when they are fifty-five years of age and another 35 percent expect to retire between the ages of 56-59.[88] Some data suggest as many as 70 percent of the nation's school administrators will reach retirement age within the next ten years.[89]

Other surveys report that approximately 94 percent of all principals are white.[90] Some anecdotal reports indicate the number of minority principals is decreasing. However, the NASSP data indicate that between 1977 and 1987 there was a very slight increase in the percentage of black (from 3 percent to 3.8 percent) and Hispanic (from .6 percent to 1.7 percent) secondary principals.[91]

Approximately 85 percent of all principals are male. Most female principals are found at the elementary level (which is not surprising, given that approximately 87 percent of all elementary teachers are female). Yet, from 1977 to 1987, the number of female secondary school principals increased from 7 to 12 percent. However, the 1987 figure represents only a slight increase since 1965 when 10 percent of the secondary principals were female.

In sum, data show that women (see table 2), and especially minorities (see table 3), are underrepresented in many educational roles when compared to student demographics and enrollment.

TABLE 2

PERCENT OF MALE AND FEMALE SUPERINTENDENTS, PRINCIPALS, AND TEACHERS

	SUPERINTENDENTS	PRINCIPALS	TEACHERS
Males	93	83	31
Females	7	15	69

Source: Superintendent and principal data from National School Boards Association, *Educational Vital Signs* (1987); teacher data from National Education Association, *Status of the American Public School Teacher* (1987).

TABLE 3

PERCENT OF WHITE AND BLACK TEACHERS, PRINCIPALS, AND STUDENTS

	TEACHERS	PRINCIPALS	STUDENTS
White	90	91	80
Black	7	4	16

Source: Student data from Center for Education Statistics, *Digest of Education Statistics 1987* (1987); principal data from National School Boards Association, *Educational Vital Signs* (1987); teacher data from National Education Association, *Status of the American Public School Teacher* (1987).

The implications of the growing racial gap between who teaches and who are taught and between who leads and who are led are profound. Minority students, especially those from the underclass, desperately need minority role models who are teachers and leaders. Moreover, the gender gap between who teaches and who leads is also critical, especially given the fact that the "moral imagination" sought in the new breed of principal[92] is most often found in the personal qualities of women administrators.[93]

Assessing Today's Evidence and Tomorrow's Prospects

We have argued that the effectiveness research, although a sound beginning for understanding successful school practices, moved from the laboratory to the real world before research identified more precise, yet context-driven procedures of effective practices. We underscored the fact that school context has a major effect on student outcomes and school effectiveness. However, the first round of educational reform, for the most part, ignored school context. Through mandated top-down prescriptions, the reforms undermined local leadership, stifled innovation, and created a situation in which "everyone has the brakes but no one has the motors" to make schools run well.[94]

We conclude that the realities of school life and teacher and principal work are unsettling and many working conditions probably would not be tolerated in other professions. Data we presented suggest that today's educators (especially teachers) are frustrated and "exhausted" from their work. Without their energy and vision, we believe, school reform may go wanting. Those teachers and principals who are tolerating the mundane and frustrating exigencies of their everyday work are not likely to have the creativity or energy to implement needed changes in school organization, curriculum, and pedagogy.

Can teachers and principals emerge from their current school realities and muster the strength to foster creative change and develop their own professions? Not likely, when teachers and administrators often attempt to educate diverse children in inadequate buildings (and with few resources) and face relentless demands from policymakers who have little understanding of their work lives. The desire has been drained from some of our educators. And it may be that those educators who tolerate poor working conditions are not the instructional talent our schools and students need.

To attract talent, policymakers will have to up the ante—both in pay and professionalized working conditions. Teachers and principals will have to be allowed to create their own effective schools. Teachers and principals must be able to create accountability systems that work for their local educational communities and, in doing so, establish and enforce the standards of their profession. Without a collaborative development of both professions simultaneously, a new vision of school improvement will be flawed. Effective schools demand the professional partnership between teachers and principals.

However, professionalism cannot develop if policymakers do not loosen the organizational, curricular, and pedagogical reins that inhibit talented teachers and principals. And if policymakers do not let go of the decision-making reins, then the talent in schools cannot be released and the talent we need to attract will continue to flock to other professions where their creativity and energy are valued, developed, and utilized.

Certainly, teachers and principals may very well need to have their basic needs taken care of prior to embarking on visionary paths to school improvement and renewal, as well as to the collaborative development of their respective professions. This seems especially salient with regard to teachers, their present working conditions, and the posture of their unions toward educational reform. In fact, in one study, it was found that reform policies cannot be substituted for traditional bread-and-butter items that regulate teachers' basic working conditions. The researchers found bread-and-butter items are, in fact, enabling conditions that must be attained before unions and teachers move on to questions of professional autonomy as well as professional accountability.[95] Thus, we can anticipate that new reforms will take hold only when satisfactory working conditions are achieved.

Over the last decade the tension between public and professional control of education has been exacerbated by increasing state dominance in educational decision making and the increasing resistance by those critics and practitioners who assert that decisions on educational issues must be made by those closest to them—i.e., principals and teachers. However, recent reforms designed to empower principals and teachers will be difficult to put in place if earlier reforms—standardized curricular and pedagogical formulas—are "permitted institutionalization."[96] Granted, some teachers and principals do not want the full responsibility that will come with professional autonomy and participation in educational decision making. But, the kinds of sweeping changes envisioned require a large pool of educators to lead the way. To a certain extent, policymakers may need to establish a venture capital fund to jump-start reform through the renewal of existing talent and the infusion of new talent.

We argue, as in the words of Thomas Green, that using state policy to fix educational problems is like using "a drop forge to quarter a pound of butter or an axe to perform heart surgery."[97] School reform needs to have a more local base with local input so that the real concerns of practicing teachers and principals can be dealt with head on.

FOOTNOTES

1. Lawrence C. Stedman, "It's Time We Changed the Effective Schools Formula," *Phi Delta Kappan* 69 (November 1987): 215-224.

2. David N. Plank, "Why School Reform Doesn't Change School: Political and Organizational Perspectives," in *The Politics of Excellence and Choice in Education*, ed. William L. Boyd and Charles T. Kerchner (Philadelphia: Falmer Press, 1988).

3. Linda Darling-Hammond, "Policy and Professionalism," in *Building a Professional Culture in Schools*, ed. Ann Lieberman (New York: Teachers College Press, 1988).

4. Plank, "Why School Reform Doesn't Change School."

5. William L. Boyd, "Rhetoric and Symbolic Politics: President Reagan's School Reform Agenda," *Education Week*, 18 March 1987, pp. 21, 28.

6. Richard Rossmiller, "Some Contemporary Trends and Their Implications for the Preparation of Educational Administrators," *UCEA Review* 27 (Winter 1986): 2-3.

7. Plank, "Why School Reform Doesn't Change School."

8. Peter Airasian, "State Mandated Testing and Educational Reform: Context and Consequence," *American Journal of Education* 95 (May 1987): 393-412.

9. Mary H. Futrell, "Restructuring Teaching: A Call for Research," *Educational Researcher* 15, no. 15 (1986): 5-8.

10. Arthur E. Wise, *Legislated Learning* (Berkeley: University of California Press, 1979).

11. Linda Darling-Hammond and Barnett Berry, *The Evolution of Teacher Policy* (Santa Monica, CA: Rand Corporation, 1988).

12. See Larry Cuban, "Transforming the Frog into a Prince: Effective Schools Research, Policy, and Practice at the District Level," *Harvard Educational Review* 54 (1984): 129-151; A. Lorri Manasse, "Improving Conditions for Principal Effectiveness: Policy Implications of Research," *Elementary School Journal* 85 (1985): 439-469; David Dwyer and L. Smith, "The Principal as Explanation of School Change: An Incomplete Story," in *Instructional Leadership: Concepts, Issues, and Controversies*, ed. William B. Greenfield (Boston: Allyn and Bacon, 1987).

13. Philip Schlechty and Victor S. Vance, "Do Academically Able Teachers Leave Education? The North Carolina Case," *Phi Delta Kappan* 63 (1981): 106-112; Timothy Weaver, *America's Quality Teacher Problem: Alternatives for Reform* (New York: Praeger, 1983); Linda Darling-Hammond, *Beyond the Commission Reports: The Coming Crisis in Teaching* (Santa Monica, CA: Rand Corporation, 1984).

14. National Center for Education Statistics, *Projections of Education Statistics to 1992* (Washington, DC: U.S. Government Printing Office, 1985).

15. Darling-Hammond and Berry, *The Evolution of Teacher Policy*.

16. Linda Darling-Hammond, "The Futures of Teaching," *Educational Leadership* 46 (November 1988): 4-10.

17. Darling-Hammond and Berry, *The Evolution of Teacher Policy*.

18. Education Commission of the States, *A Survey of State School Improvement Efforts* (Denver, CO: Education Commission of the States, 1983).

19. Darling-Hammond and Berry, *The Evolution of Teacher Policy*.

20. Darling-Hammond, "The Futures of Teaching."

21. Gary Sykes, "Contradictions, Ironies, and Promises Unfulfilled: A Contemporary Account of the Status of Teaching," *Phi Delta Kappan* 65 (1983): 87-93.

22. Lee S. Shulman, "A Union of Insufficiencies: Strategies for Teacher Assessment in a Period of Educational Reform," *Educational Leadership* 46 (November 1988): 36-41.

23. Arthur E. Wise, "States Must Create Teaching Standards Boards," *Education Week*, 11 January 1989, p. 48.

24. Adam Urbanski, "The Rochester Contract: A Status Report," *Educational Leadership* 46 (November 1988): 48-52.

25. Holly M. Houston, "Restructuring Secondary Schools," in *Building a Professional Culture in Schools*, ed. Ann Lieberman.

26. Daniel E. Griffiths, Robert T. Stout, and Patrick B. Forsyth, eds., *Leaders for America's Schools: The Report and Papers of the National Commission on Excellence in Educational Administration* (Berkeley, CA: McCutchan Publishing Corp., 1988), p. xiv.

27. R. L. Spradling, "A Comparison of Administrative Problems and Educational Issues as Perceived by First Year and Experienced Secondary School Principals" (Ph.D. diss., University of South Carolina, 1988).

28. Nancy Pitner, "School Administrator Preparation: State of the Art," in *Leaders for America's Schools*, ed. Griffiths et al.

29. Spradling, "A Comparison of Administrative Problems and Educational Issues."

30. Richard P. Gousha, Peter L. LoPresti, and Alan H. Jones, "Report on the First Annual Survey of Certification and Employment Standards for Educational Administrators," in *Leaders for America's Schools*, ed. Griffiths et al.

31. William Foster, "Educational Administration: A Critical Appraisal," in *Leaders for America's Schools*, ed. Griffiths et al.

32. Erwin Miklos, "Administrator Selection, Career Patterns, Succession, and Socialization," in *Handbook of Research on Educational Administration*, ed. Norman Boyan (New York: Longman, 1987); Paul R. Sackett, "Assessment Centers and Content Validity: Some Neglected Issues," *Personnel Psychology* 40 (1987): 13-25.

33. Erwin Miklos, "Administrator Selection, Career Patterns, Succession, and Socialization."

34. Spradling, "A Comparison of Administrative Problems and Educational Issues."

35. W. B. Greenfield, "Administrative Candidacy: A Process of New Role Learning—Part I," *Journal of Educational Administration* 15 (1977): 30-48; idem, "Administrative Candidacy: A Process of New Role Learning—Part II," *Journal of Educational Administration* 15 (1977): 170-193.

36. H. L. Sosnes, "Advice to Rookies: Do's and Don'ts for Making the First Year Successful," *Principal* (September 1982): 14-17.

37. Gary Natriello, S. M. Bornbush, and M. Hong, "A Survey of the Recent Literature on the Evaluation of Principals, Teachers, and Students," Occasional Paper no. 18 (Stanford, CA: Center for Research and Development in Teaching, Stanford University, 1977).

38. Stephen B. Peters and Naida T. Bagenstos, "State Mandated Principal Evaluation: A Report on Current Practices" (Paper presented at the Annual Meeting of the American Educational Research Association, New Orleans, 1988).

39. Stedman, "It's Time We Changed the Effective Schools Formula."

40. Larry Cuban, "Effective Schools: A Friendly but Cautionary Note," *Phi Delta Kappan* 9 (1983): 695-696; Brian Rowan, Steven Bossert, and David C. Dwyer, "Research on Effective Schools: A Cautionary Note," *Educational Researcher* 12, no. 4 (1983): 24-31.

41. Wilbur Brookover, Charles Beady, Patricia Flood, John Schweitzer, and Joe Wisenbaker, *School Social Systems and Student Achievement: Schools Can Make a Difference* (New York: Praeger, 1979).

42. Susan J. Rosenholtz, "Effective Schools: Interpreting the Evidence," *American Journal of Education* 93 (May 1985): 352-388.

43. Charles Teddlie and Robert Wimpelberg, "The Issue of Differentiated Contexts and School Effectiveness Studies" (Paper presented at the Annual Meeting of the American Educational Research Association, Washington, DC, 1987).

44. J. A. King, "Beyond Classroom Walls: Indirect Measures of Teacher Competence," in *Handbook of Teacher Evaluation*, ed. J. Millman (Beverly Hills, CA: Sage Publications, 1981); N. L. Gage, "Paradigms for Research on Teaching," in *Handbook for Research on Teaching*, ed. N. L. Gage (Chicago: Rand McNally, 1963).

45. Del Schlalock, "Research on Teacher Selection," in *Review of Research in Education*, Vol. 7, ed. David Berliner (Washington, DC: American Educational Research Association, 1979), pp. 364-417.

46. F. J. McDonald, and Patricia Elias, *Executive Summary Report: Beginning Teacher Evaluation Study, Phase II* (Princeton, NJ: Educational Testing Service, 1976).

47. Lee J. Cronbach, "The Two Disciplines of Scientific Psychology," *American Psychologist* 12 (1957): 671-684; Bruce R. Joyce and Marsha Weil, *Models of Teaching* (Englewood Cliffs, NJ: Prentice-Hall, 1972).

48. Barak V. Rosenshine, "Content, Time, and Direct Instruction," in *Research on Teaching*, ed. Penelope Peterson and Herbert J. Walberg (Berkeley, CA: McCutchan Publishing Corp., 1979).

49. Richard Shavelson and Nancy Dempsey-Atwood, "Generalizability of Measures of Teacher Behavior," *Review of Educational Research* 46 (1976): 553-612.

50. Lee J. Cronbach and Richard E. Snow, *Aptitudes and Instructional Methods: A Handbook for Research on Interactions* (New York: Irvington, 1977).

51. McDonald and Elias, *Executive Summary Report: Beginning Teacher Evaluation Study, Phase II*; N. L. Gage, *The Scientific Basis of the Art of Teaching* (New York: Teachers College Press, 1978).

52. Ken Peterson and Don Kauchak, *Teacher Evaluation: Perspectives, Practices, and Promises* (Salt Lake City, UT: Center for Educational Practice, University of Utah, 1982).

53. James M. Lipham, *Effective Principal, Effective School* (Reston, VA: National Association of Secondary School Principals, 1981).

54. William L. Rutherford, "School Principals as Effective Leaders," *Phi Delta Kappan* 67 (1985): 31-34.

55. Judith Warren Little, "The Effective Principal," *American Education* 18 (1982): 38-42.

56. Spradling, "A Comparison of Administrative Problems and Educational Issues."

57. William D. Greenfield, "Moral Imagination, Interpersonal Competence, and the Work of School Administrators," in *Leaders for America's Schools*, ed. Griffiths et al.

58. Spradling, "A Comparison of Administrative Problems and Educational Issues."

59. Rick Ginsberg, "Worthy Goal . . . Unlikely Reality: The Principal as Instructional Leader," *NASSP Bulletin* 72 (April 1988): 76-82.

60. Ibid.

61. Larry Cuban, *How Teachers Taught: Constancy and Change in American Classrooms: 1890-1980* (New York: Longman, 1983).

62. Kathleen Devaney and Gary Sykes, "Making the Case for Professionalism," in *Building a Professional Culture in Schools*, ed. Lieberman.

63. Ibid., pp. 17-19.

64. Judith Lanier and Michael Sedlak, "Teacher Efficacy and School Quality," in *Schooling for Tomorrow*, ed. Thomas J. Sergiovanni and J. T. Moore (Boston: Allyn and Bacon, 1989).

65. Ibid.

66. Devaney and Sykes, "Making the Case for Professionalism."

67. Linda McNeil, "Contradictions of Control, Part I: Administrators and Teachers," *Phi Delta Kappan* 70 (January 1988): 334.

68. National Education Association, *Status of the American Public School Teacher* (Washington, DC: National Education Association, 1987).

69. Darling-Hammond and Berry, *The Evolution of Teacher Policy.*

70. Carnegie Foundation for the Advancement of Teaching, *Report Card on School Reform: The Teachers Speak* (New York: Carnegie Foundation for the Advancement of Teaching, 1988).

71. Thomas B. Corcoran, Lisa J. Walker, and J. Lynne White, *Working in Urban Schools* (Washington, DC: Institute for Educational Leadership, 1988).

72. Ibid.

73. Rick Ginsberg et al., "Teaching in South Carolina: A Retirement Initiative," Report prepared for the South Carolina Education Association (Columbia, SC: South Carolina Educational Policy Center, 1989).

74. Ibid., p. 68.

75. Harry F. Wolcott, *The Man in the Principal's Office* (New York: Holt, Rinehart, and Winston, 1973); Kent Peterson, "Principals' Tasks," *Administrator's Notebook* 26 (1977): 1-4; Keith Goldhammer, *Elementary School Principals and Their Schools* (Eugene, OR: University of Oregon Press, 1971).

76. Rick Ginsberg and Barnett Berry, "The Folklore of Principal Evaluation" (Paper presented at the Annual Meeting of the American Educational Research Association, San Francisco, 1989).

77. William T. Martin and Donald J. Willower, "The Managerial Behavior of High School Principals," *Educational Administration Quarterly* 17 (1981): 69-90.

78. Van Cleve Morris, Robert L. Crowson, Cynthia Porter-Gehrie, and Emanuel Hurwitz, Jr., *Principals in Action: The Reality of Managing Schools* (Columbus, OH: Charles Merrill, 1984).

79. Greenfield, "Moral Imagination, Interpersonal Competence, and the Work of School Administrators," p. 209.

80. L. O. Pellicer, L. W. Anderson, James W. Keefe, Edgar A. Kelly, and Lloyd E. McCleary, *High School Leaders and Their Schools, Vol. 1: A National Profile* (Reston, VA: National Association of Secondary School Principals, 1988).

81. Daniel L. Duke, "Why Principals Consider Quitting," *Phi Delta Kappan* 70, no. 4 (1988): 308-312.

82. Pellicer et al., *High School Leaders and Their Schools.*

83. Darling-Hammond, "The Futures of Teaching."

84. David Grissmer, Gus W. Haggstrom, and Linda Darling-Hammond, *Assessing Teacher Supply and Demand* (Santa Monica, CA: Rand Corporation, 1988).

85. James Bliss, "Public School Administrators in the United States: An Analysis of Supply and Demand," in *Leaders for America's Schools*, ed. Griffiths et al.

86. National Education Association, *Status of the American Public School Teacher: 1985-86.*

87. J. C. Baratz, "Black Participation in the Teacher Pool" (Paper prepared for the Carnegie Foundation, January 1986).

88. Emily Feistritzer, "Profile of School Administrators in the United States" (Washington, DC: National Center for Educational Information, 1988) National School Boards Association, *Educational Vital Signs* (Washington, DC: National School Boards Association, 1987).

89. Education Writers Association, *Covering the Education Beat* (Washington, DC: Education Writers Association, 1987), p. 75.

90. Pellicer et al., *High School Leaders and Their Schools.*

91. Ibid.

92. Greenfield, "Moral Imagination, Interpersonal Competence, and the Work of School Administrators."

93. Charol S. Shakeshaft, "Women in Educational Administration: Implications for Training," in *Leaders for America's Schools*, ed. Griffiths et al.

94. Carnegie Foundation for the Advancement of Teaching, *Report Card on School Reform.*

95. Lorraine McDonnell and Anthony Pascal, *Teacher Unions and Educational Reform* (Santa Monica, CA: Rand Corporation, April 1988).

96. Linda McNeil, "The Co-optation of Curriculum" (Paper presented at the Annual Meeting of the American Education Research Association, Washington, DC, 1987.

97. Thomas Green, "Excellence, Equity, and Equality," in *Handbook of Teaching and Policy*, ed. Lee Shulman and Gary Sykes (New York: Longman, 1983).

CHAPTER IX

Professional Teachers and Restructured Schools: Leadership Challenges

SHARON F. RALLIS

A school is seeking a new principal. Until recently, the school had been considered a model institution with great programs and great teachers. Families often chose to relocate in the surrounding community so that their children could attend this excellent school. Since the community housed a college, education held a high priority. Various ethnic groups were represented in the community and the school reflected a multicultural environment long before most other public schools in the region. Once upon a time, teachers were seen as sensitive to the individuality of all their students.

Over the years, the school changed. The community looks much the same, but changes in the economy tightened school budgets as each tax dollar stretched to meet the newer and more critical needs. Most of the teachers, an extremely knowledgeable and well-tenured group, are tired. They seldom work together and they hardly ever talk professionally. The former principal, a kind and gentle man, retired after eighteen years.

The search committee appointed by the superintendent, as instructed by the school board, consists mostly of teachers, with one administrator and two parents.[1] The committee recognizes that most everyone in the community, when forced to face "reality" agrees the school lacks a sense of mission and teaching has become routinized and governed by bureaucratic regulations. The school needs to be renewed, if not restructured. Thus, the committee seeks someone to lead the transformation of the school.

Three finalists surfaced quickly. The first called himself an organizer. He had taught for several years, he had a doctorate in administration, and he had solid administrative experience. He talked about curriculum coordination and program budgeting; he discussed strategic planning and systems; he espoused "proactive" supervision and the need for teachers to document their successes. In general, he seemed keenly aware of the politics of running a school. The teachers and the two parents liked him. They characterized him as the "Captain" who would steer the ship back on the right course.

The second candidate labeled herself a reading expert. She felt a school should be organized around its instructional programs and she thoroughly understood curriculum and instruction. Her knowledge of the reading field was extensive. She talked about converting teachers to her philosophy of teaching, and in the final interview she baldly stated: "Once they see my way, they will want to follow." The teachers and two parents were impressed with her expertise and her energy, but they also saw a lack of administrative experience and a limited focus. They characterized her as the "Visionary" who would fight tenaciously to build the school in her own image.

The final candidate introduced herself as someone "without a prepared package to sell." She suggested that the school must serve its community and discover its own culture. She saw her role primarily as a facilitator. She used metaphors like the principal as master chef, noting that new recipes and new ingredients were sometimes not as appropriate as finding new ways to stir the pot. She encouraged developing self-evaluation strategies and pledged to be creative in finding and fighting for resources. Her background was quite eclectic. The search committee characterized her as the "Renaissance Woman" who might inspire teachers, parents, and students to undertake new challenges.

The third candidate received the recommendation of the committee. The chair summarized the committee's reasons: "We feel that she can lead us farthest forward in making some positive change. She recognizes the needs of the community and she understands that people must believe in the school. But, most important, she cares!" Then, he added, as an afterthought, "I guess the real reason we hired her is that we saw her working *with* the teachers. With her leadership, they will want to work together to improve the school."

The circumstances of this school are not unique. The search for a principal as transformational leader is not surprising. What is unusual is that the search committee recognized the need for a principal who could lead *with* those most instrumental to transformation, the teachers.

Teacher Professionalism, Restructured Schools, and Leadership

The push for restructuring American public schools reflects a global trend to rethink how humans organize themselves. "Perestroika" is happening all over the world across governmental, business, and educational organizations. Change is fueling change. If we focus on schools, we hear rhetoric for new ways to teach and learn. We see how changing demographics (e.g., the shape and color of student populations, the characteristics of households) are shaping how we organize and administer our schools. If teachers and teaching must change, then schooling and school leadership must change. In restructured schools, the traditional dichotomy between teacher and leader will be obsolete. The principal and faculty will work collaboratively to identify and solve problems related to the diverse needs of diverse student populations. The altered principal-teacher relationship unleashes a wide variety of leadership challenges. The challenge will not be to find "super" leaders, but to discover and to promote conditions that allow the process of leadership to flourish.

We must avoid the mistake made in earlier school reform efforts where every principal had to be a hero. They were to be all things to all people. Just as glory was due them when they succeeded, all blame fell on them were they to falter or fail. It is unrealistic and unfair to assume a cadre of super leaders can be cultivated to lead public schools out of the wilderness to the promised land. We must also be wary of the seductive nature of teacher empowerment rhetoric. Many reformers are now asking how teachers can be included in decision making and become more responsible for the school's progress. The call for increased professionalism is a noble goal, but let us not replace our unrealistic desire for super leaders with an equally unrealistic desire for a host of super teachers who also serve as super leaders in their spare time.

We hear considerable discussion about restructured schools. Not all principals want to be, or could be, heroes, and not all teachers want to be, or could be, leaders. We are now realizing that leadership in the effective school, while complex and multifaceted, is not obtained through the exercise of a discrete set of skills by individuals carefully chosen and duly authorized to act. School leadership cannot be broken down into separate behavioral specifications such as management or instructional supervision, each assigned to one person or group. Leadership is not a purchased commodity. It does not lie either with the principal or the teachers exclusively. Leadership involves collective decision making. Leadership might best be defined as an interactive, dynamic process drawing members of an organization together to build a culture[2] within which they feel secure enough to articulate and pursue what they want to become.

This chapter is based on the assumption that the relationship between teachers and principals is at the crux of school restructuring.[3] Moreover, it is assumed that the notion of "principal" will not disappear in the immediate future. The American public school system is too much a conservative social institution to expect a radical departure from traditional structures of authority and accountability. However, it is assumed that the concept of educational leadership will evolve dramatically over the next decade. In other words, tomorrow's schools will have principals, but the schools will be led in a much different fashion.

Educational Reform and Global Transformation

School restructuring proposals did not simply fall from space; they were at least partly shaped by societal and market conditions. As the rhetoric of *A Nation at Risk*[4] pithily reminds us, we live in a global village where economic competitiveness depends on the creation and transmission of knowledge. Technology, communication, transportation, and data processing are growing exponentially. The changing world outside schools is creating more and more demands on what goes on inside schools. Educators have not been able to ignore these changes. State departments of education and professional associations are attempting to address the "competitiveness problem" through dropout prevention, enhanced literacy, and increased achievement test scores.[5] School curriculum is asked to absorb more material in an effort to prevent or remediate problems. But these solutions can be seen as band-aids, applied here and there. The message in reports like *A Nation at Risk* is that schools are not effectively performing their major operation, which, as John Goodlad says, is to prepare young people to become functioning and contributing members of society.[6] Unfortunately, the American public school neither meets the needs of the world outside nor provides a model for the world. In fact, our schools often are separate worlds buffered from the outside. The body of teachers is predominantly white and female, middle class, born in the United States. The vast majority of school principals is white and male. Yet, the mix of youngsters is more representative of society, increasingly of color and often coming from homes where English is not the primary language. Schools are structured to limit the contact of those working inside with those outside: phones (and the time to use them) are seldom available; visitors are screened with caution; meetings are held in a lifeless cafeteria or library; nearly every minute between opening and closing bells is tightly allocated. As children must ask permission to leave a classroom, teachers in many schools must ask permission to leave the building. Isolated in their individual classrooms, most teachers have little professional interaction with and few opportunities to observe their colleagues.[7] The school environment is sequestered and controlled. As the inhabitants of Plato's cave, the teachers and students in schools learn through reflections or images of life rather than through direct experiences.

Our schools also fail to deal with global and societal transformations due to their top-down bureaucratic structures. Policies formulated at the top are passed down to become the rules and procedures all teachers must follow. Policies become schedules to be met, curricula to be followed, textbooks to be used, and strategies to group children. Those identified as leaders are forced more to maintain, control, and transmit than to build, empower, and understand. In the bureaucratic world, the need for a teacher to make professional judgments diminishes, and administrators spend much of their time buffering the internal operation from external demands. One might ask how such an isolated and controlled world can be expected to foster the dynamic instructional experiences needed to prepare students for global competitiveness. Clearly, this question has been asked by many reformers.[8] The answer tends to place the principal as the central figure in the transformation of schools and schooling.

Reform and the Principal

Simultaneously with the "excellence in education" reform movement, the effective schools paradigm grew in prominence. This new paradigm countered the message produced by studies in the 1960s that schools did not make much difference in the achievement of poor and minority children.[9] The message of school ineffectiveness supported the vision of an educational system reproducing the unequal class structure of the nation.[10] Effective schools research promoted a different message. Schools effective in teaching basic skills to poor and minority children were identified. Characteristics correlated with success seemed transferable to less-than-successful schools and were seen as a basis for improvement.[11] Some schools were, and others could be, more effective. While the impetus for this positive view was probably research on effective teaching,[12] the early literature on effective schools focused on the total learning environment, the organization as a whole. For example, Rutter and his colleagues spoke to the school's ethos, that is the values, attitudes, and behaviors characterizing the school as a whole.[13] Today, a school is more widely viewed as a small culture, a more or less loosely knit social culture,[14] and as such, no school exhibits all the effective school characteristics at all times. Essentially, each school has its own recipe for success. Yet, almost all research on effective schools mentions the importance of school leadership.

As early as 1971, there was strong research evidence that school leaders could boost reading achievement of disadvantaged urban children through consistent, school-wide emphasis on the basic skills.[15] The various other conditions necessary for effectiveness in schools (such as atmosphere, parent involvement, high expectations) are seen as dependent upon leadership. Informal leadership is mentioned, but the principal is defined as the educational leader of the school. The principal is seen as the force behind the effective school. One research study reports that elementary schools with positive learning environments and high academic achievement have principals who assume firm leadership; communicate to their staff high expectation for achievement; maintain high visibility to students; have particular competence in one area of the curriculum; have an education as elementary school teacher; are disciplinarians; allow participatory decision making by the staff; and exhibit personal characteristics of empathy, interest, and concern for others.[16]

Close on the heels of effective school research came research on successful program innovations[17] and school reform,[18] which highlighted the importance of instructional leadership. Researchers busied themselves with describing the tasks performed by an instructional leader and making connections between the execution of these tasks and effective school outcomes.[19] Instructional leadership tasks such as observing in classrooms and conferencing with teachers were differentiated from management tasks such as scheduling and budgeting.

Critics noted that the separation of leadership tasks was a somewhat specious move since routine administrative decisions such as scheduling directly influenced curriculum and instruction.[20] Anyway, the principal was expected to perform both sets of tasks. Responsibility for daily operations and long-term planning lay in the principal's hands. He needed to view the school both from the management perspective and from the educational perspective. In addition, several studies reminded principals of their role in supporting the symbolic activities, the myths, rituals, and ceremonies of the school.[21]

The principal, then, has become a primary target in the first restructured schools movement. If principals are so important to school success, surely they need more training and professional development. Certification requirements have been or are being revised to meet new conceptualizations of the principalship. The number of both professional development activities and program delivery services has grown.[22] Early in the principal development movement, centers like the Harvard Principal Center in Cambridge, Massachusetts, opened to provide a forum for exchange and support as well as additional training opportunities. Currently functional principals' centers can be found throughout the country and other countries as well.

The principal has become not only the target of great expectations but the recipient of numerous and rich resources. We expect principals to be a well-informed group with varied experience and education. The National Policy Board for Educational Administration has proposed new standards for preparing school administrators.[23] Principals are becoming a more diverse group; the numbers of females and minorities in principalships have increased somewhat in the past few years. Membership in professional organizations has increased, indicating a greater professional commitment.[24] A glance through school board literature reveals ads by personnel agencies that specialize in searching for the right principal. The chair of a 1989 search committee for a high school principal position remarked on the high qualifications of the applicant pool:

We used to see a lot of physical education teachers who had taken the required hours to be certified as a principal. Now we are looking at individuals who have doctorates and many years of teaching experience. The principal's office was a place where the incompetents in schools often hid. Today, you cannot hide in that office.

In sum, the principal's potential impact has grown; the principal is seen as the key to school improvement, and the person in the role is expected to be able to meet the challenge. There seems to be a growing unquestioned acceptance of these propositions, even though most of the effective schools research comes from the elementary level and the nature and scope of the principalship differs dramatically across school levels.

Teachers and School Restructuring

Without denying the importance of the school principal, some voices have begun to ask how one person could fulfill all the desired roles and demands.[25] The "white knight" view of leadership with its unidirectional, top-down flow of authority places all the power as well as responsibility in one person's hands.[26] The principal is expected to set schedules, communicate with parents, discipline students, handle daily crises, inspire personnel, observe classes, monitor the curriculum, supervise instruction, and articulate the institution's goals. Is it realistic to expect all this of one individual? If principals are responsible for all things, then what is a teacher's responsibility? After all, it is the teachers who must work within schedules, are the first line of contact with students, and put the curriculum into practice. They work directly with students to achieve the school's goals. To assign all functions to a principal and to attribute all school success to her leadership is to diminish the value and worth of the teaching staff. "Principals don't do it alone."[27] By assigning all hope and glory to the principal, we overlook the important role of the teacher in school improvement. Fortunately, discussion about teacher empowerment has refocused some of the reform attention on teachers.[28] *A Nation Prepared: Teachers for the 21st Century*, the report of the Carnegie Task Force on Teaching as a Profession, and the Holmes Group report, *Tomorrow's Teachers*,[29] shifted attention to the teaching profession.

The Carnegie report recommended that teachers be given more control over schools and be held more accountable for their performance. The Holmes Group report called for better conditions both for teachers to work and students to learn by altering the professional roles and responsibilities of teachers. These changes would require the establishment in schools of new authority relationships giving more autonomy to teachers.

The message of these reports was to restructure schools in order to support a true teaching profession, sharing in the responsibility as well as taking credit for school improvements. Educators at all levels have begun to design new approaches to teacher preparation and development. Institutions of higher education are revamping their teacher education programs, raising standards for admission, opening schools for staff development, and initiating collaborative efforts with local school districts. States and local districts have introduced a variety of new programs including, for example, induction activities, career ladders, differentiated staffing, teacher mentors and peer coaching, "advising teachers," and building-level teacher assistance teams for collaborative problem solving. Teacher centers have reappeared.[30] A few districts are even using committees of teachers to run the school without a principal.[31] The major teachers' unions have become a voice for teacher improvement and have assumed some responsibility for the in-service preparation of teachers as leaders.[32] For example, the American Federation of Teachers holds its annual "Quest" conference to focus on professional development and teacher leadership issues.

One organizational outgrowth of restructuring has been the initiation of school-based management teams with shared decision making.[33] Under school-based management, professional responsibility replaces bureaucratic regulation. Ideally, the school's and, in turn, the teacher's autonomy increases, as does responsibility. Teachers have a greater role in decision making about curriculum modification and personnel selection. The aim of instituting school-based management systems is to bring the authority to create better learning conditions closer to the spot where teaching and learning occur.[34]

Empowering teachers, that is, giving them more control over decisions that affect their practice, is the goal of these restructuring efforts. Teacher professionalism may be the more accurate term. Professionalism empowers teachers. Professionalism, according to Darling-Hammond, "seeks to heighten accountability by investing in knowledge and its responsible use."[35] The professional uses her knowledge to make informed judgments about what is best for her client. Knowledge—experiential, clinical, and research knowledge—gives the professional teacher the authority to control her own agenda. Thus, the individual professional is responsible for building her knowledge base and for reviewing her own practice through self-evaluation. The profession as a group is responsible for defining, transmitting, and enforcing professional standards.

One of the first hurdles in the professionalization of teaching is defining the knowledge base for teachers. The argument that teaching deserves professional status rests on the belief that a specifiable knowledge base for teaching exists and can be represented and communicated. The Holmes Group and the Carnegie Task Force claim that this knowledge base is growing and that it should shape teacher education programs and reform practice. Yet, as Shulman notes, the discussion to explicate the knowledge base has echoed in conference rooms full of educators for generations.[36] He reminds us that the knowledge base for teaching is not fixed and final and much of the proposed knowledge base remains to be discovered, invented, and refined. Thus, at the same time that reformers are calling for restructuring of schools and of teacher education programs, some researchers are presenting more complex views of what is involved in the effective teaching act. For example, Shulman talks about the processes of pedagogical reasoning and action that include comprehension, transformation, instruction, evaluation, reflection, and new perceptions.[37] Duckworth sees teaching itself as a form of research within practice; she proposes that effective teachers are active participants in answering and understanding the question of how humans learn in particular circumstances.[38] These and other interpretations of the art of teaching reflect an elevated conceptualization of teaching rather than one limited to style, presentation, and content knowledge.

Another hurdle in putting concepts of empowerment and professionalism into practice is the traditional organizational setting of schools. As knowledgeable professionals, teachers have the right to make decisions that shape their practice, but the bureaucratic structure simply does not support teacher decision making. Teaching has traditionally been considered a semiprofession because the organizational setting does not allow autonomy at all levels, nor does it ensure more than a symbolic accountability. Teachers do not need to be client-responsive because they are protected by the system. The evaluation procedures are largely meaningless for assessing actual teacher performance. Few clients withdraw if they are not satisfied with services because they usually have no other options. At the same time, teachers' ability to be client-responsive is limited because they have control over only a small part of the school's dealings with the student. While teachers are free to make decisions within the walls of their individual classrooms, the curriculum, the textbooks, the schedules, and the selection of students are usually determined by others.

School boards hesitate to give any of the power and authority of shared decision making to teachers because they do not trust the capabilities of those whom they see at the bottom, the workers. Unless boards can see evidence of the teacher knowledge base and positive results in the client, they will not trust the teacher. As professionals, teachers have both the right and obligation to demonstrate that they know what they are doing, that they care about their students, and that their efforts have merit. However, gathering and presenting the evidence in meaningful terms is not easy in the traditional school setting. The results of a teacher's performance are not always directly measurable. The inadequacies of conventional testing are part of a current debate on testing.[39] Nor is the teacher's performance regularly observed by anyone other than the learners. The learner is not necessarily the only client and in many cases is not the best judge of the teachers' performance. Administrators' observations for evaluations are mere snapshots, incapable of capturing all the forces inherent in a lesson. As a result, any discussion of teacher empowerment carries with it bedrock tensions between autonomy and control, responsibility and accountability, collaboration and isolation, group goals and individual satisfaction. Because of these unresolved tensions, teachers are judged to need a leader from outside their ranks. Traditional school organization, then, places building-level leadership in the hands of one person, the principal.

The traditional perspective of school organization and structure also tends to inhibit professionalism by separating its personnel—from each other, across levels, and from the external environment. Teachers are isolated physically, and instructional programs are fragmented. Even when teachers share a mutual problem, getting together to work on a solution is nearly impossible. They do not have access to each other on an informal basis for extended periods of time, and formal meetings follow established agendas. Because teachers do not have ways to recognize and articulate shared goals, they see little reward in making time to work with colleagues. Trained to think in terms of "my classroom" and "my children," a teacher does not think in terms of organizational goals. They teach a grade or a subject, and one level or subject area seldom speaks with another except on district-wide committees.

Teachers also are separated from administration. A principal or department head, while still responsible for evaluating the teacher, sees only glimpses of a teacher's performance; they can seldom produce a thick or rich description of what actually occurs in a given teacher's classroom. Communication is generally conducted through memos or brief encounters in the hall.[40] Few legitimate channels exist for teachers to feed back information or criticism or reactions to the principal. Moreover, since administration seldom has the opportunity (and, for some, the interest) to instruct students themselves, teachers often are skeptical if the principal can understand them or be trusted on matters of instructional improvement.

The organization and control of public schools isolates teachers from the community. For safety and legal reasons, today more than ever, many schools cannot be open to the general public. People without legitimate purposes have never been welcome to walk into a school building. Moreover, unions have fought residency requirements for teachers, so many who do not live in the community in which they teach may not have knowledge about their students' cultural and ethnic backgrounds. At the same time, considerable money is being spent to increase parent involvement in schools.[41] Without some form of direct intervention, school and community partnerships tend not to grow.

The major effort teachers have made to connect with one another—the formation of labor unions—has been a source of greater separation from the administration and the community. Contracts include explicitly described limits on work hours and duties, which limits community access to teaching and teacher access to the community. Collective bargaining often creates an adversarial relationship between teachers and administration, and, at times, the community. Grievances on the negotiation table are not necessarily the most positive setting for shared decision making or collaborative problem solving. In recent years, unions have begun to work on professional development and defining and enforcing professional standards,[42] but the primary effort is still in response to their need to control their own environments and to protect their constituents from external demands.

Since 1970, fewer qualified graduates have chosen to become teachers. The numbers of those defecting from teaching have increased[43] while union membership has risen and collective bargaining is widespread. The job of teaching has taken on new configurations. Public Law 94-142 demanded the identification and servicing of special needs students by the local education agency, so a teacher became labeled either "regular ed" or "special ed" and considerable resources have been allocated to special education programs. English as a second language and bilingual programs created more separateness. Basic education plans and state mandates have largely defined what is taught, while the ever-present threat of a lawsuit has built clear boundaries around what teachers can and cannot do with their students. Negotiated contracts between union and management have grown to define a teacher's responsibilities and duties. Contract language has established a standard for teacher behavior and involvement (e.g., "Teachers will not be required to attend more than one evening meeting per year; teachers will not be asked to use their lunch periods for committee meetings."[44])

To be a teacher in today's schools has more limitations, as well as more demands, and the separation from administration has been extensive and profound.

New Relationships and New Forms of Leadership

Research now suggests that schools improve significantly when teachers stop functioning in isolation and start solving problems together with other teachers and their principals.[45] From this research comes a glimpse of what may be beyond the lionizing of the principal, the instructional leadership debate, and the barriers to teacher empowerment in the reform and restructuring journey schools are taking. Leadership is collaborative. Effective schools have always existed; the way we are seeing effective schools now reveals different organizational conditions. The new effective schools build organizational culture with structures fostering connections between personnel rather than promoting separations. Teacher assistance teams, mentor teachers, and school-site management teams are examples of collaborative leadership. The restructured school places great demands on teachers and principals, but it provides professional rewards to both. As professionals, the teachers and principals define their relationship to maximize organizational effectiveness. They enter a dialogue about what is to be taught and how it is to be taught, as well as how the teaching is to be judged.

In the new vision of school leadership, teachers are viewed differently. Darling-Hammond notes that:

Effective teaching is not routine, students are not passive, and questions of practice are not simple, predictable, or standardized. Consequently, instructional decisions cannot be formulated on high, then packaged, and handed down to teachers.[46]

She points out that teacher leadership need not conflict with principal leadership. Rather, the teacher with a strong knowledge base must participate in any decision that may affect his instructional efforts. Working together, teachers can discover new ways to solve problems and to lead school reform and improvement.

A variety of new models for teacher work are developing in the United States. Some models give teachers alternative schedules to allow more time for working together. Other models create structures for shared decision making and school-based management. Every member of the faculty participates and teams work out implementation strategies. Still other models create differentiated staffing where designated teachers assume leadership roles with increased responsibility, higher pay, and greater, more flexible accountability.[47]

Many schools use school leadership teams to develop and implement school improvement or staff development plans.[48] School leadership teams are assembled so teachers, and often community members, may share with the principal the responsibility for innovation. They differ from principals' advisory councils because they are actually involved in decision making. These leadership teams were created in response to the school change research that recognized the need to link the realities of teaching with the realities of schools as organizations.[49] Teachers and administrators who share the burden of design and implementation through school improvement teams develop mutual ownership and enhance understanding of their own practice. The presence of both teachers and administrators on the teams offers a means of reducing suspicions, promoting accessibility, and building trust. While the teams do have a chairperson, the role is not necessarily filled by the principal.

One example of a small but functional restructuring commonly applied throughout the country is the building-level teacher assistance team. The purpose of these teams may vary in specifics, but their primary goal is to provide a forum for teachers to bring classroom-related problems to a group of their colleagues for collaborative problem solving. The teams usually are trained in processes such as problem definition, brainstorming, and solution generation. Whatever the original incentive behind the formation of the team, school personnel recognize it as "an official legitimization of the necessary network that exists amongst teachers in those schools that work."[50] Chairpersons report that intervention assistance teams have played a significant role in improving professionalism, curriculum options, perceptions of students with learning difficulties, teachers' roles, and faculty dynamics. Specifically, they attributed the following changes to the intervention assistance teams:

- increasing communication among staff,
- improving sensitivity to individual student needs,
- establishing priorities in the list of necessary curriculum and material options,
- encouraging flexibility in programming, assessment, and use of instructional techniques,

- increasing teacher confidence,
- providing leadership roles for teachers,
- formalizing and documenting previously informal conversations between teachers ("talks over coffee"),
- recognizing and remediating teacher isolation,
- demonstrating teachers' needs for discussion of common issues,
- raising the overall level of professionalism in the building, and,
- encouraging teachers to talk about students in a positive way.

These models of participatory decision making offer new ways for teachers to work together and improve their in-school lives. For example, one principal credits the teacher support team as "saving a teacher's career by giving her a place to go, an outlet where she was supported and assured she wasn't a bad teacher." Intervention assistance teams recognize teachers as professionals and offer opportunities for professional judgments on what is best for children. In schools with functioning teams, the principals, team members, and referring teachers embrace the opportunity to shape school practice by recognizing, affirming, and utilizing the collective expertise of the faculty.

Schools having success with these models are building a culture where norms are defined by professionalism. The primary aim is meeting the clients' (the students') needs, so all participants must work together. Characteristics of a professional educator culture are continued personal growth, enhanced collaboration, and constant self-evaluation.

Professional Culture and School Leadership

The first step toward a more professional culture is the development of collegiality among teachers. Collaboration must replace the old norms of isolation and defensiveness. Working together, teacher, principal, and staff developer all "share equally in the obligations and the risks, invest equally in the hard work of applying ideas in practice, and get credit equally for the accomplishment."[51] When all knowledge for professional growth flows from the "expert," a teacher's development of confidence and competence is hindered.[52] But moving off the old norms is not easy. Teacher leaders must organize nonthreatening ways of working to encourage group and individual learning.

Collaboration means teachers assume leadership and are willing to work longer hours, to work effectively with adults, to increase their expertise in their subject areas, and to evaluate their own work. To have an extensive knowledge base, a teacher's training must be thorough, and in-service professional development must be an integral part of her work. Preservice teacher training is facing major reform efforts and in-service programs are beginning to be remodeled as well. For example, some school improvement programs train teachers so they may train others. The training-of-trainers model is used extensively to develop a cadre of teachers who can conduct in-service activities in their own buildings. Using in-house teachers to teach others about new practices takes advantage of the existing craft nature of teaching.[53] Such an in-service strategy is based on the idea that "similar experiences, and a common collegial bond with other teachers tends to increase credibility."[54] In addition to teacher-led programs, new forms of in-service training must provide professional development to help teachers establish a culture of professionalism.

Since establishing a professional culture will require great commitment on the part of teachers, unions must be involved. Just as the negotiating table has produced contracts that limit the time and responsibility the organization is able to ask of its teachers, it also can be the most effective means to establish new work norms. Through the power of collective bargaining, teachers can achieve more flexible schedules and more flexible accountability systems. The union can build acceptance and support for changes aimed at the enhancement of the profession. Recent research by the Rand Corporation reveals that plans for school change do not become real classroom changes without the participation of a powerful, well-led teachers' union.[55] The cohesion and structure of an effective union enables teachers to have a constructive influence on reform. The union serves as a major conduit for information transmission and compliance pressure. The bargaining power of a strong union can shape the improvement strategy and ensure that the agreed-upon strategy will be implemented. Union leadership can transform school leadership. In his commentary on the Rand report, AFT President, Albert Shanker, suggests that education reform is a new form of union militancy.[56]

Equally important in the building of a professional culture is the role of the principal. Just as restructured schools yield a new image of the teacher, so do they yield a new image of the principal. In order to grow, collaborate, and self-evaluate, all members of the organizational culture must feel they belong in such a way that they feel secure enough to take risks and to create. The principal leads by working with teachers to build a safe but innovative school culture. The principal recognizes and reafffirms those rituals and ceremonies that draw together the members in celebration at success and self-reflection at failure.

While not the lion, hero, or white knight, which represent the popular image of the corporate head,[57] the principal is still the key figure in the school. The principal is often the only person who has access to all the varied systems operating more or less independently in the loosely coupled school. The principal has been viewed as an engineer keeping the school's machinery working through symbolic, facilitative, or political strategies.[58] Whatever the strategy, the principal is important because she can see the total picture and can make sense out of it. At the same time, she is the buffer between those working within the school and the environmental conditions. For instance, parents usually visit a principal first when they have a concern or complaint about a teacher or a program; reporters tend to call the principal about salient school issues.

Research on school-based teams also recognizes the key role the principal plays in professional innovation; the principal is seen as one of the necessary conditions for positive change.[59] In every instance where some innovative program is reaping positive results, a principal is, in some way, supporting the change. The principal may not always be an active participant in the innovation, but is always willing to put voice as well as resources behind the endeavor. For example, even in schools where the principal was not a member of the teacher assistance team, he or she arranged schedules or hired substitutes to allow meeting time, located funds to compensate teachers for extra hours, or identified resources to enable teachers to implement interventions they designed. Conversely, principals were also capable of sabotaging the innovation in spite of faculty support. Thus, it is the principal who can foster the spirit of belonging to the team; it is the principal who can "make things work."

The effective principal in the restructured and professionally oriented school will need a broad knowledge base.[60] This knowledge base should include not only understanding of children and child development, of educational history and philosophy, of administrative skills and competence, but also understanding of adult development and of techniques to work with adults. Seldom does traditional administrative training require these competencies in principals.

Principals must be able to work with groups of independent and growing adults; they must be able to facilitate, articulate, collaborate, communicate, and buffer. Because truly professional teachers cannot lead lives of mechanical routine relegated to the obscurity of their isolated classrooms, they will need leaders who can manipulate time, space, resources, and personnel. Leaders in these settings will be effective not because they make decisions and are ultimately accountable, but because they encourage a process which symbolically, politically, and structurally enables teachers to act and grow professionally. Again, the principal leads by facilitating the process of belonging so team members feel free and secure to collaborate.

If we view the leader as the catalyst, guide, interpreter, and facilitator for a process, then "what the leader stands for and communicates to others is more important than how he or she behaves given any particular set of circumstances."[61] The effective principal establishes organizational conditions, such as creating and enabling cohesive work groups that substitute for direct, more autocratic leadership.[62] The principal supports experimentation and risk through symbolic acts, like finding a small reward for a successful task force; political acts, like asking the union president to speak at a meeting; structural acts, like providing substitutes to cover the classes of teachers who are on a personnel search committee. These acts serve to establish a collaborative and professional atmosphere, keeping the school moving forward. These acts legitimize teachers' actions; they say, "your work is important and accepted, you belong."

The professional teacher will need a principal who can infuse organizational routines with educational meaning.[63] For example, one routine in need of educational meaning is traditional staff development. A professional teacher needs continued in-service development and while schools provide in-service days those days seldom have value for the individual professional. The overwhelming failure of in-service activities is probably due to a faulty design that assumes all staff have identical in-service needs to be serviced at the same time.[64] The process of leadership in a school with a professional culture must allow for a variety of individual growth activities instead of mass sessions offered as panaceas for the total faculty. The principal helps individuals find their own places and means for growth.

Another important organizational routine is the process of performance evaluation. It is of paramount importance in the restructured school because the professional must be able to demonstrate the quality of her own performance. The principal can facilitate professional growth by shaping the development of meaningful evaluation processes. Faculty members need to move beyond the clinical supervision model to develop strategies essential for self-evaluation. Teachers who claim the right to set their own agenda must assess the results of their work and demonstrate success. Simultaneously, they must have the knowledge as well as freedom to choose and build their own assessment strategies. First, they must feel safe to look critically at themselves. If change is needed, the principal might use the "pat and nudge" approach because the teacher's competence and confidence are at stake. Again, the principal can facilitate this process by providing teachers access to knowledge about evaluation, by forming task forces that allow teachers an opportunity to develop evaluation strategies collectively, and by treating the results fairly and sensitively. The principal can further enhance these efforts by remaining flexible enough to accept a range of self-evaluation techniques or methods and by spreading the word about teacher success. In short, the principal encourages professional development by her demonstrated commitment to policies and procedures that enable the teacher to take greater control over her own practice.

Since many of these routines are tied to teacher rights and security, they often are defined by negotiated contracts. The principal, in her role as facilitator, might also need to serve as a bridge between labor and management. In tomorrow's schools, the priorities of labor and management must become more similar. For example, in those schools with shared decision making in school-site management, teachers are looking beyond salary issues into policy decisions while board members are rising above budgets to examine working conditions. The principal must be a leader who can speak both languages, that of managers and management and that of instructors and instruction.

Even in the world of shared decision making, the budget still is the ultimate determiner of what actually happens. While teachers' primary responsibility is not (nor do teachers have the time) to develop and balance budget items in the detail required to meet fiscal needs and to pass board and taxpayer review, their input as to how funds should be allocated and in setting fiscal priorities is essential if resources are to be chosen and distributed in an effective manner. Again, it is the principal who facilitates professional input by informing the faculty about the budgeting process and by creating legitimate structures for participation.

Because the important behaviors of a principal are not always directly observable, technical in nature, or tightly linked to curriculum and instruction, drawing up a list of specific behaviors a principal can be trained to perform is unrealistic. For example, a principal's policy initiatives, such as setting and promulgating high academic standards, may have more effect than conducting regular classroom observations.[65] Principals themselves report that they rely primarily on informal, indirect, and facilitative strategies.[66] In fact, most principals' interactions with teachers are informal, brief, and fragmented.[67] Put simply, the school that encourages collaboration between the principal and teachers and among teachers still will require management, but the principal's behaviors will not be limited to those traditionally defined as middle management. Rather, they will include facilitative, interpretive, and guiding behaviors. The relationship between teachers and the principal will be the central part of the school leadership process.

Leadership Challenges

If restructuring schools means changing the conditions of teaching and learning, it also means taking up the challenge of changing the conditions of leadership. The metaphors of steward, captain, visionary, evangelist, manager, or instructional leader are inadequate because they suggest leadership is confined to a role or described by a set of skills or tasks to be accomplished. Relying on behavioral specifications for persons in leadership roles without grounding these behaviors in the context of the school organization has produced a simplistic and unrealistic formulation of leadership. For example, Murphy points out the false dichotomy between the concepts of educational management and instructional leadership, two potentially reinforcing constructs.[68] He talks about traditional behaviors labeled as managerial (such as assigning students to classes) that may really be instructional. A similar problem exists with the overemphasis on the personal aspects of leadership. Donmoyer cites the "fundamental attribution error—the tendency to attribute causality to personal characteristics rather than structural or organizational factors."[69] School leadership too often is seen as a functional activity assigned to people and often solely to one person, the principal.

If schools operate under the norms of a strong professional culture with teachers and principals operating in an interdependent, connected relationship, a reconceptualization of leadership is required. Under the traditional view of building leadership, the principal defines the desired changes, the roads to be taken. The reconceptualized view of leadership is more context-oriented than person- or role-specific. Leadership is a process of bringing people together, helping them to belong, so they may do the work of the organization. They belong by accepting and sharing the norms, values, and beliefs of the organizational culture, however large or small it may be.[70] Only when participants belong do they feel secure enough to experiment and care enough to do their best. The principal who understands the school and its environment can facilitate this belonging. Clearly, the dynamics of belonging vary across school levels. Working with grade-level teams in an elementary school is distinctively different from working with subject area departments in a high school. What it takes to help an elementary teacher feel a sense of belonging will not be the same for a high school teacher. Perhaps the greatest challenge for educational leadership is how to be sensitive to the distinctive characteristics of culture building between elementary and secondary schools. The preparation process for school leaders must pay particular attention to this issue as well.

The challenge of leadership as a culture-specific process and the role of the principal in the process is illustrated by the Classroom Alternative Support Team. We saw the principal as key both to successful teams and to nonfunctioning teams. Her importance to the team's functioning was due not to her authority or directives (in some cases of thriving teams, the principal was not even a member), but to her ability to cultivate conditions for collaborative leadership. The teams that worked believed in their own knowledge and judgments; they believed their decisions were important and could transform a student and his teacher; they believed they were valued. They also worked with a principal who allocated time and located space for their meetings, provided them with ample information, followed through on the team's interventions, saw that resources were available or obtained. In short, the principal gave them security as a group so they could collaborate, take risks, and create solutions.

The school at the beginning of the chapter needed a principal who would secure a supportive culture for the faculty again, one who would reestablish a strong sense of belonging. A teacher stated the leadership need succinctly:

I hope this new principal can draw us back together again. Right now we are each going our own way. We're not fighting, but we don't care about each other. There is even some fear. I sure want to feel like I am a part of a family— you know, safe—again, the way we used to be.

This school needs collaborative leadership; it requires a process through which it may build a strong culture with shared values and beliefs and traditions to celebrate together. It needs such a culture so people in the organization can get on with their important work.

FOOTNOTES

1. The details of the case are based on my actual participation on a search committee for an elementary school principal in the spring of 1989.

2. My working definition of culture comes from the classic anthropological one formulated by A. L. Kroeber and Clyde Kluckhohn in *Culture: A Critical Review of Concepts and Definitions* (Cambridge, MA: The Museum, 1952): "Patterns, explicit and implicit, of and for behavior acquired and transmitted by symbols . . . including their embodiments in artifacts; the essential core of culture consists of traditional (i.e., historically derived and selected) ideas and their attached values" (p. 181). I add Erickson's emphasis on "relatively tight organization of patterns, coherence in the meaning system, and identical (or at least closely shared) understanding of symbols across diverse members of the social group." See Frederick Erickson, "Conceptions of School Culture," *Educational Administration Quarterly* 23, no. 4 (1987): 13.

3. Many of the assertions in this chapter emerge from the results of a four-year evaluation study I have conducted of the impact on participating schools of the Classroom Alternative Process (CAP), which aimed to establish building-level teacher assistance teams in schools. Both project implementation and the accompanying evaluation study were funded through the Rhode Island Department of Education (RIDE). The CAP was introduced in 1985 and by spring, 1989, training had been completed in all school districts in the state. Ongoing formative evaluation reports have preceded the summative report to be available in August 1989. Anne DeFanti of RIDE is the Project Director. The Center for Evaluation and Research of Rhode Island College, Providence, Rhode Island, has the evaluation contract. Judith Beckman has assisted me with the evaluation study.

4. National Commission on Excellence in Education, *A Nation at Risk: The Imperative for Educational Reform* (Washington, DC: U.S. Department of Education, 1983).

5. The Rhode Island Department of Education offers one example in its K-2 Literacy Initiative, which began in school year 1987-88 and requires the local education agency to set aside 3 percent of its allocated state aid to support literacy activities in the early grades. For an example of a professional association's work in these areas, see the annual resolutions of the Association of Supervision and Curriculum Development.

6. John Goodlad, *A Place Called School* (New York: McGraw-Hill, 1984).

7. For more complete discussion of these issues, see Madeleine R. Grumet, "Dinner at Abigail's: Nurturing Collaboration," *NEA Today* 7 (January 1989): 20-25.

8. See National Science Board Commission on Precollege Education in Mathematics, Science, Technology, *Education for Americans for the 21st Century* (Washington, DC: National Science Foundation, 1983); Task Force on Education for Economic Growth, *Action for Excellence: A Comprehensive Plan to Improve Our Nation's Schools* (Denver, CO: Education Commission of the States, 1983); Task Force on Federal Elementary and Secondary Education Policy, *Making the Grade* (New York: Twentieth Century Fund, 1983).

9. James S. Coleman, E. G. Campbell, C. J. Hobson, J. M. McPartland, A. M. Mood, F. D. Weinstein, and R. L. York, *Equality of Educational Opportunity* (Washington, DC: U.S. Department of Health, Education, and Welfare, 1966).

10. Samuel Bowles and Herbert J. Gintis, *Schooling in Capitalist America: Education Reform and the Contradictions of Economic Life* (New York: Basic Books, 1976).

11. Ronald R. Edmonds, "Some Schools Work and More Can," *Social Policy* 2, no. 2 (1979): 288-32; Wilbur B. Brookover and Lawrence W. Lezotte, *Changes in School Characteristics Coincident with Changes in Student Achievement* (E. Lansing, MI: Institute for Research in Teaching, Michigan State University, 1979); Stewart Purkey and Marshall Smith, "Effective Schools: A Review," *Elementary School Journal* 83, no. 4 (1983): 427-452; Michael Rutter, Barbara Maughan, Peter Mortimore, Janet Ouston, and Alan Smith, *Fifteen Thousand Hours: Secondary Schools and Their Effects on Children* (Cambridge, MA: Harvard University Press, 1979); George Weber, *Inner City Children Can Be Taught to Read* (Washington, DC: Council for Basic Education, 1971).

12. See, for example, Barak V. Rosenshine, "Recent Research on Teaching Behaviors and Student Achievement," *Journal of Teacher Education* 27 (1976): 61-65; Thomas L. Good and Douglas A. Grouws, "Teaching and Mathematics Learning," *Educational Leadership* 37 (1979): 39-45; Carolyn Denham and Ann Lieberman, eds., *Time to Learn* (Washington, DC: Program on Teaching and Learning, National Institute of Education, 1980).

13. Rutter et al., *Fifteen Thousand Hours*.

14. Stewart Purkey and Marshall Smith, "Too Soon to Cheer? Synthesis of Research and Effective Schools," *Educational Leadership* 40, no. 3 (1982): 64-69.

15. Weber, *Inner City Children Can Be Taught to Read*.

16. *Why Do Some Urban Schools Succeed?: The Phi Delta Kappa Study of Exceptional Urban Elementary Schools* (Bloomington, IN: Phi Delta Kappa, 1980), pp. 132-135.

17. See, for example, Peter Berman and Milbrey McLaughlin, *Federal Programs Supporting Educational Change, Vol. 8: Implementing and Sustaining Innovations* (Santa Monica, CA: Rand Corporation, 1978).

18. Ernest Boyer, *High School: A Report on Secondary School Education in America* (New York: Harper and Row, 1983); Goodlad, *A Place Called School*; Arthur G. Powell, Eleanor Farrar, and David K. Cohen, *The Shopping Mall High School: Winners and Losers in the Educational Marketplace* (Boston: Houghton-Mifflin, 1985).

19. For a critical review of research on instructional leadership, see Joseph Murphy, "Methodological, Measurement, and Conceptual Problems in the Study of Instructional Leadership," *Educational Evaluation and Policy Analysis* 10 (Summer 1988): 117-139.

20. Ibid., pp. 127, 128.

21. Terrence E. Deal and Lynn D. Celotti, "How Much Influence Do (and Can) Educational Administrators Have on Classrooms?" *Phi Delta Kappan* 61 (March 1980): 471-473; William A. Firestone and Bruce L. Wilson, "Using Bureaucratic and Cultural Techniques to Improve Instruction: The Principal's Contribution," *Educational Administration Quarterly* 21, no. 2 (1985): 7-30; Thomas J. Sergiovanni, "Ten Principles of Quality Leadership," *Educational Leadership* 39, no. 5 (1982): 330-336.

22. See Murphy, "Methodological, Measurement, and Conceptual Problems," p. 118.

23. National Policy Board for Educational Administration, *Improving the Preparation of School Administrators: An Agenda for Reform* (Charlottesville, VA: National Policy Board for Educational Administration, 1989).

24. The statement on diversity is based on nationwide surveys reported annually in *The Executive Educator*, a monthly journal of the National School Boards Association; the membership increases are revealed in the annual reports of the National Association of Elementary School Principals and the National Association of Secondary School Principals.

25. Sharon F. Rallis and Martha C. Highsmith, "The Myth of the Great Principal: Questions of School Management and Instructional Leadership," *Phi Delta Kappan* 68, no. 4 (1986): 300-304.

26. See, for example, Edwin M. Bridges, "The Nature of Leadership," in *Educational Administration: The Developing Decades*, ed. Luvern Cunningham, Walter Hack, and Raphael Nystrand (Berkeley, CA: McCutchan, 1977).

27. Shirley M. Hord, Gene E. Hall, and Susan M. Stiegelbauer, "Principals Don't Do It Alone: The Role of the Consigliere" (Paper presented at the Annual Meeting of the American Educational Research Association, Montreal, 1983). See also, Shirley M. Hord and Leslie Huling-Austin, "Effective Curriculum Implementation: Some Promising New Insights," *Elementary School Journal* 87 (September 1986): 97-115.

28. See, for example, Albert Shanker, "The Revolution That's Overdue," *Phi Delta Kappan* 66 (January 1985): 311-315; idem, "Our Profession, Our Schools: The Case for Fundamental Reform," *American Educator* 10, no. 3 (1986): 10-17.

29. Task Force on Teaching as a Profession, *A Nation Prepared: Teachers for the 21st Century* (New York: Carnegie Forum on Education and the Economy, 1986); Holmes Group, *Tomorrow's Teachers: A Report of the Holmes Group* (E. Lansing, MI: Holmes Group, 1986).

30. Many of these approaches to teacher development are examined in Susan Loucks-Horsley, Catherine K. Harding, Margaret A. Arbuckle, Lynn B. Murry, Cynthia Dubea, and Martha K. Williams, *Continuing to Learn: A Guidebook for Teacher Development* (Andover, MA: Regional Laboratory for Educational Improvement of the Northeast and Islands, 1987).

31. An example of a school operating by teacher committee without a principal since fall 1987 is the Second Avenue School in Woonsocket, Rhode Island.

32. The American Federation of Teachers operates several innovative in-service programs such as its Educational Research and Dissemination Program. The National Education Association sponsors the Mastery in Learning Project.

33. See, for example, *A Historical Perspective: School Based Management/Shared Decision Making: A Pilot Program* (Miami, FL: Office of School Board Management, Dade County Public Schools, 1987); Patrick O'Rourke, "Shared Decision Making at the School Site: Moving toward a Professional Model," *American Educator* 11, no. 1 (1987): 10-17; Linda Turrelli-Shiver, "New Roles for Administrators in Rochester," *Educational Leadership* 46, no. 3 (1988): 52-55.

34. For a discussion of authority in schools, see Richard F. Elmore, "Reform and the Culture of Authority in Schools," *Educational Administration Quarterly* 23, no. 4 (1987): 60-78.

35. Linda Darling-Hammond, "Accountability and Teacher Professionalism," *American Educator* 12, no. 4 (1988): 8-13.

36. Lee S. Shulman, "Knowledge and Teaching: Foundation of the New Reform," *Harvard Educational Review* 57, no. 1 (1987): 1-22.

37. Ibid.

38. Eleanor Duckworth, "Teaching as Research," *Harvard Educational Review* 55, no. 4 (1986): 481-495.

39. See, for example, the special section on testing in *Phi Delta Kappan* 70, no. 9 (1989): 683-722, and the issue of *Educational Leadership* 46, no. 7 (1989) on assessment.

40. See Barbara McEvoy, "Everyday Acts: How Principals Influence Development of Their Staffs," *Educational Leadership* 44 (February 1987): 73-77.

41. For example, the Ford Foundation has completed a second year of funding programs in twenty-one cities throughout the country for prevention of school dropouts.

42. See, for example, Susan Moore Johnson, "Pursuing Professional Reform in Cincinnati," *Phi Delta Kappan* 69, no. 10 (1988): 746-751.

43. See Linda Darling-Hammond, *Beyond the Commission Reports: The Coming Crisis in Teaching* (Santa Monica, CA: Rand Corporation, 1984).

44. Paraphrased from a 1989-92 contract with a local National Education Association union.

45. See, for example, Ann Lieberman, ed., *Building a Professional Culture in Schools* (New York: Teachers College Press, 1988); Susan J. Rosenholtz, *Schools, Social Organization, and the Building of a Technical Culture* (New York: Longman, 1989). See also, the work of the Coalition of Essential Schools, c/o Brown University, Providence, RI.

46. Linda Darling-Hammond, "Who Should Be Schools' Instructional Leaders? Professionalism Requires Strong Teacher Voice," *Education Week*, 4 August 1987.

47. See, for example, Adam Urbanski, "The Rochester Contract: A Status Report," *Educational Leadership* 46, no. 3 (1988): 48-52.

48. See, for example, Jeffrey W. Eiseman and Leslie F. Hergert, *The Role of School Leadership Teams in Implementing School Improvement Plans* (Andover, MA: Regional Laboratory for Educational Improvement of the Northeast and Islands, forthcoming). See also, the work of the Coalition of Essential Schools.

49. See Ann Lieberman, "Is School Improvement Possible?" in *Excellence in Our Schools: Making It Happen* (New York: College Entrance Examination Board, 1985), pp. 68-76.

50. This quote and the following data come from Sharon F. Rallis and Judith Beckman, *The Impact of the Classroom Alternative Project on Participating Schools in Rhode Island: A Summary Report* (Providence, RI: Center for Evaluation and Research, Rhode Island College, 1989).

51. Judith Warren Little, "Seductive Images and Organizational Realities in Professional Development," in *Rethinking School Improvement: Research, Craft, and Concept*, ed. Ann Lieberman (New York: Teachers College Press, 1986).

52. A. Lin Goodwin and Ann Lieberman, "Effective Assistance Personnel Behavior: What They Brought and What They Learned" (Paper presented at the Annual Meeting of the American Educational Research Association, Washington, DC, 1987).

53. Jack Kreuger and Ralph Parish, "We're Making the Same Mistakes: Myth and Legend in School Improvement," *Planning and Change* 13 (Fall 1982): 131-140.

54. David P. Crandall, "The Teacher's Role in School Improvement," *Educational Leadership* 41 (November 1983): 9.

55. Paul T. Hill, Arthur E. Wise, and Leslie Shapiro, *Educational Progress: Cities Mobilize to Improve Their Schools* (Santa Monica, CA: Rand Corporation, 1989).

56. Albert Shanker, "Why a Strong Union is Essential to Reform," *On Campus* (May 1989): 5.

57. Jerome T. Murphy, "The Unheroic Side of Leadership: Notes from the Swamp," *Phi Delta Kappan* 69, no. 9 (1988): 654-659.

58. Terrence E. Deal, "Effective School Principals: Counselors, Engineers, Pawnbrokers, Poets . . . or Instructional Leaders?" in *Instructional Leadership: Concepts, Issues, Controversies*, ed. William Greenfield (Boston: Allyn and Bacon, 1987).

59. Rallis and Beckman, *The Impact of the Classroom Alternative Project*.

60. See, for example, work emerging from the project between the University of Houston (Patricia Holland, Renee Clift, Mary Lou Veal) and several independent school districts. The project, funded in part by the Danforth Foundation, is examining the role of the principal as teacher educator.

61. Sergiovanni, "Ten Principles of Quality Leadership," p. 334.

62. Nancy J. Pitner, "Substitutes for Principal Leader Behavior: An Exploratory Study," *Educational Administration Quarterly*, 22, no. 2 (1986): 23-42.

63. Daniel L. Duke, "The Aesthetics of Leadership," *Educational Administration Quarterly* 22, no. 1 (1986): 7-27; McEvoy, "Everyday Acts."

64. Daniel L. Duke, "Fitting Teacher Evaluation to the Complexities of Teaching" (Presentation at the AFT QUEST Conference, Washington, DC, 1987).

65. William A. Firestone and Robert E. Herriott, "Prescriptions for Effective Elementary Schools Don't Fit Secondary Schools," *Educational Leadership* 40, no. 3 (1982): 51-53.

66. Barbara Guzzetti and M. Martin, "A Comparative Analysis of Elementary and Secondary Principals' Instructional Leadership Behavior" (Paper presented at the Annual Meeting of the American Educational Research Association, San Francisco, 1986).

67. McEvoy, "Everyday Acts."

68. Murphy, "Methodological, Measurement, and Conceptual Problems," p. 127.

69. Robert Donmoyer, "Cognitive Anthropology and Research on Effective Principals," *Educational Administration Quarterly* 21, no.2 (1985): 31-57.

70. Terrence E. Deal and Allan A. Kennedy, *Corporate Cultures: The Rites and Rituals of Corporate Life* (Reading, MA: Addison-Wesley, 1982.

CHAPTER X

The Evolution of Educational Management: Eroding Myths and Emerging Models

JAMES W. GUTHRIE

School systems and the strategies by which they are governed and managed are shaped forcefully by the interaction of practical events (e.g., demography, technology, and economics) and public values (e.g., equality, efficiency, liberty, and community). The consequences of social and technological innovation formerly manifested themselves over centuries. However, the pace of change has now accelerated dramatically, and already it is possible for an institution, a process, or a product to evolve and become extinct in a relatively short period of time. This may increasingly be the case for schools. Societal expectations regarding education continue to have deep roots in the past; however, what people want of their schools is also now evolving. Educators need to be keenly sensitive to this evolution so that they can assist in shaping the future rather than being controlled by it. This essay raises questions about the nature and direction of this administrative challenge.

The twentieth century is drawing to a close, and the historical dominance of the currently widespread bureaucratic model of school management may be doomed to disappear with it. Worldwide information services and an insatiable quest for technological innovation increasingly interact to shape the foundations of modern economies. The significance of education has intensified dramatically as a consequence. Developing human capital now outstrips natural resources, inexpensive labor, merchant fleets, and powerful armies as a means to enhance a nation's economic and civic well-being. The

This paper was originally prepared for the International Conference on Cultural Traditions and Contemporary Education held at Chinese University of Hong Kong, October 14, 1988. The conference is sponsored jointly by the School of Education of the Chinese University of Hong Kong and the Goethe Institute. The author wishes to acknowledge the useful comments and criticisms of Charles Achilles, Guy Benveniste, Geraldine J. Clifford, John W. Evans, Mark Hanson, Julia Koppich, Judith Warren Little, Brad Mitchell, and Edward G. Wynne. Errors of fact or interpretation are the responsibility of the author alone.

educated intelligence and creativity of its citizenry are becoming a nation's most significant economic assets.

Worldwide education reforms are increasingly evident. Democratic education systems are occupied with problems of *quality*, setting higher standards for student performance. Elite systems are occupied with problems of *quantity*, elevating the numbers of individuals who receive higher levels of education. The policy instruments they select to achieve their various ends may differ from nation to nation. Nevertheless, their objectives are similar—a wider swath of more intensely schooled citizens and workers.

Out of necessity, school management strategies are beginning to adapt to these changing societal conditions and popular expectations. This evolution is nowhere complete, nor is the transition anywhere smooth and fluid. Alternative school management models are evolving. However, change cannot be measured in terms of an even flow forward toward a new strategy. No perfect vision of a new management model yet exists.

Consequently, various localities, provinces, states, and nations design different strategies, sometimes experimenting with the new, sometimes reverting to the past. However, throughout the world it is possible to see fundamental components of the formerly unquestioned bureaucratic model begin to erode under the pressure to deliver different and more intense kinds of instruction than their original design allowed.

The purposes of this chapter are to (1) describe the fundamental public sector management strategies and their historic application to United States education; (2) analyze assumptions contained in the currently dominant, bureaucratic management strategy and specify why those assumptions increasingly may fail to make sense; (3) speculate regarding the models that appear to be evolving to compete with pyramidal bureaucracy as a dominant mode of school management; and (4) project the consequences of a shift in management strategies for administrator practice and preparation and systematic inquiry about educational administration.

Public Sector Management Strategies

Public sector organizations (health, sanitation, transportation, police, education, etc.) can be managed by any one of four strategies, either singly or in combination. These four strategies, or models, for purposes of description and discussion will be labeled "political," "pyramidal" (or "bureaucratic"), "professional," and "private" (or "market-driven").

Because of the complexities that accompany much of modern-day life, these four models seldom exist in pure form. It is far more common to find them in combination. Nevertheless, the following description treats them separately, in an effort to distill the distinctive characteristics of each. Also, the development of these management models should not be taken as linear or smooth. There is no teleology involved, nor should any specific model automatically be presumed more effective than another. Each has developed to fit evolving social and economic conditions.

POLITICAL MANAGEMENT AND A VIEW OF THE PAST

Political management is most often found either in small jurisdictions, where there are relatively few individuals employed to provide services to relatively few clients, or in developing, preindustrialized nations.

An essential component of this model is that one political official or a team of officials, however authorized and selected,[1] directly manages the organization. Those authorized to govern manage the system themselves. No cadre of executives, trained administrators, or civil servants sits interposed between those who govern and those who deliver services to clients. The line of administrative authority is direct from the politically selected leader, or governing board, to workers engaged to deliver services. If any intervening individuals do exist, they will be few in number and devoid of initiating authority. Their role almost certainly will be simply to facilitate communication between politically empowered managers and direct providers of services.

Political managers personally perform all three functions of government: rule making, rule implementation, and rule adjudication. Thus, employees of a politically managed organization frequently owe their positions to having been selected directly by the political leader(s). Communication is generally immediate between the political leader and the employee. A political manager delegates little authority.

Typically, there is little reliance upon specialized personnel. Occasionally, an employee may concentrate upon a particular or narrowly defined task. More likely, however, politically managed organizations will depend upon relatively low levels of skilled labor and regard workers as highly interchangeable across positions.

Politically managed systems typically have few codified or systematically derived rules. Managerial control tends to be exercised personally through direct supervision of employees by the political leader. The employee's discretionary power is variable, depending upon the rules and relationships established personally by the political manager(s). Codes of employee conduct are relatively simple and enforced in an individual manner by the political leader or leaders. Salary schedules, job descriptions, employment contracts, accounting procedures, performance evaluation, retirement plans, and so forth, are rudimentary or do not exist at all.

In the purest form of this model, there is no civil service job protection, no tenure, no job rights, and no grievance or process. The system is closed to most outside influence, including employee appeals to higher authority. Terms and conditions of employment and work expectations are seldom negotiated. Such features are almost always specified by the political manager and accepted, with various degrees of willingness, by workers.

Politically managed organizations are often tribal in nature.[2] They are highly idiosyncratic. They are analogous to small, family-owned neighborhood businesses; however convenient and immediately useful, they are limited in their ultimate size and the range of products or services they can deliver. It is difficult for them to expand or adapt to complexity. When these latter conditions—growth and complexity—arise, they promote a pyramidal, bureaucratic management model.

Public schooling in the United States was established initially under a political management model. Legal authority for the operation of schools came to be vested constitutionally in state governments. Nevertheless, the operational reality of locally dominated, lay-controlled, special government agencies dedicated to schooling spread from New England throughout most of the nation, and, as a governance format, has prevailed to the present.[3]

Historically, locally elected school board members were almost totally responsible for rule making, rule implementation, and rule adjudication. The overwhelming majority of the organizations they managed were one-room, one-school local districts. Acting directly as managers, school boards arranged for the building or themselves constructed and furnished the school, determined the curriculum, employed and evaluated the teacher, established rules for student discipline, ensured there was firewood, etc. Whatever rules existed were simple, barely codified, and personally interpreted and applied.

This political management model prevailed for more than two centuries in the United States. In the last quarter of the nineteenth century, population growth, efforts to achieve economic efficiencies, and political reform efforts began to alter this model, primarily by imposing managerial layers between political leaders and workers, school board members and teachers. These changes are explained in the subsequent section. Suffice it to state here that such changes were the initial stages in the transition to a pyramidal management model.[4]

PYRAMIDAL (BUREAUCRATIC) MANAGEMENT MODELS: THE CURRENTLY DOMINANT MODE

Large size and complexity stimulate reliance upon hierarchically arrayed management models. In these instances, authority, while perhaps emanating from one or a few at the top of an organization, cascades through tiers to those who deliver services or manufacture material products at the bottom of the pyramid. In contrast to a politically managed organization, bureaucracies are characterized by multiple intervening levels separating those with ultimate managerial authority from those at the bottom who directly deliver services or manufacture goods. Authority of those at the top may stem from political processes. However, those at the bottom of the pyramid are guided by elaborate sets of rules developed by mid-level managers with the approval of those at the top.

Pyramidal organizations prevail or flourish when at least three threshold conditions exist: (1) there is a necessity to encompass a wide span of organizational control, i.e., there are many individual workers to be supervised; (2) it is possible to specify within relatively narrow operational boundaries the work tasks of individual employees, i.e., employees can become specialists; and (3) when end users of the organization's products or services can all be regarded similarly, i.e., there is little necessity to tailor services or products to clients' and customers' individual preferences.

Control is a critical component of bureaucracies. Control is needed for coordination, to ensure that individual activities of numerous employees are directed toward accomplishing the organization's purposes. A superior's personalized judgments of employee performance, so typical of politically managed organizations, are generally eschewed by pyramidal bureaus in favor of the application of universalized performance standards. Employee evaluation, undertaken by superordinates in the hierarchy, tends to be a judgment of worker behavior relative to codified standards and job expectations.

An employee's performance is likely to be judged relative to a set of rules rather than relative to the manufacture of a high calibre crafted product or the satisfaction of a client. These rules, while subject to the approval of those at the top of a pyramidal organization, are likely to have been devised by mid-level managers.

Similarly, employees are themselves expected to avoid personalized interpretations in their manufacture of products or their delivery of services to clients. All products of a type are expected to be manufactured to a uniform standard. All interactions with a bureau's clients are expected to be depersonalized, undertaken consistent with a set of previously established, universally applicable organizational procedures, and absent any untoward employee favoritism. Indeed, employees who display undue personal initiative in tailoring a product or a service may be subject to organizational discipline or dismissal.

Bureaucratic instruments, emphasis on universal standards and organizational rules, task specialization for workers, and the priority given to depersonalized production of products and services are the means by which mid-level managers control employees in pyramidal organizations. Over time, through collective activities such as unionization and political lobbying for civil service regulations, employees have gained a reciprocal measure of control over bureaucratic managers. Protections afforded employees are one of the major distinctions between politically managed models and modern bureaucracies.

In many pyramidal organizations, managerial discretion is curtailed through union contracts and government-enacted civil service procedures which are every bit as codified, depersonalized, and standardized as are the work rules promulgated by the bureau to control the behavior of its employees. In short, rules promoted by employees to protect their interests frequently are quid pro quo mirror images, reflected back up the levels of a pyramidal hierarchy, of the downwardly focused rules promoted by managers to carry out the purposes of the organization.

Pyramidal limitations. Pyramidal models have displayed a substantial ability to conquer challenges posed by large organizational scale. Nevertheless, they exhibit limitations. Organizational emphasis upon employee coordination and control through specialization, codification, and standardization convey at least three major operational impediments: (1) inability to respond and adapt quickly to complex change, (2) awkwardness in adapting to complicated personal interactions and technological transactions, and (3) insensitivity to the personal preferences and individual circumstances of clients and customers.

Under circumstances where change, complexity, and personalization of products and services are desirable, added attention is given to professionalized or participatory management models.

Public schools in the United States began their shift toward pyramidal organizations during the last quarter of the nineteenth century. Enrollment growth in school systems, particularly in large East Coast cities, was a prime stimulus for the transition from political to pyramidal management. However, the evolution was additionally fueled by widespread policy efforts at economic and political restructuring. The school-related effects of these last-mentioned reform efforts, the so-called scientific management movement, rural school district consolidation, and "Progressive Era" government reform, extended well into the twentieth century. Nevertheless, by the mid-1920s, bureaucracy was the dominant management mode for the overwhelming majority of schools in the United States, and such remains the case today.

The onset of professional school administration. By the middle of the nineteenth century, the United States had made a transition from an agricultural to an industrialized economy. The majority of the population was following economic opportunities and moving from rural areas into the large manufacturing and commercial centers, the eastern and midwestern cities. Public school systems in these cities were becoming unusually large. Also, they were deluged by waves of new immigrants. Many of these new citizens did not speak English and had to be socialized to the norms of American government and culture.[5]

Schools were also undergoing a transformation of purpose. They no longer were expected merely to inculcate a primary school level of literacy into citizen farmers and prepare a small economic or scholarly elite to progress to higher education. Economic changes, greater emphasis upon manufacturing and commerce, necessitated a more highly educated workforce. To be sure, requirements of the time were not the equal of today's even more intense educational expectations. Nevertheless, in nineteenth- and early twentieth-century America to be an accounting clerk, secretary, salesman, factory foreman, etc., increasingly meant an individual had to possess a minimum comprehension of mathematics and a broader cultural understanding than had previously been acceptable.

Increasingly, schools were also asked to facilitate upward

mobility, to overcome disadvantaged social backgrounds and assist youngsters in rising a step or two higher than their parents on the economic ladder. In order to improve the lives of individuals, schools were now expected to assume functions previously conducted by families, churches, settlement houses, and other community agencies. To meet these intensified expectations and simultaneously accommodate vastly greater numbers of new immigrants to the cities, both from abroad and from rural America, meant an alteration in the manner in which schools were managed.[6]

The management shift was to build pyramidal organizations, i.e., bureaucracies. It is unlikely that school authorities consciously set about to construct impersonalized, rule-driven, work-specialized, managerial hierarchies. Rather, they were experiencing increasing problems of scale, control, and complexity. To meet the imperatives of the new economics and demographics, they were driven to bureaucratic procedures. What high-ranking school authorities believed they needed were managers who could begin to sort out the booming, buzzing confusion and impose order. Thus came the establishment of school managerial pyramids, however mindless and with whatever subsequent dysfunctional consequences. These "bureaus" began to separate schools from conventional political management through the employment of cadres of professional managers.

The first hiring of school superintendents occurred in large East Coast cities—New York, Baltimore, Boston, and so forth.[7] The idea spread rapidly and by the beginning of the twentieth century, most city and suburban school districts had a professional manager, interposed between politically empowered boards of directors, the school board, and teachers. Because of the overwhelming size of many city systems, these superintendents rapidly employed tiers of supporting managers to operate components of the school system, e.g., business, maintenance, instruction, testing, textbook purchase, and personnel. Two decades into the twentieth century, school bureaucracies were firmly established with many of them having four or five levels of management intervening between the school board and classroom teachers.

Pyramidal management was furthered by three additional conditions. Efficiency advocates claimed that small rural schools were economically costly to maintain and educationally ineffective. Thus, by using the bully pulpit and gaining enactment of state legislative mandates and incentives, literally thousands of local school districts were consolidated into larger governing units. It is not clear that either of the twin objectives, efficiency or effectiveness, was ever accomplished. Nevertheless, from a twentieth-century high point of 128,000 local school districts nationwide, the pool has been reduced to today's 15,000. While the number of governmental units declined, the nation's total population increased. The result was ever larger school districts, schools, and ever larger managerial bureaucracies.[8]

Coinciding with the school district consolidation effort was the so-called "scientific management" movement. Beginning at the turn of the twentieth century and continuing for two decades, the American private sector, particularly manufacturing, undertook a dramatic effort to enhance efficiency. This was the era of efficiency experts, time-and-motion studies, and Taylorism, named after a highly visible industrial engineer of the day, Frederick Taylor.

Taylor and his followers analyzed production procedures in order to minimize workers' time and efforts, and thus reduce labor costs and enhance profit. This led to intensified specialization of manufacturing production tasks. Public school educators, who have never enjoyed the professional security of a scientific or technological base for their efforts, and who frequently attempt to gain added legitimacy in the eyes of the public by encasing themselves in the mantle of private-sector fads, were quick to trumpet for schools the virtuous applicability of scientific management.

Schools of education trained and certified growing numbers of novitiates steeped in the litany of scientific management, and they were eager to apply their new knowledge religiously to public schools. Scientific management, in this context, had many manifestations.[9] Crucial for the concerns described here, however, was the stress given to the separation between policymaking, presumably the prerogative of the school board, and administration, the sanctified domain of school managers. School board members were admonished to be particularly careful not to transgress this boundary, however blurred the borderline might appear.

In this process, the influence of professional school managers was enhanced, and their control over growing bureaucracies solidified. However, the legitimacy and discretion of previously powerful political managers, school board members, was further eroded.

The fading presence of the political management model was accelerated by yet another turn-of-the-century restructuring effort, this time in the realm of politics and government. "Muckrakers," a group subsequently to be dignified by the occupational label "investigative reporters," uncovered rampant corruption in state and local government, particularly in large cities. School boards were found to be no exception in this period of poor public judgment and weak civic morality. Elected school board members were found guilty of illegal actions such as nepotism, cash kickbacks on supply and construction contracts, and extortion of employees. The widely proffered solution was to remove schools from politics. By insulating public education from partisan political efforts, it was thought that corruption could be dampened and schools better managed.

The political reforms of this "Progressive Era" involved the appointment, instead of election, of school board members in many large cities, ensuring where elections were held that school board candidates were unaligned with partisan political parties, and the abandonment of small local electoral districts, wards, in favor of city-wide, at-large elections. "Good government" reformers were successful in breaking the link between city political machines and public schools. School board members became electorally ever more remote representatives of their constituents, had even less leverage with other city officials, and were relegated to an even lower political status. All these changes further fed the growing influence of professional school managers, and growing school bureaucracies.[10]

The yawning organizational gap between the top (school board members) and the bottom of the pyramid (classroom teachers) eventually contributed to teacher unionization. Following World War II, teachers, initially in New York City and subsequently throughout the entire United States, banded together into two powerful unions, the American Federation of Teachers and the National Education Association. The legitimacy of their organizing efforts was subsequently confirmed in the 1970s by widespread enactment of collective bargaining statutes by state legislatures.[11]

Thus, by the third quarter of the twentieth century the governing authority of school board members was badly diluted. They not only had to manage through cadres of professional administrators, they also had to share decision-making discretion at the bargaining table with the very individuals, the teachers, they had initially employed professional managers to control. Bureaucratization was complete. Employees were controlled by managers' rules, and managers were controlled by employees' rules. The resulting organization, while perhaps appropriate for delivering instruction of a level and intensity sufficient to meet twentieth-century expectations, was increasingly proving clumsy at satisfying emerging twenty-first century economic and social needs.

PROFESSIONALIZED MANAGEMENT MODELS:
A WIDELY PROPOSED CHANGE

Modern services delivery in particular (but technologically sophisticated material production as well) increasingly demands individual judgments by those at the bottom of an organizational pyramid, regardless of the number of levels in the hierarchy. The most clear-cut examples are physicians employed in large hospitals or health maintenance organizations and attorneys, architects, management consultants, and engineers in large firms. Here, however broad the span of organizational control, it is unreasonable rigidly to proscribe employee behavior through multitiered managerial levels and codified rules. Standardized products and performance are precisely the opposite of what end users of the services desire. Moreover, depersonalized behavior frequently conflicts with the norms of behavior inculcated into professionals through their advanced training. Professionalized management models have evolved to accommodate these conditions.

Professionalized management strategies are characterized by two features that stand in substantial contrast both to political and pyramidal management models. These two features are (1) employee participation in the establishment, implementation, and adjudication of the organizations' rules, and (2) a far wider realm of individual discretion regarding the manner in which each employee performs assigned tasks.[12] Indeed, on selected dimensions of organizational activity, "workers" are themselves a part of professionalized management.

Professionalized management is necessary when the product to be manufactured or the service to be delivered is complicated, individual judgment is needed in tailoring the product or service to the preferences of the user, and the underlying technology for the production process or service is incompletely developed. It is this latter condition that particularly reinforces the necessity for the "worker" to utilize individual discretion and judgment in shaping the service activity or product.

Professionally managed organizations may also be large, and thus the need for control remains. However, neither the idiosyncratic and personalized controls of politically managed systems nor the universalized and depersonalized rules of a pyramidal organization facilitate appropriate employee discretion. Standardized rules inhibit the expression of professional judgment and impede the ability of an organization to tailor a service or product to the tastes of a client.

Consequently, professionally managed organizations engage workers in the development of the rules needed for control. Gaining worker adherence to rules is thus accomplished more through collegial participation than through authoritative imposition and hierarchical supervision.[13]

Professionally managed organizations not only engage workers in the development of rules applicable to the entire organization, but also permit, indeed encourage, employee participation in the design and conduct of their own specific work tasks. Workers are clearly not free to do anything they want any time they want. Such could lead to organizational chaos. However, the "envelope"[14] of professional discretion available to a worker in a professional organization is substantially wider than in a politically or pyramidally managed setting.

Employee evaluation in professionally managed organizations relies heavily upon the judgments of workers' peers and clients. The personal views of those in immediate authority, as with a political management model, or comparisons of worker behavior to a previously codified, universally applicable template of directives, as in a pyramidal model, are given relatively little weight. Under such conditions, the role of those in the highest levels of organizational authority shifts from a heavy emphasis upon supervision of underlings to greater attention to selection and assignment of entry-level workers and judgments regarding their reward and promotion.

Peer and, to some degree, client participation in worker evaluation is much less efficient in terms of time consumption than is the political or pyramidal model for employee evaluation. However, this short-run inefficiency is judged an acceptable trade for greater long-run organizational ability to achieve production or service goals.

As with each of the previously described management models, participatory strategies also have limitations. In a partial or complete client monopoly setting, it is possible for a professionally managed organization to lose sight of its goals—consumer satisfaction and serving client interests. Peer review and professional standards may prove insufficient for evaluation purposes, in the absence of any choice of alternatives or any avenue for "voice" by clients.[15]

In the last quarter of the twentieth century, signs of a global economic transformation are becoming clearly evident. Electronic communication now quickly transcends national boundaries. Ideas, including technology, flow worldwide, as does capital. International trade competition has intensified dramatically. No nation can long expect to hold an economically advantageous position simply by virtue of its natural resource base, abundant supply of inexpensive labor, or strategic geographic location. Constant technological and productive creativity has become the only means for ensuring economic survivability. In the absence of an ability to pursue technological innovation, a nation risks loss of jobs, trade deficits, and eventually a lower standard of living for its citizens.

Under such conditions of international economic competitiveness, nations are coming to rely with growing intensity upon the educated capacity of their citizenry. Far more than ever before in history, formal schooling is critical for national well-being. The organizational arrangements that evolved two centuries ago to deliver educational services to industrializing economies are proving insufficient to meet the expectations of new industries and services now dominated by information and the need for technological innovation. Consequently, there is hardly a nation that currently is satisfied with its education system.

School reform is virtually a global mission. The United States, characterized by the absence of a national system of schooling and by a political system better geared to preventing rather than passing legislation, is slower than many to undertake reform. Nevertheless, America has begun the cumbersome process of restructuring its education system. This was launched most visibly with the 1983 publication of a federal government report entitled *A Nation at Risk*. In 1988, England launched a similar effort with passage of the Thatcher government's proposed Education Reform Act. Though in different forms and on different scales, other nations—Canada, Australia, Israel, France, Scandinavian countries, New Zealand, Singapore, Hong Kong, Japan, USSR, Belgium, etc.—are engaged in comparable efforts.

The present character and past development of a nation's education system influences the details of proposed policy reforms. Nations with elite systems of schooling, often steeped in the British tradition, are frequently eager to expand educational services to a broader segment of the population. In effect, they are concerned with matters of quantity. Nations with highly democratized systems of schooling, e.g., the United States, are frequently concerned with elevating standards of student performance. They are intent on enhancing quality. Yet other nations (e.g. Japan), seemingly satisfied with the quality and quantity components of their education systems, may be concerned with the degree to which individual creativity is fostered.

These widespread attempts to tailor schooling more productively to the needs of newly developing economic forces are frequently accompanied by remarkably similar rhetoric. Inevitably reform advocates assert that dropout rates are too high and test scores are too low, creativity is stifled, or human talent is wasted. Comparisons are made with the education systems of other nations and the spectre of economic subjugation to a foreign industrial juggernaut is projected.

Pyramidal organizations with their conventional fixation upon control mechanisms are ill suited for the transmission of technical knowledge increasingly expected by nations to enable them to participate in contemporary economic developments. Higher-order thinking skills, the creative processes necessary for invention and technological innovation, and intensified quantitative and scientific reasoning do not lend themselves easily to instruction in a standardized, depersonalized regulatory environment. The highly educated persons necessary to convey such knowledge effectively are not easily adaptable to conventional bureaucratic settings. Also, given the added intensity of such instruction, it increasingly is necessary to permit instructors to tailor their tactics to their students' characteristics. In short, a level of professional discretion and personal attention beyond what a standard bureaucracy is capable of delivering may be instructionally necessary.

Unlike the arguments put forward to gain their enactment, the education reform proposals themselves are not everywhere the same. The proposals rely on a wide range of tactical educational changes, intensified high school graduation requirements and college-entry criteria, extended periods of schooling, more rigorous curricula offerings and textbook standards, higher teacher entry qualifications, expansion of secondary and tertiary school places, added discretion for school heads, national curriculum, added parent discretion, more achievement testing, etc. Despite such apparent tactical variety, there are a limited number of underlying strategies. Common among them is a growing attention to altering the conventional management model, moving away from pyramidal organizations and toward added professionalization or "worker" empowerment.

In the United States, empowerment advocates hope to restructure schools such that teachers will be involved in a wider spectrum of decisions than has conventionally been the case. The decisions discussed are curriculum design, textbook selection, participation in the employment of new teachers, evaluation of colleagues eligible for tenure, and consultation regarding the overall operation of a school.[16] Many teacher leaders are also advocates of substantially elevated standards for entering into and remaining in the teaching "profession."

Professionalization of management also involves devolving greater decision discretion not simply to teachers, but to schools as operating units. "School based management" is described as a means for placing resources and decisions closer to the clients that educators serve—the parents and students at individual school sites.[17] In the United States, states as far flung as Washington and Florida have enacted legislation to allocate resources to schools, rather than to school districts, and to promote far wider decision making at the school than was possible under the strict bureaucratic management model. In England, the previously mentioned Education Reform Act has as one of its crucial components bypassing local education authorities for many purposes and permitting the Head to become a chief executive officer responsible for operating his or her school. (It should be noted, however, that the Thatcher government is not proposing, at least at this juncture, the professional empowerment of teachers, beyond what school based management might strictly necessitate.)[18] Similar proposals for restructuring have been enacted or are being considered in New Zealand, Australia, and Singapore.

These modern reforms, although clearly appearing as a worldwide trend, are nowhere solidified, and it is too early to proclaim a movement, much less a paradigm shift from pyramidal to professional management models. Nevertheless, given the substantial incongruities between fundamental components of pyramidal management schemes and the evolving educational needs of nations, the eventual development of these trends into more complete versions of participatory management seems highly probable.

PRIVATIZATION MANAGEMENT MODELS: POSSIBLY ON THE HORIZON

This management strategy is characterized by the degree to which "authority" to influence the organization is consciously extended to end users, customers, and clients. It can operate on a continuum extending from modest dependence upon user feedback (opinion surveys of client and customer satisfaction) to intense reliance on market mechanisms, deliberately encouraged competition among providers of products and services. Whatever the mechanisms utilized for empowering end users, the intent is the same: render producers more sensitive to the preferences of clients, hence enhancing the effectiveness of the organization.

Privatization can be grafted onto any one or a combination of the previously described management strategies. Certainly pyramidal and professionally oriented organizations can solicit client opinion. For that matter, even if seldom motivated to do so, politically managed organizations can do the same. Almost all organizations can be placed by government in a market-oriented environment wherein they possess no guaranteed clientele and must compete for customers.

A trade-off is thought to exist between serving the public interest and the efficiency benefits of private provision. Thus, in monopoly or quasi-monopoly organizational settings (for example, local telephone service) privatization may be restricted and regulated in order to avoid inefficient competition (i.e., having to install the instruments of multiple telephone companies in one's home). However, even here reasonable individuals can disagree regarding where the appropriate balance in the trade-off occurs. Some free market advocates would go so far as to privatize national defense. Others with an opposite point of view would nationalize, or socialize, almost all manufacturing and services. There are few scientific principles, only political ideology or practical experience, to guide judgments regarding where to limit or how to balance privatization.

Proposals for educational privatization have existed literally for centuries. Nineteenth-century political economist John Stuart Mill advocated such a management scheme. Intellectual longevity by itself, however, is no guarantee of reality, and privatization advocates have yet to make much headway in convincing the policymakers of any nation to convert schooling into a full-blown consumer choice arrangement. However, change often occurs slowly, and it may be that privatization will be accepted incrementally as a component of an evolving management model.

For example, several states in the United States (e.g., Minnesota and California) have already expanded the range of parent choice among local public school districts. Policymakers in California, Massachusetts, Hawaii, and in other states are now discussing the even more radical idea of permitting "open enrollment" of students across all public school district lines. Proposals continue to be made in the U.S. Congress to permit parents of students in schools that have a record of overall low performance to choose an alternative public school for their child. The alterations to English education sponsored by Prime Minister Thatcher also permit an expansion of parent choice. If another local school has space, a household may choose to transfer a child into it from the assigned neighborhood school. It would take only a small twist of the policymaking dial to convert this arrangement into a much wider parent choice education system.

Privatization, while possibly consistent with a participatory or professionalization management model, is nevertheless regarded in most policy circles as a more radical alteration to an education system. Consequently, while possibly occurring eventually, one would expect elements of client empowerment to be grafted onto any evolving management model at a relatively slow pace. This is particularly true if a nation's need for "community" becomes strong. For example, increasingly global flows of labor through migration from one region or one nation to another may intensify demands for citizenship education, social cohesion, or building a common core of values. Under such conditions pyramidal management models become more attractive and policymakers may be less predisposed toward empowering clients.

There are numerous dimensions on which the management models described above can be compared and analyzed, e.g., delegation of authority, communication patterns, worker satisfaction, employee evaluation, and consumer sensitivity. However, for the thesis under consideration here, the important point is the systematic extension of authority from those immediately empowered to govern in a political model, to managerial intermediaries in a pyramidal model, to employees themselves in a professionalized model, through to end users in a privatized model.

The extension of authority may be a common metric with which to measure the evolution of educational management. If so, it is highly likely that the engine propelling change will be global alterations to the economy in terms of modern technology and means of production. An essential evolutionary conservatism may operate, however. *It seems likely that organizational ontogeny will recapitulate managerial phylogeny.* That is, the resulting or eventual management model may well continue to possess characteristics from each of its preceding stages. This condition has important consequences for the preparation of educational administrators and the conduct of research about educational administration. These are the topics to which we next turn.

Consequences for Practice, Preparation, and Research

If school management significantly evolves to place added emphasis upon professional or client empowerment, or both, then there are several fundamental consequences for administrator practice and preparation, and for research. These changes are triggered by the extension of authority and decision discretion to added groups of actors, primarily teachers and parents. In general, these changes will result in fewer centrally prescribed organizational rules, greater uncertainty about the external environment and future conditions, and a greater need for planning and analysis. In short, educational administrators will have to add to their portfolio the skills of a statesman and an entrepreneur.

Many of these skills will be in addition to the capabilities managers currently are expected to possess. In effect, expectations will be added but few if any will be deleted. The following sections illustrate skill additions likely to be necessary.

PRACTICAL CONSEQUENCES

Team building. Building and inspiring a team will become a primary leadership activity. It is a much more difficult and dynamic process than conveying and enforcing decision rules made by central authorities. Changing roles for administrators will have all the insecurity that typically accompanies newly found freedoms.

Added professional empowerment will entail teacher participation in activities such as hiring and promotion, curricular and instructional innovation and implementation, and decisions regarding standards, e.g., student admission, graduation, and grading. This departure from conventional bureaucratic procedures will surely be distressing to some administrators. No longer will they be able easily to invoke the authority of a centrally promoted set of rules to guide behavior. Rather, many more decision rules will have to be developed within their own organizations by administrators as leaders of professional teams. Such activities will occupy enormous amounts of time for virtually all administrators. However, to be successful, administrators will have to develop and sustain a culture of professional collegiality, and encourage risk taking among their teaching staff.

Financial management. Most educational administrators presently possess only minimal budgetary responsibility. They may have discretion over supply and expense accounts generated from a per-student allocation formula and federal government categorical aid programs, e.g., funds for handicapped students. Generally there is little budgetary discretion over personnel and almost never discretion over major capital accounts.

New management models often define the school as the

fundamental operating unit in an educational system. The consequence is to empower school administrators with greater budgetary discretion than is typically the case in bureaucratized models. Where teachers are empowered, this may entail not only possessing financial management capability, but also sharing even greater authority than was referred to above in connection with "team building."

Performance appraisal. Administrators have always had responsibilities for evaluating individual and institutional performance. However, a quid pro quo is developing whereby greater professional discretion is permitted in exchange for greater attention to outcome accountability. Statewide and nationwide outcome assessment procedures are being more widely developed and implemented.[19] Generally these procedures rely upon the school site as the unit of analysis. Administrators will no longer easily be able to rely upon experts in testing and measurement to analyze and interpret performance data for their schools or their districts. They will have to understand the techniques and outcomes sufficiently to be able to use assessment results for managerial decisions, as well as to explain the outcome to interested constituencies, such as parents.

Enterprise. Where clients are empowered (for example, in a system where parents can select their children's schools) administrators will also have to be capable of market analysis and other means for determining the preferences and satisfaction levels of clients and prospective clients. If market mechanisms come into play, and schools are no longer guaranteed a client base, then entrepreneurial activity will be rewarded and selling clients on the virtues of one's school and continuing to assess their preferences and opinions will be an additional crucial capability for administrators. Those who do not possess such skills may find themselves in the awkward posture of not having sufficient clients to justify continued operation.

Instructional understanding. In order to be perceived as a "leader" in a school where teachers are themselves empowered, or see themselves as equals with leaders, principals will have to be instructional experts. They will not only have to know about instruction, they also will have to possess credentials as outstanding instructors. Simply being a good manager will no longer suffice in an environment wherein one is expected to interact with instructors about teaching. A "manager" principal will no longer possess legitimacy in such circumstances.

ADMINISTRATOR PREPARATION

The preparation of professional educational administrators is one of the weakest components of United States education. Too little attention is paid to standards, either admission or completion, evaluations are almost always only on academic criteria, and even these are typically slighted. Virtually no serious attention is given to techniques of team building, financial management, and the other added skills listed in the preceding section. Clearly, this must change in order effectively to administer schools in which professional teachers and possibly clients play ever larger roles.

In addition to more rigorous preparation, and added attention to the dimensions listed above, administrators increasingly will have to provide evidence that they are outstanding instructors. It may develop, for example, that school districts will require administrators responsible for instruction to possess certification from the newly formed National Board of Professional Teaching Standards.

RESEARCH

There is a long record of criticism regarding research in educational administration. It generally is viewed as being of low utility to practitioners, poorly conducted, and based in an inappropriate methodological paradigm.[20] There is no need here to repeat these often cited and quite valid criticisms.

What is of added note is that research will need to expand to encompass those dimensions associated with employee and client empowerment. The two dimensions that will be most noticeable are governance and efficiency. For example, attention will need to be given to the development and assessment of governance mechanisms for resolving tensions between client's individual choices and societal imperatives. For example, if given a choice, will households choose schooling patterns at odds with racial desegregation?

Also, greater discretion in decision making at school sites should be accompanied by greater disaggregation of revenue and expenditure data. This in turn can lead to the kinds of microeconomic analyses of instruction that have long been needed but, to this point, have been impeded by financial data aggregated at an inappropriate level, i.e., the school district. In this way, more can be known about the cost of instruction and added progress can be made toward an educational production function. Research of this nature will eventually permit the design of management strategies that extend authority beyond professionals and parents, and actually empower pupils.

FOOTNOTES

1. "Political" officials may include a range of types from divinely inspired monarchs and military despots to democratically elected representatives. They may draw their authority from a variety of sources: election, appointments, inheritance, charisma, etc. What matters for purposes of this discussion is not how they came to possess authority, but rather that workers or employees in their organizations accept them as legitimate leaders.

2. See David Tyack, *The One Best System: A History of American Urban Education* (Cambridge, MA: Harvard University Press, 1974).

3. The historical evolution of United States school governance is described in James W. Guthrie, Diana K. Thomason, and Patricia A. Craig, "The Erosion of Lay Control," in National Committee for Citizens for Education, *Public Testimony on Public Schools* (Berkeley, CA: McCutchan, 1975), chapter 5.

4. Michael B. Katz, *The Irony of Early School Reform: Educational Innovation in Mid-nineteenth Century Massachusetts* (Cambridge, MA: Harvard University Press, 1968), and idem, *Class, Bureaucracy, and Schools: The Illusion of Educational Change in America* (New York: Praeger, 1971).

5. For a history of these developments, see Diane Ravitch, *The Great School Wars: New York City, 1805-1973* (New York: Basic Books, 1974); Stanley Schultz, *The Culture Factory: Boston Public Schools, 1789-1860* (New York: Oxford University Press, 1973); Carl Kaestle, *The Evolution of an Urban School System: New York City, 1750-1850* (Cambridge: Harvard University Press, 1973); and Selwyn Troen, "Popular Education in Nineteenth Century St. Louis," *History of Education Quarterly*, no. 13 (Spring 1973): 23-40.

6. The history of this period is chronicled by Lawrence C. Cremin in *The Transformation of the School* (New York: Knopf, 1961).

7. The history of the urban school superintendency is contained in Theodore Lee Reller, *The Development of the City Superintendency of Schools in the United States* (Philadelphia: Theodore Lee Reller, 1935) and Raymond E. Callahan, *The Superintendent of Schools: An Historical Analysis* (Washington, DC: U.S. Office of Education, 1967).

8. Most of the 128,000 "school districts" existing in 1928 were classic one-room schools. By 1988, there were approximately 600 one-room public schools. In 1960, there were 20,213. The high point was 149,282 in 1930. *Education Week*, 1 February 1989, p. 3.

9. The history of the scientific management in education is captured by Raymond E. Callahan, *Education and the Cult of Efficiency* (Chicago: University of Chicago Press, 1962), and Tyack, *The One Best System.*

10. David Tyack and Elisabeth Hansot, *Managers of Virtue: Public School Leadership in America 1820 to 1980* (New York: Basic Books, 1982).

11. Edgar B. Wesley, *NEA, The First One Hundred Years: The Building of the Teaching Profession* (New York: Harper and Brothers, 1957), and Willard S. Elsbree, *The American Teacher: Evolution of a Profession in a Democracy* (New York: American Book Co., 1939).

12. Because of the sharing of authority between those in authority and workers, this strategy is sometimes characterized in the manufacturing sector as "participatory management."

13. Rosabeth Moss Kanter, *The Changemasters: Innovation and Entrepreneurship in American Corporations* (New York: Simon and Shuster, 1982).

14. The concept of an "envelope" of worker discretion is explained by Guy Benveniste in *Professionalizing the Organization: Reducing Bureaucracy to Enhance Effectiveness* (San Francisco: Jossey-Bass, 1987).

15. For a discussion of client or customer feedback and its consequences for organizational productivity and sensitivity, see Albert O. Hirschman, *Exit, Voice, and Loyalty* (Cambridge, MA: Harvard University Press, 1970).

16. Charles Achilles notes that those proposed arrangements promote the possibility of an interesting organizational paradox. At a time when speed to adapt to changing conditions in the external environment is increasingly important, widespread teacher participation in decisions may actually slow an organization's ability to respond. Personal letter, Achilles to Guthrie.

17. See James W. Guthrie, "School Based Management: The Next Needed Education Reform," *Phi Delta Kappan* 68 (December 1986): 305-309.

18. See Hymel Thomas and Stewart Ranson, "Education Reform in Britain" (Paper prepared at the Center for Education Management and Policy Studies, University of Birmingham, 1988).

19. U. S. Department of Education, "Creating Responsive and Responsible Accountability Systems: Report of the Office of Educational Research and Improvement (OERI) State Accountability Study Group" (Washington, DC: OERI, 1988).

20. See Rodney Muth, "Reconceptualizing Training for Administrators and Leaders: Focus on Inquiry" (Paper presented at the annual meeting of the University Council on Educational Administration, Cincinnati, 1988).

Section Five
IMPLICATIONS FOR RESEARCH
AND PRACTICE

CHAPTER XI

Preparing School Administrators for the
Twenty-First Century: The Reform Agenda

JOSEPH MURPHY

School administration is currently facing vociferous demands for change and improvement.[1] The profession is responding by engaging in the most comprehensive analysis and overhaul of its basic operating structure since the behavioral science revolution of the 1950s and 1960s.[2] A number of factors suggest that this current era of pointed criticism and political turbulence may lead to fundamental changes in the preparation of school administrators and in the organization and management of schools. As late as 1985, Peterson and Finn reported:

At a time when the nation is deeply concerned about the performance of its schools, and near-to-obsessed with the credentials and careers of those who teach in them, scant attention has been paid to the preparation and qualifications of those who lead them.[3]

In the most recent wave of school reform and studies of the 1980s (1985-1988), much more attention has been directed to issues of school administration and leadership. Yet, to date, no comprehensive analysis of these calls for changes in school administration has been undertaken. The purpose of this chapter is to provide such a review by examining reports dealing specifically with educational administration and with studies that consider management and leadership within the scope of more comprehensive reform suggestions.

The specific goals of this chapter are threefold. The first is to explain the reasons for the calls for reform of school administration that have become an important component of the current educational reform movement. A comprehensive treatment of the rationale supporting these reform proposals is presented in the first part of the chapter. The conceptual framework employed for this first objective was developed by Murphy and Hallinger.[4] Based upon a review of the literature on school improvement, educational leadership, and administrative preparation and professional development, the six-part, macro-level framework developed by these authors is used to explain current demands for specific, micro-level changes in the area of school administration.

The second objective is to review the major studies and reports on educational reform from 1982 to 1988 to uncover their messages for the improvement of school administration. Thirty-two major reports and studies that served as catalysts for the current educational reform movement have been identified and classified, consistent with reports separating reform activities of the 1980s into two eras.[5] Reports have been classified as being concerned with the reform of either education in general or school administration in particular. In addition, the major treatises written during the 1980s on the reform of school leadership and administration were examined. Document analysis—coding and the use of recording matrices—was used to draw information from the reports and studies. The categories used on the matrices were established by the coding labels and generally corresponded to specific calls for reform, e.g., the recruitment of women and minorities into administration preparation programs and administrative roles.

The third objective, based on the two earlier goals, is to discuss educational administration reform issues that need further attention, e.g., the superintendency and the role of the school district. By casting a wide net, we are able to shed light upon a number of topics that have not been fully explored.

Underlying Pressures for Reform

Reform proposals in the area of school administration are buttressed by analyses of current conditions, beliefs about education and the schooling process, and folklore. Collectively, these supporting elements can be classified into four underlying trends that have fueled the proposals for improvement—both those flowing from reform reports (discussed in the next section) as well as from initiatives being undertaken by states, colleges and universities, and school districts.[6] In this section we explore these trends. Two general conditions and two conditions specific to educational administration are discussed.

School administration and the larger reform debate. It was inevitable that the lenses being used to examine the general educational problems of the 1980s—declining economic competitiveness and increasing indicators of school failure such as plummeting test scores, poorly educated and unskilled graduates, high student dropout rates—would focus somewhat on the quality of educational leadership and management:

Although teachers bore the brunt of accountability demands, administrators did not get off scot-free. If students were not achieving enough, teachers must not be teaching well enough, and logically, administrators must not be doing enough either.

Problem assumptions about educational leadership relate primarily to the school productivity decline manifested in falling test scores. As policymakers addressed the problem of declining achievement they first criticized teacher performance then school administration.[7]

Once the reform spotlight was directed to the preparation of school administrators and their performance on the job, many of the same problems discovered in the teaching profession surfaced—lack of entry standards for all rungs of the professional career ladder (i.e., recruitment, preparation, selection, advancement); poor, and perhaps dysfunctional, training; the absence of personal accountability; and limited, if not weak, appraisal of performance. While there are some notable differences in solutions proposed for the problems of teaching and administration, it is clear that many central concerns about educational quality relate to efforts to reform school administration.

Rethinking of the appropriate organizational structure for schools. Many believe the most prevalent organizational school structure in the United States—the bureaucracy—is an impediment to addressing the most important, difficult, and intransigent problems in our schools. A number of influential analysts have concluded that, if substantial educational improvement is to occur, fundamentally different organizational arrangements will be required.[8] Three arguments have converged to push the restructuring debate to the forefront of the educational reform agenda. First, there are analyses of the dysfunctions accompanying bureaucracies.[9] These treatments show how reforms that depend on hierarchical linkages or reinforce existing organizational structures are not only unlikely to succeed, but will probably spawn additional problems.[10]

Second, coupled to the antibureaucracy argument are calls for the professionalization of teaching.[11] The message in these reports is that real educational reform will occur only when a professional teaching corps is created to guarantee it. The corollary for restructuring schools has been laid out by the Holmes Group: "If the construction of a genuine profession of teaching is to succeed, schools will have to change."[12]

The third argument for school restructuring emanates from current decentralization trends in business organizations,[13] from school effects research[14] and from school improvement studies.[15] The importance of substantial autonomy for site-level staffs is quite a popular concept:

The more control a school has over those aspects of its organization that affect its performance—the articulation of goals, the selection and management of teachers, the specification of policies—the more likely it is to exhibit the qualities that have been found to promote effectiveness.[16]

The growing acceptance of the need to alter the basic organizational structure of schools puts tremendous pressure for change on school administration. New forms of governance and control, with concomitant shifts in both the distribution of authority in the system and the bases for influence, require new models of leadership.[17] New perspectives on educational leadership suggest important changes in the preparation of prospective principals and superintendents and of other men and women to fill many yet to be defined leadership roles. Two of these potential new roles—head teachers for individual schools, and headmistresses or headmasters for a senior high school and its feeder schools—have been described by John Goodlad in his book *A Place Called School*. In addition, the growing acceptance of: (a) school-based management teams and building leadership teams; (b) notions of leadership as a function rather than a role; and (c) organizational substitutes for leadership functions, has important implications for training programs and professional development experiences in school administration.

PRESSURES SPECIFIC TO SCHOOL ADMINISTRATION

Dissatisfaction with the status quo. With some notable exceptions, demands for the reform of school administration are supported by a pervasive sense of the inadequacy of current operations. University programs have come under severe criticism for the way they conduct business and the results they produce.[18] There is a growing conviction that current preparation programs are dysfunctional. Some argue that, in their quest to gain respectability in the wider university community, programs were molded to fit an arts and sciences model rather than a professional model of preparation. The behavioral sciences in turn became the structure and deductive theory became the soul of the new model.[19]

Over the last ten to fifteen years, researchers pointed to how social science frameworks failed to deliver on their promise to yield powerful understandings of the business of school administration.[20] Others showed how the arts and sciences model contributed to the use of processes and procedures that conflict with those emphasized on the job.[21] Still others revealed how the profession, driven by the "behavioral science theory engine,"[22] directed administrative attention away from the study of technical core operations and issues of educational productivity and toward generic issues of management.[23] Finally, and most seriously, analysts documented the failure of the theory movement to produce real improvements in the practice of school administration and the functioning of school organizations.[24]

Lessons from successful schools. The dissatisfaction with the status of educational leadership is accompanied by reform pressure of a more positive sort—a growing body of research showing that school administrators can have an important influence on organizational outcomes, especially on measures of student performance. At the same time that deficiencies in programs for preparing administrators are being uncovered, studies are confirming the connection between school administrators, especially principals, and effective schools:

> For years now, studies have been pointing to the pivotal role of the principal in bringing about more effective schools. Our own field studies bear out these findings. In schools where achievement was high and where there was a clear sense of community, we found, invariably, that the principal made the difference.[25]

Researchers are discovering that principals in "effective" schools act differently than their counterparts in average schools.[26] Thus, there is growing pressure to change university preparation programs and to create alternative systems to produce school administrators who are prepared to function more like the principals of these effective schools—and less like social scientists.

Reform Reports and Messages for
Educational Leaders

Not surprisingly, there are some differences among the various reform reports concerning the appropriate scope and nature of school administration reform. At the same time, however, the reports share some important consistencies in terms of philosophy and action. In particular, the reports proposed similar points of view on basic notions of leadership, professionalism, and quality standards.

Leadership is the coin of the realm in virtually all reform reports related to school administration. Of the thirty-two documents examined (see table 1), two-thirds proposed improving schools by strengthening management or leadership skills, or both. Of these twenty-one, seventeen dealt overwhelmingly with the leadership dimension of administration, two focused primarily on management skills, and two others gave roughly equal emphasis to both. Most of the reports also shared a vision about the direction and focus of educational leadership. The following statements from some of the reports illustrate the common concern about leadership:

We urge that administrative training programs in higher education be examined and modified to provide for explicit educational leadership skills in existing and potential administrators. We further urge local education agencies to recognize that building principals will have to delegate some managerial duties in order to assume the leadership role we propose. Building principals may need additional personnel to assist in managing their schools so that they have time to provide educational leadership.[27]

These things being so, the head of the school—its administrator—should not be solely or even primarily concerned with running the school efficiently or economically, or merely keeping the peace of the community. Keeping the peace, doing justice, balancing budgets, enforcing laws is the main business of the political community at any level; they are not the *main business* of the school community. Its main business is teaching and learning. The head of the school—its principal—should, therefore, administer all other affairs in ways that facilitate the *main business*.[28]

Reform of school administration in the 1980s has been synonymous with reform of the principalship. Sixteen reports deal almost exclusively with this role. The emphasis seems to be on increasing the leadership capacity of current and prospective school-site administrators. Yet, remarkably little attention has been given either to superintendents specifically or to district level operations in

TABLE 1
REFORM REPORTS AND SCHOOL ADMINISTRATION:
AN ANALYTIC LOOK

Wave 1 of School Reform (January 1983-October 1985)

GENERAL REFORM REPORTS

A Nation at Risk (1983)	National Commission on Excellence in Education
Academic Preparation for College: What Students Need to Know and Be Able to Do (1983)	College Board
Educating Americans for the 21st Century (1983)	National Science Board Commission
Action for Excellence (1983)	Education Commission of the States
A Call for Change in Teacher Education (1985)	National Commission for Excellence in Teacher Education

EDUCATIONAL ADMINISTRATION: SPECIFIC REFORM REPORT

Selecting American School Principals (1983)	National Institute of Education (D. C. Baltzell and R. A. Dentler)

EDUCATIONAL STUDIES

The Paideia Proposal (1982)	Mortimer Adler
High School: A Report on Secondary Education in America (1983)	Carnegie Foundation (Ernest Boyer)
Action in the States (1984)	Education Commission of the States
A Place Called School (1984)	John Goodlad
Horace's Compromise: The Dilemma of the American High School (1984)	Theodore Sizer

Wave 2 of School Reform (November 1985-December 1988)

GENERAL REFORM REPORTS

Tomorrow's Teachers (1986)	Holmes Group
School Boards: Strengthening Grass Roots Leadership (1986)	Institute for Educational Leadership
What Works: Research about Teaching and Learning (1986)	U.S. Department of Education
Time for Results: The Governors' 1991 Report on Education, Chairman's Summary (1986)	National Governors' Association

First Lessons: A Report on Elementary Education in America	U.S. Department of Education (William J. Bennett)
A Nation Prepared: Teachers for the 21st Century (1986)	Carnegie Forum
School Reform Policy: A Call for Reason (1986)	Association for Supervision and Curriculum Development
American Democracy: Making It Work (1988)	U. S. Department of Education

EDUCATIONAL ADMINISTRATION: SPECIFIC REFORM REPORTS

Performance-Based Preparation of Principals (1985)	National Association of Secondary School Principals
Principal Selection Guide: A Framework for Improvement (1987)	U. S. Department of Education/Office of Education Research and Improvement
Leaders for America's Schools (1987)	National Commission on Excellence in Educational Administration
Speaking for Leadership (1987)	Education Commission of the States (Bill Clinton)
School Leadership Preparation: A Preface for Action (1988)	American Association of Colleges for Teacher Education

EDUCATIONAL STUDIES

The Shopping Mall High School: Winners and Losers in the Educational Marketplace (1985)	Arthur Powell, Eleanor Farrar, and David Cohen
Keeping Track: How Schools Structure Inequality (1985)	Jeannie Oakes
The Last Citadel: American High Schools Since 1940 (1986)	Robert Hampel
Selling Students Short: Classroom Bargains and Academic Reform in the American High School (1986)	Michael Sedlak et al.
Time for Results: The Governors' 1991 Report on Education (1987)	National Governors' Association
Report Card on School Reform (1988)	Carnegie Foundation (Ernest Boyer)
Schools Matter: The Junior Years (1988)	Peter Mortimore et al.
What Price Democracy: Politics, Markets, and American Schools (1988)	John Chubb and Terry Moe

general. Two factors help explain the preoccupation with the principalship. First, a focus on principals fits well with efforts to decentralize governance and to bolster leadership in schools. Moreover, this logic connects with the recent emphasis on decentralized management in the private sector and the widespread lobbying for a school-by-school improvement model in education. Second, there has been a historical neglect of the superintendency as an area of analysis.[29] Thus, it is not surprising that reformers in the 1980s have largely overlooked the central office.

Calls for strengthening leadership tend to center administrative attention on internal school operations rather than on the management of school-environmental interactions, a pattern consistent with reform proposals in other areas as well. Eleven of the seventeen relevant reports have a primarily internal focus, five have a mixed internal– external focus, and one directs principals' attention to issues external to the school. There appears to be a clear shift away from the predominant concern devoted to environmental issues related to the behavioral science model of administrator preparation in the 1960s. That last major era of administrative reform opened the eyes of school leaders to the wider world in which their schools operated. Current reform refocuses vision on internal school operations, especially on the teaching-learning process.

Consistent with the redirection of attention toward internal operations, reform proposals have exhorted administrators to develop a better understanding of the core technology of education and to devote more attention and authority to the instructional mission of the school:

Without a thorough grounding in the realities of the classroom, principals will continue to feel uncomfortable and inadequate in educational leadership roles. Moreover, they will continue to lack credibility in instructional matters with their teachers.[30]

What of the school principal? He or she is the *principal teacher*. Schools need business management, and there should be executives for this. But the *principal* is the lead teacher and needs to be among colleagues and students, as that is where the most vital judgments in the life of a school must be made.[31]

The status and authority of school administrators will shift. Their authority will derive more directly from their expertise in the core functions of schooling than from hierarchical positions in the school bureaucracy.[32]

Keeping in mind that there are certain rather serious flaws in study designs used to measure the instructional leadership activities of administrators,[33] the cumulative results from this line of investigation reveal that, before the onslaught of the reform proposals of the 1980s, principals were spending between 5 and 20 percent of their time managing technical core operations and superintendents were devoting even less time to curricular and instructional matters.[34] If the reform proposals of the 1980s are influential in shaping preservice preparation programs and administrative behavior, there should be a dramatic shift in the attention administrators devote to the core technology of schooling.

The professionalization of school administration is a second major theme in numerous reform reports. While a similar theme characterizes proposals to improve teaching, there are important differences between the two areas in the strategies employed to promote professionalism. The professionalization of teaching focuses on standards, working conditions, salaries, autonomy, and involvement in school decisions.[35] With the exception of standards and autonomy, these strategies for enhancing the status of teachers are not major components of the reform literature for school leadership. Rather, methods to strengthen the profession of school administration have focused primarily on two interrelated issues—the development of a professional knowledge base and the use of a preparation system based on a professional school model, rather than on a classic model of graduate education. ·

As noted earlier, the 1960s brought the behavioral sciences model to preparation programs for educational leaders. Frameworks from various social science disciplines became the knowledge base and deductive theory became the preferred method of inquiry. Lessons from practice were dismissed as "cookbook recipes" that were incompatible with the scientific perspective and intellectual rigor of this new context for training. The behavioral science frameworks, although readily accepted by university departments of educational administration, never generated much enthusiasm in the field.[36] Neither did they live up to the expectation that they would lead to meaningful improvements in administrative practice:

The once-glowing promise of a Theory Movement in educational administration—rooted in the academic disciplines and the scientific method, bringing theory-based research to the improvement of practice, striving mightily to develop a profession well grounded in reliable and affirmed knowledge— seems to have been unfulfilled.[37]

While growing discontent with the behavioral science model was surfacing, practitioners and professors alike were seeking powerful new frames of knowledge that would lead to a unification of the preparation and delivery arms of the profession and to real improvements in the management and organization of schools. The focus of both groups has come to rest on the type of knowledge base that underlies other professions such as law and medicine:

In order to accomplish *their* charter, however, schools of education must take the profession of education, not academia, as their main point of reference. It is not sufficient to say that the greatest strength of schools of education is that they are the only places to look at fundamental issues from a variety of disciplinary perspectives. They have been doing so for more than half a century without appreciable effect on professional practice. It is time for many institutions to shift their gears.[38]

The new knowledge base proposed by today's reformers is different from the old behavioral science frameworks in a number of ways. Most importantly, due to the emphasis on inductive methods of knowledge development, the realities of the workplace are much more accurately portrayed. As noted earlier, the emerging administrative knowledge base is grounded on internal school operations and technical core issues, thus reversing the previous preoccupation with environmental issues and with the generic aspects of administrative roles. Moreover, recent thinking about educational leadership patterns has been shaped by information about administrator effects on organizational outcomes, especially on student learning. Finally, because newer views of school administration emanate more directly from the study of practice, skill-based knowledge has been relegitimated.

Reformers in the area of school administration have become disgruntled with current preparation programs that are: (a) often little more than collections of diverse and poorly integrated classes lacking clear focus and purpose;[39] (b) delivered to prospective administrators with little thought or regard for sequence of skills and knowledge;[40] and (c) provided to students at times and through instructional approaches least conducive to learning.[41] In seeking a more appropriate system to deliver the new knowledge base they envision, reformers have again turned toward professional schools for examples:

Schools of education, and particularly departments of educational administration, must turn back to the schools and establish relationships such as exist between professional schools in the university and their practitioners. We should be proud to become the professional backbone of the schools. Schools of education must become full-fledged professional schools, not pseudo arts and science colleges. . . . Once we accept the idea that schools of education must become *professional* schools granting *professional* degrees, we can get squared away on the job of preparing professional school administrators.[42]

The model explicated by reformers clearly separates the Ph.D. (research) and the Ed.D. (professional) degrees. The latter program is designed to "differ from that of researchers because it must emphasize the application of knowledge and skills in clinical rather than academic situations."[43] A further objective of the new preparation model is the codification of knowledge into a sequential body of understandings and skills. Educational administration students would progress through these knowledge continuums like students in other professions; that is, in the proper sequence, in cohorts, and in full-time study.[44] Instructional approaches emphasized in other professional schools would become integral components of the delivery model. In addition, the professional delivery model offers hope for overcoming two of the most intransigent problems in educational administration— the absence of robust clinical preparation[45] and the lack of integration between the training and delivery arms.[46]

A third theme that colors almost every aspect of administrative reform is the need to raise standards. From recruitment of students, to program quality, to the selection of men and women for administrative positions, the profession's standards have been found wanting.

Reform reports that address the recruitment and selection procedures used by educational administration programs have found them to be either absent, pro forma, or ineffective.[47] Processes are often informal, haphazard, and casual.[48] Because leader recruitment programs are often lacking, prospective administrators are often self-selected.[49] Few efforts are made to attract women and minorities.[50] Entry is not competitive and completion of programs is easy. The results of low standards for recruitment and selection have been amply documented: prospective administrators of considerably below average ability compared to peers in other graduate school departments;[51] reduced standards in other phases of preparation programs;[52] men and women who are politically conservative and averse to risk-taking and personal accountability;[53] and a lack of minorities in administrative roles at every level of the profession.[54]

The reports of the National Association of Secondary School Principals and the National Commission on Excellence in Educational

Administration pointed to outdated content, lack of sequenced coursework, and the absence of meaningful clinical experiences. Clark concluded that course content, in addition to being outdated, is often banal.[55] The American Association of Colleges for Teacher Education noted that there is much redundancy in coursework. Overall assessments of the quality of preparation programs are not flattering. The California Commission on the Teaching Profession[56] labeled training for the administrative credential as "hopelessly inadequate." Peterson and Finn reported that many graduates consider their programs "to have been easy, boring, and only intermittently useful to them in their work."[57]

The lack of entry requirements and content standards is reinforced by a delivery structure—part-time, evening coursework—that promotes low expectations on the part of professors and students. Clark has made explicit what others have feared to verbalize: "We have given up holding tired, end-of-the-day students to graduate level performance."[58] This self-reinforcing cycle of diminished expectations often leads professors to ask less and less of students and students to become more and more cynical about their university preparation for administrative jobs. Compounding this problem is a professoriate in educational administration that: (a) is unwilling or unable to improve the delivery structure (and content);[59] and (b) has bargained away expectations and standards in exchange for high enrollments and compliant student behavior.[60]

It is not surprising that programs which are easy to enter and do not require much of students should also have low standards in the area of monitoring student progress. Assessments of student progress at the key junctures of their programs are either absent or conducted in a perfunctory fashion. Meaningful competency tests on needed skills are conspicuous by their absence in most preparation programs. The assumption is that rigorous and appropriate standards will be applied at later stages in the process of moving toward administrative employment—especially at the dissertation, certification, and job-selection steps. Unfortunately, this assumption is inaccurate.[61]

In many states, certification "is little more than a pro forma requirement"[62] and it does not provide rigorous standards for the licensure of prospective administrators. The National Commission on Excellence in Educational Administration concluded that "it is difficult to think of another profession in which [certification] screening is so poorly executed."[63]

A number of the major reform reports have reported that the

standards employed to screen job applicants are no higher than those used in the major steps leading to this activity. Boyer labeled the selection process as "quixotic" and subject to a cloudy "set of local and custom-bound criteria."[64] The most damaging assessment of standards employed in the selection of school leaders was provided by Baltzell and Dentler in a study conducted for the National Institute of Education. Specifically, they found that neither educational leadership, merit, nor equity criteria characterized the selection process.[65] Rather, they reported candidates were selected in terms of goodness of fit with local values and image.

Reform reports suggest the quality of programs for the professional development of practicing school administrators leaves much to be desired. This area has been the subject of more reform initiatives during the 1980s than any other topic in school administration. The lack of time to study, the absence of systematic professional development opportunities, and the need for greater district support and enhanced incentives have all been noted time and time again.

A Review of the Reform Agenda
Related to Educational Leadership

In this chapter we have outlined the scope and nature of calls for reform in school administration in the 1980s. We began by examining the forces that raised problems to the surface and sustained reform efforts. We reported how the larger reform debate has contributed to illuminating school administration issues and helped spawn leadership improvement proposals more tightly integrated with other important areas of education. We revealed how the reexamination of the appropriate operating structures for schools has raised fundamental questions about leadership and management. We also saw how factors endemic to educational administration were contributing to the school leadership reform agenda. Specifically, we examined how the widespread dissatisfaction with the status quo in school administration—especially the estrangement between the training and delivery arms of the profession—has influenced the debate about needed changes. We developed the link between reform initiatives and lessons from successful schools, especially in terms of ideas for how administrators should work with the teaching core and how they should spend their time.

Next we turned our attention to the major reform reports and studies of the 1980s to see what commonalities they contained for improvement of the profession. Three major themes were uncovered—leadership, professionalism, and standards. We discussed how calls for more and better leadership have dominated the reform literature. We reported that there is much consistency in suggestions that administrators, particularly principals, turn more of their attention to the internal workings of their schools, especially to the central mission of teaching and learning. The second major reform theme, the professionalization of school administration, was distilled from calls to reshape preparation programs in the mold of other professional schools—through both the development of a knowledge base grounded in practice and the establishment of a professional school preparation model. We noted how the unification of the academic and field components of the profession is a central tenet of professionalization. Finally, we viewed an array of issues that illustrated the third theme of the reform proposals—the establishment of more rigorous standards at every phase of the profession, from recruitment of students into preparation programs to employment selection.

On the surface, the reforms being proposed—raising the intellectual and educational capital in the profession and moving toward practice-driven models of knowledge development and delivery—offer much promise for improving not only educational administration but the whole of schooling as well. Yet, as with most treatments of educational issues, the easiest job is the analysis of problems. Real work, like plotting appropriate directions for improvements based on these analyses, is more difficult. Completion of the activities to ensure that the new visions are realized will be exceedingly difficult business indeed. The "theory movement" produced so little, compared with expectations, not because of inappropriate specification of problems (e.g., the naked empiricism of the 1940s and 1950s), nor because the direction it charted was flawed. It failed to reach its potential because the difficult day-in-and-day-out work of developing and translating theory was not done well enough by sufficient numbers of professionals. The same fate may lie in store for the "professional movement" if a large enough number of professors and practitioners do not carry forward with the sometimes tedious, sometimes exhilarating work of authentic transformation.

I close with a note about two expansions in this new professional movement in school administration. The first is to bring educational administration programs and views of school leaders in line with the latest wave of educational reform in the 1980s. Scholars like Michael Kirst at Stanford and Willis Hawley at Vanderbilt have pointed to the need to expand reform beyond standards (wave one) and the restructuring of schools (wave two). They have called for a child-centered reform agenda (wave three). I believe that this agenda provides a robust framework to develop, organize, and unpack the appropriate content to be employed in professional schools of education generally and in departments of educational administration specifically. It is a framework that is consistent with the philosophy and content of this yearbook.

A second expansion is drawn from the work of Luvern Cunningham at Ohio State University. Cunningham and his colleagues are engaged in efforts to apply interprofessional lenses (as opposed to the interdisciplinary frames from the theory movement) to the solution of important problems in education.[66] This approach, especially in conjunction with a child-centered educational agenda, offers much hope for enhancing the profession of school administration and the wisdom of the men and women who lead our schools.

FOOTNOTES

1. Daniel Griffiths, Robert Stout, and Patrick Forsyth, eds., *Leaders for America's Schools: The Report and Papers of the National Commission on Excellence in Educational Administration* (Berkeley, CA: McCutchan, 1988).

2. National Commission on Excellence in Educational Administration, *Leaders for America's Schools* (Tempe, AZ: University Council for Educational Administration, 1987).

3. Kent Peterson and Chester Finn, "Principals, Superintendents, and the Administrator's Art," *Public Interest*, no. 79 (Spring 1985): 42.

4. Joseph Murphy and Philip Hallinger, eds., *Approaches to Administrative Training* (Albany, NY: State University of New York Press, 1987).

5. The designation of a reform report as "wave 1" or "wave 2" has more to do with the nature of the suggestions than with the date of publication. However, given this caveat, there is a very strong correlation between publication date of the major reform reports and the underlying principles and content of their recommendations. See J. Green, *The Next Wave: A Synopsis of Recent Education Reform Reports* (Denver, CO: Education Commission of the States, 1987). See also, Willis Hawley, "Missing Pieces of the Educational Reform Agenda: Or Why the First and Second Waves May Miss the Boat," *Educational Administration Quarterly* 24 (November 1988): 416-437.

6. See R. P. Gousha, A. H. Jones, and P. L. LoPresti, "Where Are We and Where Are We Going in School Administration Preparation in the United States?" (Paper presented at the Annual Meeting of the American Educational Research Association, San Francisco, 1986); National Governors' Association, *Time for Results: The Governors' 1991 Report on Education, Chairman's Summary* (Washington, DC: National Governors' Association, 1986); idem, *Time for Results: The Governors' 1991 Report on Education* (Washington, DC: National Governors' Association, 1987); J. Underwood, "State Legislative Responses to Educational Reform Literature," in *Recent Advances in Educational Administration*, Vol. 1, ed. Linda Lotto and P. W. Thurston (Greenwich, CT: JAI Press, 1988).

7. Association for Supervision and Curriculum Development, *School Reform Policy: A Call for Reason* (Alexandria, VA: Association for Supervision and Curriculum Development, 1986), pp. 32, 34.

8. See American Association of Colleges for Teacher Education, *School Leadership Preparation: A Preface for Action* (Washington, DC: American Association of Colleges for Teacher Education, 1988); John E. Chubb, "Why the Current Wave of School Reform Will Fail," *Public Interest*, no. 90 (Winter 1988): 28-49; David Clark and J. M. Meloy, "Renouncing Bureaucracy: A Democratic Structure for Leadership in Schools," in *Schooling for Tomorrow: Directing Reforms to Issues That Count*, ed. Thomas Sergiovanni and J. H. Moore (Boston: Allyn and Bacon, 1989); National Governors' Association, *Time for Results*; Michael W. Sedlak, Christopher W. Wheeler, Diana C. Pullin, and Philip A. Cusick, *Selling Students Short: Classroom Bargains and Academic Reform in the American High School* (New York: Teachers College Press, 1986); Theodore Sizer, *Horace's Compromise: The Dilemma of the American High School* (Boston: Houghton-Mifflin, 1984).

9. Anthony Downs, *Inside Bureaucracy* (Boston: Little, Brown, 1967); Jack Frymier, "Bureaucracy and the Neutering of Teachers," *Phi Delta Kappan* 69 (September 1987): 9-14; Sizer, *Horace's Compromise*.

10. Chubb, "Why the Current Wave of School Reform Will Fail"; Sedlak et al., *Selling Students Short*.

11. See Carnegie Task Force on Teaching as a Profession, *A Nation Prepared: Teachers for the 21st Century* (New York: Carnegie Forum on Education and the Economy, 1986); Carnegie Foundation for the Advancement of Teaching, *Report Card on School Reform: The Teachers Speak* (New York: Carnegie Foundation for the Advancement of Teaching, 1988); Holmes Group, *Tomorrow's Schools: A Report from the Holmes Group* (E. Lansing, MI: Holmes Group, 1986); National Commission for Excellence in Teacher Education, *A Call for Change in Teacher Education* (Washington, DC: American Association of Colleges for Teacher Education, 1985); Arthur E. Wise, "Professional Teaching: A New Paradigm for the Management of Education," in *Schooling for Tomorrow*, ed. Sergiovanni and Moore.

12. Holmes Group, *Tomorrow's Teachers*, p. 67.

13. David Kearns, "A Business Perspective on American Schooling," *Education Week* 7 (April 20, 1988): 32, 34; idem, "An Education Recovery Plan for America," *Phi Delta Kappan* 69 (April 1988): 565-570.

14. Chubb, "Why the Current Wave of School Reform Will Fail"; Peter Mortimore et al., *Schools Matter: The Junior Years* (London: Open Books, 1988).

15. Ernest Boyer, *High School: A Report on Secondary Education in America* (New York: Harper and Row, 1983); John I. Goodlad, *A Place Called School* (New York: McGraw-Hill, 1984); Sizer, *Horace's Compromise*.

16. Chubb, "Why the Current Wave of School Reform Will Fail," p. 37.

17. Clark and Meloy, "Renouncing Bureaucracy"; Ann Lieberman, "Teachers and Principals: Turf, Tension, and New Tasks," *Phi Delta Kappan* 69 (May 1988): 648-653; National Commission on Excellence in Educational Administration, *Leaders for Tomorrow's Schools*.

18. See David Clark, "Charge to the Study Group of the National Policy Board of Educational Administration" (Unpublished manuscript, 1988); William Gerritz, Julie Koppich, and James Guthrie, *Preparing California School Leaders: An Analysis of Supply, Demand, and Training* (Berkeley, CA: Policy Analysis for California Education, 1984); Murphy and Hallinger, *Approaches to Administrative Training*; Peterson and Finn, "Principals, Superintendents, and the Administrator's Art."

19. Norman Boyan, "Follow the Leader: Commentary on Research in Educational Administration," *Educational Researcher* 10 (February 1981): 6-13, 21; Jack Culbertson, "Antecedents of the Theory Movement," *Educational Administration Quarterly* 17 (Winter 1981): 25-47; Erwin Miklos, "Evolution in Administrator Preparation Programs," *Educational Administration Quarterly* 19 (Summer 1983): 153-177.

20. Roald Campbell, "The Professorship in Educational Administration: A Personal View," *Educational Administration Quarterly* 17 (Winter 1981): 124; F. Carver, "The Evaluation of the Study of Educational Administration" (Paper presented at the EAAA Allerton House Conference, University of Illinois at Urbana-Champaign, 1988); Bruce Cooper and William Boyd, "The Evolution of Training for School Administrators," in *Approaches to Administrative Training*, ed. Murphy and Hallinger; Robert Crowson and R. Bruce McPherson, "The Legacy of the Theory Movement: Learning from the New Tradition," in *Approaches to Administrative Training*, ed. Murphy and Hallinger.

21. Edwin Bridges, "The Nature of Leadership," in *Educational Administration: The Developing Decades*, ed. Luvern Cunningham, Walter Hack, and Raphael Nystrand (Berkeley, CA: McCutchan, 1977); Dale Mann, "What Peculiarities in Educational Administration Make It Difficult to Profess: An Essay," *Journal of Educational Administration* 13 (May 1975): 139-147; Peterson and Finn, "Principals, Superintendents, and the Administrator's Art"; Nancy Pitner, *Training of the School Administrator: State of the Art*, Occasional Paper (Eugene, OR: Center for Educational Policy and Management, 1982).

22. Carver, "The Evaluation of the Study of Educational Administration," p. 1.

23. William Boyd, "What School Administrators Do and Don't Do: Implications for Effective Schools," *Canadian Administrator* 22 (March 1983): 1-4; Murphy and Hallinger, *Approaches to Administrative Training*.

24. Arthur Blumberg, "The Craft of School Administration and Some Other Rambling Thoughts," *Educational Administration Quarterly* 20 (Fall 1984): 24-40; Edwin Bridges, "Research on the School Administrator: The State of the Art," *Educational Administration Quarterly* 18 (Summer 1982): 12-33; Keith Goldhammer, "Evolution in the Profession," *Educational Administration Quarterly* 19 (Summer 1983): 249-272; Daniel Griffiths, *Educational Administration: Reform PDQ or RIP*, Occasional Paper No. 8312 (Tempe, AZ: University Council for Educational Administration, 1988).

25. Boyer, *High School*, p. 219.

26. Joseph Murphy, "Principal Instructional Leadership," in *Recent Advances in Educational Administration*, vol. 1, ed. Lotto and Thurston.

27. National Commission on Excellence in Teacher Education, *A Call for Change in Teacher Education*, p. 34.

28. Mortimer Adler, *The Paideia Proposal* (New York: Macmillan, 1982), pp. 63-64.

29. Bridges, "Research on the School Administrator."

30. Boyer, *High School*, p. 223.

31. Sizer, *Horace's Compromise*, p. 198.

32. American Association of Colleges for Teacher Education, *School Leadership Preparation*, p. 1.

33. Joseph Murphy, "Methodological, Measurement, and Conceptual Problems in the Study of Instructional Leadership," *Educational Evaluation and Policy Analysis* 10 (Summer 1988): 117-139.

34. Murphy, "Principal Instructional Leadership."

35. See Carnegie Task Force on Teaching as a Profession, *A Nation Prepared*; Carnegie Foundation for the Advancement of Teaching, *Report Card on School Reform*; Green, *The Next Wave*.

36. Goldhammer, "Evolution in the Profession"; National Association of Secondary School Principals, *Performance Based Preparation of Principals: A Framework for Improvement* (Reston, VA: National Association of Secondary School Principals, 1985).

37. Crowson and McPherson, "The Legacy of the Theory Movement," p. 46.

38. Geraldine Clifford and James Guthrie, "Strategies for Reforming Schools of Education," *Education Week* 7 (June 8, 1988): 32.

39. Charles Achilles, "Forecast: Stormy Weather Ahead in Educational Administration," *Issues in Education* 2 (Fall 1984): 127-135; Cooper and Boyd, "The Evolution of Training for School Administrators"; National Association of Secondary School Principals, *Performance Based Preparation of Principals*; U. S. Department of Education, *American Education: Making It Work* (Washington, DC: U. S. Department of Education, 1988).

40. Peterson and Finn, "Principals, Superintendents, and the Administrator's Art"; Pitner, *Training of the School Administrator*.

41. American Association of Colleges for Teacher Education, *School Leadership Preparation*; David A. Erlandson and L. Witters-Churchill, "The Texas NASSP Study" (Paper presented at the annual meeting of the National Association of Secondary School Principals, March 1988); Michael Y. Nunnery, "Reform of K-12 Educational Administrator Preparation: Some Basic Questions," *Journal of Research and Development in Education* 15, no. 2 (1982): 44-52; U. S. Department of Education, *American Education: Making It Work*.

42. Griffiths, *Educational Administration: Reform PDQ or RIP*, p. 10.

43. National Commission on Excellence in Educational Administration, *Leaders for America's Schools*, p. 19.

44. Clark, "Charge to the Study Group"; Griffiths, *Educational Administration: Reform PDQ or RIP*.

45. John Daresh, "The Practicum in Preparing Educational Administrators: A Status Report" (Paper presented at the annual meeting of the Eastern Educational Research Association, Boston, 1987); David Erlandson, "Language, Experience, and Administrator Preparation," *Planning and Changing* 10 (Fall 1979): 150-156; John Peper, "Clinical Education for School Superintendents and Principals: The Missing Link," in *Leaders for America's Schools*, ed. Griffiths et al.

46. Carver, "The Evaluation of the Study of Educational Administration"; Goldhammer, "Evolution in the Profession"; National Commission on Excellence in Educational Administration, *Leaders for America's Schools*.

47. National Commission on Excellence in Educational Administration, *Leaders for America's Schools*.

48. Cooper and Boyd, "The Evolution of Training for School Administrators"; Gerritz et al., *Preparing California School Leaders*; Goodlad, *A Place Called School*.

49. Achilles, "Forecast: Stormy Weather Ahead in Educational Administration"; Clark, "Charge to the Study Group"; National Commission on Excellence in Educational Administration, *Leaders for America's Schools*.

50. American Association of Colleges for Teacher Education, *School Leadership Preparation*.

51. Griffiths, *Educational Administration: Reform PDQ or RIP*; Richard A. Rossmiller, "Some Contemporary Trends and Their Implications for the Preparation of Educational Administrators," *UCEA Review* 27 (Winter 1986): 2-3.

52. Cooper and Boyd, "The Evolution of Training for School Administrators."

53. Achilles, "Forecast: Stormy Weather Ahead in Educational Administration"; U. S. Department of Education, *American Education: Making It Work*.

54. Griffiths, *Educational Administration: Reform PDQ or RIP*.

55. Clark, "Charge to the Study Group."

56. U. S. Department of Education, *American Education: Making It Work*.

57. Peterson and Finn, "Principals, Superintendents, and the Administrator's Art."

58. Clark, "Charge to the Study Group," p. 4.

59. Martha McCarthy, "The Professoriate in Educational Administration: Current Status and Challenges Ahead," *UCEA Review* 28 (Winter 1987): 2-6.

60. Mann, "What Peculiarities in Educational Administration Make It Difficult to Profess."

61. D. C. Baltzell and R. A. Dentler, *Selecting American School Principals: A Sourcebook for Educators* (Washington, DC: U. S. Department of Education, 1983).

62. U. S. Department of Education, *American Education: Making It Work*, p. 17.

63. National Commission for Excellence in Educational Administration, *Leaders for America's Schools*, p. 25.

64. Boyer, *High School*.

65. Baltzell and Dentler, *Selecting American School Principals*.

66. Luvern L. Cunningham, Mark H. Spencer, and Sarah Battison, "Expanding Professional Awareness: The Commission on Interprofessional Education and Practice," *Quarterly Report of the Mershon Center, Ohio State University* 7, no. 4 (Summer 1982): 1-7.

CHAPTER XII

Reform from the Center

WILLIAM R. TORBERT

The contributions to this volume attack the problem of providing quality mass education from all sides.

From Cunningham's review in chapter 1 of previous yearbooks of the National Society for the Study of Education, through Mitchell's sardonic reflections on educators' fixation with the prefix "re" in chapter 3, to Murphy's listing of thirty-two reform reports issued during the 1980s in chapter 11, the foregoing chapters repeatedly document the ongoing and intensifying—but at the same time faltering and despairing—attempts to provide quality mass education in the United States.

Educational reform attempts to attack the problem from all sides, but the situation continues to grow worse.

One reason for the current state of affairs is that, contrary to our continuing lullaby to ourselves, we are no longer a young nation. In fact, not only is our population aging, but, as a system of government, the United States is virtually the oldest on the planet. Old age inevitably brings decay and often brings decadence as well.

The only specific that wards off decadence is a moral, religious, and educational vision that locates each participant—whether person, family, faction, profession, or organization—as serving, and as responsible to, some higher calling than one's own comfort, pleasure, or self-interest. Democratic capitalism is an ideology without any such vision of superordinate, common good.[1] It is an ideology that releases youthful vigor from constraint; it is an ideology that guards against spurious and totalitarian definitions of a "common" good; but it is also an ideology that, with increasing age, invites decadent self-absorption and a preoccupation with entitlement rather than service. Such is the cultural condition of the United States political economy today.

A second reason for the current state of affairs and the relative failure of educational reform stems directly from the first. The decadent approach to problem solving is to keep the process as removed from oneself as possible. The implicit reasoning is something like "I am not part of the problem, but part of the solution. It's good of me to care at all, and this in itself indicates that my position is beyond reproach. It would certainly, therefore, be unjust to threaten my entitlements or to suggest any solution that creates any significant inconvenience for me and mine." Of course, to state such an attitude explicitly is to make it sound more suspicious than it does when felt implicitly. In any event, the eventual outcome of such an approach to problem solving is to attack the problem ineffectually from all sides, while all centers (all selves and social units felt from within) remain protected against significant reform. Thus, the educational problem continues to grow worse *precisely because* we are attacking it from all sides and not from the center.

Reform from the Center

Significant educational reform can only come from the center, from all centers.

Each social unit—person, family, faction, profession, or organization—with a stake in quality mass education must, first and foremost, study and reform its own actions. Each social unit within the educational process must become truly self-educating in its practice. To do so, each must generate within itself a community of inquiry that tests, in an ongoing, real-time fashion, the relationships among its vision, strategies, practices, and outcomes.[2] Discovering significant incongruities among these qualitatively different layers (and there *are* always such incongruities to be discovered, even in the most high-performing of organizations) will motivate experiments and reforms toward greater awareness, efficacy, and integrity. From time to time, such incongruities will suggest even more profound changes for the person or organization engaging in self-study: a developmental transformation whereby the fundamental assumptions under which the unit has been operating are revealed and overturned when necessary. A true community of inquiry within an ongoing community of social practice will be one that can accept such fundamental change within itself. This overall conception relates closely to Mitchell's proposals at the end of chapter 2.

Once such a process of reform from the center is well underway, that social unit becomes capable of creating liberating structures within its sphere of action and authority. Liberating structures are organizational systems (whether within a particular classroom, a particular school, or a particular profession) that simultaneously motivate high performance and develop a capacity for reform from the center on the part of participants.[3] Obviously, such structures must be profoundly complex and ironic, and hence supremely challenging to create and manage, for it would be contradictory to speak of a "structure" that forces "self-reform."

There will always be many pressures directed against reform from the center, never more so than in a decadent society where the dominant ideology subtly obscures the possibility of such self-reform. Although these pressures must be recognized and responded to, they do not constitute a rational argument against the process of self-reform, for self-reform is the process for generating increasingly efficacious and responsible initiatives. At the outset of self-reform, the social unit typically feels overwhelmed by divergent pressures and virtually incapable of sustained, focused initiative. The process of self-reform generates the capacity to withstand and overcome the very pressures that incapacitate otherwise comparable social units.

This perspective on reform helps to organize many of the otherwise puzzling findings within educational research, as well as many of the proposals advanced in the earlier chapters of this book. As Thomas Hoffer and James Coleman show in many ways in chapter 6, individual schools and subgroups within schools can influence students' behaviors independently of aggregate community effects and even of the students' own individual predispositions. In other words, positive educational quality can be generated at all points (all centers) in the system, irrespective of external conditions and pressures.

This recognition relates directly to the many proposals for increasing the empowerment of individual teachers, principals, and school buildings, proposals reiterated throughout this volume and especially in chapters 8, 9, and 10. The dilemma is how to accomplish such empowerment while simultaneously raising standards. Only an individual and institutional process of self-reform in the midst of ongoing practice can simultaneously accomplish these dual objectives.

Obviously, this process of self-reform must somehow be difficult at both the personal and organizational levels, or else its practice would be widespread and recognizable. Why and how it is difficult will also seem immediately obvious to many readers from the very term "self-reform." Self-reform implies a continuing vulnerability to inquiry, criticism, and the turbulence of transformation. To most persons, such vulnerability connotes, in turn, discomfort, disequilibrium, and pain. Hence, it is natural for persons and organizations to shy away from reform from the center.

According to Piaget's and Kegan's developmental theory,[4] however, it is also natural (but a long, slow, and uncertain process) for persons to reform themselves from the center, dethroning their reigning assumptions at any given stage of development and relegating these to explicit and manageable variables within a wider system of assumptions at the next stage. Why, then, does the tendency to shy away from reform from the center seem to supercede the attractiveness of such reform?

Why We Shy Away from Reform from the Center

The first reason why adults and educational institutions shy away from reform from the center, or self-reform, is that virtually no leaders or organizations support such a strategy. Piaget's stages of development refer to childhood development. At each childhood developmental transformation there are adults and contexts supportive of the qualitatively new kind of meaning the child begins to make of self and world. By contrast, we are here speaking of development within those very adults and those very contexts toward stages beyond Piaget's final "formal operations" stage.[5] Although these later stages are inherently self-reforming once they are reached, transformation *toward* these stages is a delicate process that requires help over extended periods from mentors and organizational systems already at these stages. Yet research finds very few adults (e.g., teachers, administrators) or organizational contexts operating beyond the "formal operations" stage.[6] School personnel and schools that edge toward such self-reform find virtually no models or support for the qualitatively new kind of meaning they begin to make.

This new kind of meaning is characterized by strong paradox, that is, by opposites that require one another rather than mutually excluding one another. For example, late stage educational leaders (e.g., Gandhi, Pope John XXIII, Lech Walesa) exhibit passionately held theories *and* the artistic practice of inquiry, with strong theory and strong practice mutually reforming one another through their interaction.[7]

A second reason why people are more likely to shy away from than embrace self-reform is that the general culture of discourse does not point toward the existence of strong paradox. This reason interacts with the first reason in a chicken and egg fashion. Because there are few adults and institutions at postformal stages, postformal discourse characterized by strong paradox is rare. And, vice versa, because of the rarity of postformal discourse, operational concepts that are fundamental to organizing and educating become reified in ways that obstruct adult and organizational development beyond formal operations.

For example, the terms "power" and "freedom" have lost virtually all vestiges of their original postformal, paradoxical meaning and are usually viewed today as mutually exclusive opposites. "Power" has come to mean unilateral, unidirectional causation of change in another,[8] reducing the other's freedom. Mitchell has explored closely in chapter 2 how this impoverished notion of power creates a caricature of educational authority in many of our schools. In a parallel but opposite loss of meaning, "freedom" has come to mean merely freedom from constraint (freedom from external powers that unilaterally control one's behavior).

Power, today, rarely refers to the mutual, dialectical self-reforming causation inherent in the educational power of Plato's dialogues, of Nietzsche's self-overcoming will to power, of liberating structures, and of the process of development itself. (Piaget and Kegan both show how developmental causation is interactional, not unilateral.) Freedom, today, rarely refers to the positive, postformal developmental freedom to act with "virtuosity," that is, virtuously, excellently, and effectively all at once (Plato's concept of *arete*,[9] Nietzsche's notion of "Caesar with the soul of Christ"[10]).

Any truly educational organization that supports development will in fact intertwine power and freedom in a form that I have named "liberating structure." (See above and footnote 3.) But such structures, which are simultaneously capable of reforming themselves and of engaging their participants in self-reform, become impossible to imagine—let alone implement—so long as "power" and "freedom" are assumed to be opposites.

There is yet a third reason why the tendency to shy away from reform from the center seems to supercede its attractiveness. This reason concerns the scholarly climate today surrounding the conduct of social science in general and of educational research in particular. Reform from the center, or self-reform, requires an integration of ongoing action and ongoing inquiry amidst real-time organizational pressures. The scientific issues of reliability, validity, and generalizability must be faced amidst such pressures, not apart from them. Such an integration of action and inquiry—whether it be called "action inquiry," "collaborative inquiry," "action science," or "reflective practice"[11]—represents a fundamentally different approach to social science than either the quantitative, empirical approach or the qualitative, phenomenological approach. Like the ironic, dialectical process characteristic of "liberating structures," the dialectic of "action inquiry" is virtually impossible to imagine, let alone implement, within the world of research and scholarship today. Yet educational research and colleges of education will remain fundamentally uneducational—not supporting adult and organizational self-reform and development and not responding to James Guthrie's criticisms at the end of chapter 10—unless they explore the paradoxical demand of action inquiry.

In other words, we tend to shy away from reform from the center, not because of a lack of external resources or a surfeit of external pressures, but because of a lack of leaders, institutions, and methods that model, support, and generate reform from the center. Reform from the center during the 1990s is a developmental challenge, not just for particular persons and organizations, but for our society as a whole. Cunningham's chapter on reconstituting local government suggests one way to approach reform from the center.

John Dewey's Practice as an Incomplete Illustration of Self-Reform

A backward glance at John Dewey's practice can provide us with a slightly more concrete illustration of what reform from the center means; of how difficult reform from the center is to recreate by imitation; of how easily someone dedicated to self-reform passes beyond the understanding of others; and of how easily that person's process of self-reform can cease, even when he is as explicitly and intelligently dedicated to such a process as was John Dewey.

We all know—at varying degrees of distance—that John Dewey is quite probably the foremost philosopher produced by this continent. We call his philosophy "pragmatism," know that it had something to do with learning the truth by active experimentation, and that it led to an educational reform movement called "progressive education."

Fewer know that Dewey himself directed a school that embodied this mode of education—the laboratory school at the University of Chicago. Even fewer know that the practice of this school was not to implement any particular ideology, such as what later came to be known as "progressive education," but rather to observe constantly and discuss the practice of the individual teachers and the community as a whole.[12]

In short, what was so dynamic, provocative, and powerful about

Dewey's practice was that it constituted an institutionalized and individualized process of self-reform. Precisely this element of his practice was lost, however, when it was translated first (by Dewey) into a fully explicit, didactic philosophy and then (by readers) into an ideology. Gradually, a caricature of the original practice spread widely: in place of the positively empowering process of active experimentation, many progressive schools and teachers offered students a negative freedom from constraint that came to be called "permissiveness."

In the meantime—and this is even less known—Dewey in his late fifties, while at Columbia's Teachers College, for a time worried that his formal philosophy, for all that it rhetorically espoused the importance of practice, was in fact so distant from a description of self-reforming practice that it lent itself to misinterpretation. Why was his theory so shaded a window to his practice? Why had he himself put more store by his philosophizing than by his practicing, when his practice was in fact perhaps closer to his essential genius? How might this incongruity be rectified?

Prompted by questions like these, Dewey began working with a man named Alexander who helped persons experience the relationship between their bodies and their heads through various breathing, posture, and eye-hand coordination exercises. Dewey found these exercises "the most humiliating experience of my life, intellectually speaking. For to find that one is unable to execute directions . . . in doing such a seemingly simple act as to sit down, when one is using all the mental capacity which one prides oneself upon possessing, is not an experience congenial to one's vanity."[13] Dewey was discovering that, despite his devotion to reflecting about practice (not to mention reflecting about reflecting about practice), there was at each moment a yawning gap of which he had heretofore been unaware between his mind and his body.

Dewey gradually came to feel how his head, too, was embodied— how thought occurs within the context, always, of one's daily practice, how true thought is not general, context-free philosophy or science, but rather poetry, thought reformed from the center by an awareness of its relation to one's current breath, passion, and action. Dewey produced considerable poetry in the years following the beginning of his work with Alexander, especially during a passionate, secret (and perhaps not physically consummated) love affair with the Polish immigrant novelist Anzia Yezierska.[14]

That these events at least verged on the transformational for him is repeatedly suggested by the critical significance and passion with which his own references imbued them. Prior to meeting Alexander and Yezierska, Dewey had intellectually hated any philosophical dualism between thought and action, but had recognized in himself the predominance of intellectuality ("a onesidedness I regret but am too old to rectify"[15]) as well as a certain affectlessness. Of Alexander's subsequent influence, Dewey would write, "My theories of mind-body, of the coordination of the self and of the place of ideas in inhibition and control of overt action required contact with the work of F. M. Alexander . . . to transform them into realities."[16] Of Yezierska's influence, he would write, poetically, "I am overcome as by thunder/ Of my blood that surges/ From my cold heart to my clear head" and "Had not rich fall[17] her ripe fruit brought/ As proof of time's fulfilled good/ Life's inner speech I had not caught."[18]

But if, through his relationship to Yezierska, Dewey caught something of "life's inner speech," the awareness of how passion interrelates thought and action, he may soon have let go his tenuous grip. At least, he soon ended his relationship with her. In her *Love in the Promised Land*, Mary Dearborn calls this development "tragic emotional cowardice" on Dewey's part.[19] The circumstances are fascinating. Dewey hired the Polish immigrant Yezierska to participate in a study of Polish immigrants in Philadelphia, along with a number of his leading doctoral students. But he increasingly distanced himself from her as she became increasingly critical of the parallel distance that the study's scientific methods created between the researchers and the immigrants. In the end, Dewey reclaimed the correspondence between the two of them, threw his poems in the trash (whence they were recovered and eventually published twenty-five years after his death), and took a trip to the Orient that lasted several years. Instead of discovering a new type of engaged social research, as would later be named "collaborative inquiry" or "action science," Dewey took the conventional academic route toward objectivity — greater distance.

As difficult as such things are to judge at a distance, it appears that Dewey stopped short of a developmental transformation from the "Strategist" stage (a stage that few enough adults reach, where one seeks intellectually to bridge the gap between theory and practice) to the "Magician" stage (an extremely rare position, reached perhaps by Gandhi and Pope John XXIII, where one maintains an ongoing experiential alertness to the interplay of thought, passion, and practice in oneself and others).[20]

However, even Dewey's early efforts to integrate his theory and practice more profoundly through an ever self-awakening and self-reforming awareness were unpalatable to his peers, students, and emulators. They viewed his interest in the Alexander techniques as a peculiar eccentricity rather than as a "progressive" development on his part and as a potential aim for themselves. Most did not know about his relationship with Yezierska at all.

So, Dewey—one of the most practical philosophers since Socrates walked the streets of Athens and certainly the philosopher with the greatest impact on the American educational scene—was emulated widely in theory, but hardly at all in his practice of reform from the center at the University of Chicago laboratory school. Later, he himself would verge upon, but not complete, a further developmental transformation—a further reform from the center. This reform was so far removed from most people's conventional views of the practical that this time he was not emulated at all, despite his prior widespread influence and his continuing conviction that the entire corpus of his work pointed toward the experiential integration of mind and body. He himself discontinued his developmental transformation when its direction contradicted the norms of mainline social scientific method.

Conclusion

This version of the story of John Dewey suggests how seminal the challenge of reform from the center is.

First, individuals seeking to lead reform from the center must cultivate a self-study and self-reform process that generates an active awareness of their own intuitions, theories, ongoing actions, and effects on the environment and of the gaps among them. As we have seen, Dewey in his later life recognized his own incompleteness in this regard and began to explore, but evidently stopped short in the pursuit of, an experiential awareness that can listen to "life's inner speech."

Second, schools and other institutions that seek to model reform from the center in their operations must cultivate an analogous self-study or self-reform process, like the process at Dewey's University of Chicago laboratory school. But this process has proven difficult, if not impossible, to imitate. In a sense, it must be rediscovered through an experimental process in each institutional setting, yet few of us are oriented to value and to endure the struggles involved in such ongoing experimentation.

Finally, at the center of reform from the center, communities of inquiry based on a profoundly different model of social science than is current today must develop. I leave it to readers of this piece to judge how likely it is that such communities of inquiry will develop within our current university structures!

A major dilemma emerges. On the one hand, this essay and this volume as a whole suggests that only a process that can be named reform from the center will respond to the challenges to education and human development in the United States during the 1990s. On the other hand, all the evidence and reason we can adduce suggests that widespread reform from the center is highly improbable. The existence of such a sharp incongruity can be interpreted either as a sign that this counsel ought to be dismissed as impractical, or as a deflating counsel of despair, or as an invitation to transformational self-study with others. This chapter and other chapters in this volume have highlighted the invitation to self-study. This chapter has emphasized, further, that true educational leadership revels in paradox, rising to its challenge.

Reform from the center *is* an improbable future. But reform from the center *creates* improbable futures.

FOOTNOTES

1. Among the many authors to offer a similar argument are Robert Heilbronner, *The Making of Economic Society* (Englewood Cliffs, NJ: Prentice-Hall, 1980), and Richard Pascale and Anthony Athos, *The Art of Japanese Management* (New York: Simon & Schuster, 1981), and Lester Thurow, *The Zero Sum Society* (New York: Basic Books, 1980).

2. This notion of self-study in practice is presented in William Torbert, "The Role of Self-Study in Improving Managerial and Institutional Effectiveness," *Human Systems Management* 2 (1981): 72-82, and idem, "Interpersonal Competence," in *The Modern American College*, ed. Arthur Chickering (San Francisco: Jossey-Bass, 1981). The notion of creating communities of inquiry within communities of social practice, as an aim not just for educational organizations, but for all organizations and for social science as well, is presented in Chris Argyris, Robert Putnam, and Diana Smith, *Action Science* (San Francisco: Jossey-Bass, 1985). The openness to change at the center, characteristic of such communities, is illustrated by analogy in the Roman Emperor Hadrian's architectural masterpiece, the Pantheon, with its curved dome culminating at the center in an opening to the heavens above.

3. William Torbert, "Educating toward Shared Purpose, Self-Direction, and Quality Work: The Theory and Practice of Liberating Structure," *Journal of Higher Education* 49, no. 2 (1978): 109-135.

4. In *The Evolving Self* (Cambridge, MA: Harvard University Press, 1982), Robert Kegan has reinterpreted and expanded Piagetian theory in the most provocative and pedagogically useful formulation of the dynamics of development yet produced.

5. These "postformal" stages begin to receive definition and description in Charles N. Alexander and Ellen J. Langer, eds., *Higher Stages of Human Development* (New York: Oxford University Press, 1989), in Ken Wilber, *The Atman Project: A Transpersonal View of Human Development* (Wheaton, IL: Quest Books, 1980), and in William R. Torbert, *Managing the Corporate Dream: Restructuring for Long-Term Success* (Homewood, IL: Dow Jones-Irwin, 1987). See also, Michael L. Commons, Francis A. Richards, Cheryl Armon, eds., *Beyond Formal Operations: Late Adolescent and Adult Cognitive Development* (New York: Praeger, 1984).

6. Robert Kegan and Lisa Lahey, "Adult Leadership and Adult Development: A Constructivist View," in *Leadership: Multidisciplinary Perspectives*, ed. Barbara Kellerman (Englewood Cliffs, NJ: Prentice-Hall, 1984) and William R. Torbert, "Leading Organizational Transformation," in *Research in Organizational Change and Development*, Vol. 3, ed. Richard Woodman and William Pasmore (Greenwich, CT: JAI Press, 1989). The research presented in these studies suggests, very broadly, that no more than one in twenty adults and one in a hundred organizations evolve to a postformal stage.

7. For discussion of Gandhi, see Erik Erikson's *Gandhi's Truth* (New York: Norton, 1969). For discussion of Pope John XXIII, see Torbert, "Leading Organizational Transformation." For discussion of Walesa, see idem, "Executive Mind, Timely Action," *ReVision* 6, no. 1 (1983): 1-23.

8. In *Models of Man* (New York: Wiley, 1957), Nobel prize winner Herbert Simon illustrates this concept of power (and its close relationship to one kind of science) in the following definition: "For the assertion, 'A has power over B,' we can substitute the assertion 'A's behavior causes B's behavior.' If we can define the causal relationship, we can define . . . power. . . . [It is] a problem of giving operational meaning to the asymmetry of the relationship between independent and dependent variable" (p. 5). Here power and causality are both assumed to be, and defined as, unilateral and unidirectional.

9. For discussion of *arete* see Alasdair MacIntyre, *After Virtue* (Notre Dame, IN: University of Notre Dame Press, 1981), p. 115.

10. Friedrich Nietzsche, as quoted in Martin Heidegger, *What Is Called Thinking?* (New York: Harper Torchbook, 1968), p. 69.

11. Early attempts to define and illustrate an approach to social science that integrates action and inquiry include Donald Schon, *The Reflective Practitioner* (San Francisco: Jossey-Bass, 1983); Chris Argyris, *Inner Contradictions of Rigorous Research* (New York: Academic Press, 1980); Argyris, Putnam, and Smith, *Action Science*; William R. Torbert, "Why Educational Research Has Been So Uneducational: The Case for a New Model of Social Science Based on Collaborative Inquiry," and "Collaborative Metropolitan Desegregation," in *Human Inquiry: A Sourcebook of New Paradigm Research*, ed. Peter Reason and John Rowan (Chichester, England: Wiley, 1981); idem, "Executive Mind, Timely Action"; idem, *Learning from Experience* (New York: Columbia University Press, 1972); idem, *Creating a Community of Inquiry* (Chichester, England: Wiley, 1976); idem, *Managing the Corporate Dream*.

12. See the description of Dewey's school in Seymour Sarason, *The Culture of the School and the Problem of Change* (Boston: Allyn and Bacon, 1971).

13. From Dewey's "Introductory Word" in F. Mathias Alexander's *Man's Supreme Inheritance: Conscious Guidance and Control in Relation to Human Evolution in Civilization* (New York: Dutton, 1918), p. xvii.

14. As recently documented in Mary Dearborn's *Love in the Promised Land* (New York: Free Press, 1988).

15. Ibid., p. 110.

16. Ibid., p. 97. Quoted from Jane Dewey, "Biography of John Dewey," in *The Philosophy of John Dewey*, Vol. 1, ed. Paul Schilp (Evanston, IL: Northwestern University Press, 1939), p. 35.

17. A reference to Yezierska, whose birthday was in the autumn.

18. From Jo Ann Boydston, ed., *The Poems of John Dewey* (Carbondale, IL: Southern Illinois University Press, 1977), as quoted in Dearborn, *Love in the Promised Land*, pp. 110-111. The lines are from the poems entitled "Two Weeks" and "Autumn."

19. Dearborn, *Love in the Promised Land*, p. 119.

20. For further discussion of these late and rare adult developmental positions and of how Gandhi's and Pope John XXIII's practices reflect them, see Torbert, *Managing the Corporate Dream*, and idem, "Leading Organizational Transformation."

Name Index

Subject Index

INFORMATION ABOUT MEMBERSHIP IN THE SOCIETY

Membership in the National Society for the Study of Education is open to all who desire to receive its publications.

There are two categories of membership, Regular and Comprehensive. The Regular Membership (annual dues in 1990, $25) entitles the member to receive both volumes of the yearbook. The Comprehensive Membership (annual dues in 1990, $45) entitles the member to receive the two-volume yearbook and the two current volumes in the Series on Contemporary Educational Issues. For their first year of membership, full-time graduate students pay reduced dues in 1990 as follows: Regular, $20; Comprehensive, $40.

Membership in the Society is for the calendar year. Dues are payable on or before January 1 of each year.

New members are required to pay an entrance fee of $1, in addition to annual dues for the year in which they join.

Members of the Society include professors, researchers, graduate students, and administrators in colleges and universities; teachers, supervisors, curriculum specialists, and administrators in elementary and secondary schools; and a considerable number of persons not formally connected with educational institutions.

All members participate in the nomination and election of the six-member Board of Directors, which is responsible for managing the affairs of the Society, including the authorization of volumes to appear in the yearbook series. All members whose dues are paid for the current year are eligible for election to the Board of Directors.

Each year the Society arranges for meetings to be held in conjunction with the annual conferences of one or more of the major national educational organizations. All members are urged to attend these sessions. Members are also encouraged to submit proposals for future yearbooks or for volumes in the series on Contemporary Educational Issues.

Further information about the Society may be secured by writing to the Secretary-Treasurer, NSSE, 5835 Kimbark Avenue, Chicago, IL 60637.

RECENT PUBLICATIONS OF THE NATIONAL SOCIETY FOR THE STUDY OF EDUCATION

1. The Yearbooks

Eighty-ninth Yearbook (1990)

Part 1. *Textbooks and Schooling in the United States*. David L. Elliott and Arthur Woodward, editors. Cloth.

Part 2. *Educational Leadership and Changing Contexts of Families, Communities, and Schools*. Brad Mitchell and Luvern L. Cunningham, editors. Cloth.

Eighty-eighth Yearbook (1989)

Part 1. *From Socrates to Software: The Teacher as Text and the Text as Teacher*. Philip W. Jackson and Sophie Haroutunian-Gordon, editors. Cloth.

Part 2. *Schooling and Disability*. Douglas Biklen, Dianne Ferguson, and Alison Ford, editors. Cloth.

Eighty-seventh Yearbook (1988)

Part 1. *Critical Issues in Curriculum*. Laurel N. Tanner, editor. Cloth.

Part 2. *Cultural Literacy and the Idea of General Education*. Ian Westbury and Alan C. Purves, editors. Cloth.

Eighty-sixth Yearbook (1987)

Part 1. *The Ecology of School Renewal*. John I. Goodlad, editor. Cloth.

Part 2. *Society as Educator in an Age of Transition*. Kenneth D. Benne and Steven Tozer, editors. Cloth.

Eighty-fifth Yearbook (1986)

Part 1. *Microcomputers and Education*. Jack A. Culbertson and Luvern L. Cunningham, editors. Cloth.

Part 2. *The Teaching of Writing*. Anthony R. Petrosky and David Bartholomae, editors. Paper.

Eighty-fourth Yearbook (1985)

Part 1. *Education in School and Nonschool Settings*. Mario D. Fantini and Robert Sinclair, editors. Cloth.

Part 2. *Learning and Teaching the Ways of Knowing*. Elliot Eisner, editor. Paper.

Eighty-third Yearbook (1984)

Part 1. *Becoming Readers in a Complex Society*. Alan C. Purves and Olive S. Niles, editors. Cloth.

Part 2. *The Humanities in Precollegiate Education*. Benjamin Ladner, editor. Paper.

Eighty-second Yearbook (1983)

Part 1. *Individual Differences and the Common Curriculum.* Gary D Fenstermacher and John I. Goodlad, editors. Paper.

Part 2. *Staff Development.* Gary Griffin, editor. Paper.

Eighty-first Yearbook (1982)

Part 1. *Policy Making in Education.* Ann Lieberman and Milbrey W. McLaughlin, editors. Cloth.

Part 2. *Education and Work.* Harry F. Silberman, editor. Cloth.

Eightieth Yearbook (1981)

Part 1. *Philosophy and Education.* Jonas P. Soltis, editor. Cloth.

Part 2. *The Social Studies.* Howard D. Mehlinger and O. L. Davis, Jr., editors. Cloth.

Seventy-ninth Yearbook (1980)

Part 1. *Toward Adolescence: The Middle School Years.* Mauritz Johnson, editor. Cloth.

Part 2. *Learning a Second Language.* Frank M. Grittner, editor. Cloth.

Seventy-eighth Yearbook (1979)

Part 1. *The Gifted and the Talented: Their Education and Development.* A. Harry Passow, editor. Paper.

Part 2. *Classroom Management.* Daniel L. Duke, editor. Paper.

Seventy-seventh Yearbook (1978)

Part 1. *The Courts and Education.* Clifford B. Hooker, editor. Cloth.

Seventy-sixth Yearbook (1977)

Part 1. *The Teaching of English.* James R. Squire, editor. Cloth.

The above titles in the Society's Yearbook series may be ordered from the University of Chicago Press, Book Order Department, 11030 Langley Ave., Chicago, IL 60628. For a list of earlier titles in the yearbook series still available, write to the Secretary, NSSE, 5835 Kimbark Ave., Chicago, IL 60637.

2. The Series on Contemporary Educational Issues

The following volumes in the Society's Series on Contemporary Educational Issues may be ordered from the McCutchan Publishing Corporation, P.O. Box 774, Berkeley, CA 94702.

Boyd, William Lowe, and Walberg, Herbert J., editors. *Choice in Education: Potential and Problems.* 1990.

Case, Charles W., and Matthes, William A., editors. *Colleges of Education: Perspectives on Their Future.* 1985.

Eisner, Elliot, and Vallance, Elizabeth, editors. *Conflicting Conceptions of Curriculum.* 1974.

Erickson, Donald A., and Reller, Theodore L., editors. *The Principal in Metropolitan Schools.* 1979.

Farley, Frank H., and Gordon, Neal J., editors. *Psychology and Education: The State of the Union.* 1981.

Fennema, Elizabeth, and Ayer, M. Jane, editors. *Women and Education: Equity or Equality.* 1984.

Griffiths, Daniel E., Stout, Robert T., and Forsyth, Patrick, editors. *Leaders for America's Schools: The Report and Papers of the National Commission on Excellence in Educational Administration.* 1988.

Jackson, Philip W., editor. *Contributing to Educational Change: Perspectives on Research and Practice.* 1988.

Lane, John J., and Walberg, Herbert J., editors. *Effective School Leadership: Policy and Process.* 1987.

Levine, Daniel U., and Havighurst, Robert J., editors. *The Future of Big City Schools: Desegregation Policies and Magnet Alternatives.* 1977.

Lindquist, Mary M., editor. *Selected Issues in Mathematics Education.* 1981.

Murphy, Joseph, editor. *The Educational Reform Movement of the 1980s: Perspectives and Cases.* 1990.

Nucci, Larry P., editor. *Moral Development and Character Education.* 1989.

Peterson, Penelope L., and Walberg, Herbert J., editors. *Research on Teaching: Concepts, Findings, and Implications.* 1979.

Pflaum-Connor, Susanna, editor. *Aspects of Reading Education.* 1978.

Purves, Alan, and Levine, Daniel U., editors. *Educational Policy and International Assessment: Implications of the IEA Assessment of Achievement.* 1975.

Sinclair, Robert L., and Ghory, Ward. *Reaching Marginal Students: A Prime Concern for School Renewal.* 1987.

Spodek, Bernard, and Walberg, Herbert J., editors. *Early Childhood Education: Issues and Insights.* 1977.

Talmage, Harriet, editor. *Systems of Individualized Education.* 1975.

Tomlinson, Tommy M., and Walberg, Herbert J., editors. *Academic Work and Educational Excellence: Raising Student Productivity.* 1986.

Tyler, Ralph W., editor. *From Youth to Constructive Adult Life: The Role of the Public School.* 1978.

Tyler, Ralph W., and Wolf, Richard M., editors. *Crucial Issues in Testing.* 1974.

Walberg, Herbert J., editor. *Educational Environments and Effects: Evaluation, Policy, and Productivity.* 1979.

Walberg, Herbert J., editor. *Improving Educational Standards and Productivity: The Research Basis for Policy.* 1982.

Wang, Margaret C., and Walberg, Herbert J., editors. *Adapting Instruction to Student Differences.* 1985.

Warren, Donald R., editor. *History, Education, and Public Policy: Recovering the American Educational Past.* 1978.